AF566735

How to Enter & Win Fine Arts & Sculpture Contests

How to Enter & Win Fine Arts & Sculpture Contests

By
ALAN GADNEY

Executive Editor
CAROLYN PORTER

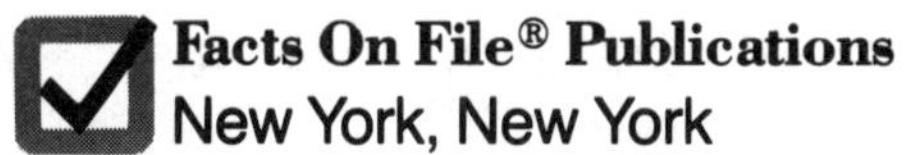
Facts On File® Publications
New York, New York

How to Enter and Win Fine Arts & Sculpture Contests

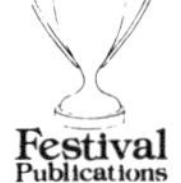

Published by Facts On File, Inc.
460 Park Ave. South, New York, N.Y. 10016

In cooperation with Festival Publications

Library of Congress Cataloging in Publication Data

Gadney, Alan.
How to enter and win fine arts contests.

Includes index.
1. Art—Competitions. 2. Sculpture—Competitions.
I. Title.
N393.G3 707'.9 81-12580
ISBN 0-87196-573-9 AACR2
ISBN 0-87196-579-8 (pbk.)

PRINTED IN THE UNITED STATES OF AMERICA
9 8 7 6 5 4 3 2 1
Computer Programming and Typesetting by Datagraphics Inc.

TO MARY M. GADNEY
whose confidence, love, and hard work
helped to make this series possible.
Thanks Mom.

EDITORIAL STAFF

CONTENTS

INTRODUCTION ix

How the Books Began
About the Fine Arts & Sculpture Book
How to Use this Book
How to Analyze an Event
Yearly Planning Guide
Helpful Hints on How to Win
A Word About Grants
Why Enter Contests
A Few Closing Thoughts

FINE ARTS & SCULPTURE

Amateur, Student, Youth 1
Animal, Nature, Wildlife 7
Art History Fellowships, Internships 10
Drawing 16
Drawing, Painting, Mixed Media 17
Drawing, Painting, Prints 20
Drawing, Painting, Prints, Collage, Mixed Media 25
Drawing, Painting, Prints, Sculpture 29
Drawing, Painting, Prints, Sculpture (Regional-State) 41
Drawing, Painting, Prints, Sculpture, Collage, Mixed Media 51
Drawing, Painting, Prints, Sculpture, Collage, Mixed Media (Regional-State) 57
Drawing, Painting, Sculpture 66
Drawing, Prints 69
Drawing, Sculpture 72
Grants, Loans (General) 74
Grants (Regional-State) 83
Graphics, Painting 87
Graphics, Painting, Sculpture, Mixed Media 89
Historical, Scenic 94
Miniature 98
Painting (All Media) 101
Painting (Watercolor, Water Media) 106
Painting, Sculpture 112

Prints 116
Residence Grants, Scholarships, Fellowships 120
Scholarships, Fellowships 133
Sculpture 140
Small Works 144
Visual Arts (General) 146
Visual Arts (Regional-State) 154
Other, Theme 161
Art Fairs, Festivals (All Media) 164
Art Fairs, Festivals (Specific Media) 173

ALPHABETICAL EVENT, SPONSOR, AWARD INDEX 189

SUBJECT-CATEGORY INDEX 203

INTRODUCTION

WELCOME . . . to How to Enter and Win FINE ARTS & SCULPTURE CONTESTS, an all new, completely up-to-date sourcebook for the contest competitor and grant seeker in the fine arts and sculpture fields (drawing, painting, prints, sculpture and collage) . . . one of an ongoing series of contest-grant books covering art and other related arts fields.

Each book in the series focuses in detail on an individual art or medium (Fine Arts & Sculpture, Design & Commercial Art, Color Photography, Black & White Photography, Film, Video-Audio-TV/Radio Broadcasting, Fiction Writing, Nonfiction Writing & Journalism, Crafts, and so on).

And each book in the series lists complete entrance information for anyone wanting to:

- Enter their work in national and international contests, festivals, competitions, salons, shows, exhibitions, markets, tradefairs, and other award events and sales outlets.
- Apply for grants, loans, scholarships, fellowships, residencies, apprenticeships, internships, training and benefit programs, and free aids and services.

The books also have: ALPHABETICAL INDEXES listing each event, sponsor, and award by its various names. SUBJECT/CATEGORY INDEXES to the entrants' specific areas of interest. Extensive CROSS-REFERENCES and DEFINITIONS throughout. And introductory HELPFUL HINTS on how to analyze and enter the events, and possibly come up a winner!

HOW THE BOOKS BEGAN

This series of contest-grant guides actually began several years ago with the first release print of *West Texas* (a one-hour featurette I made while completing my graduate work at the USC Cinema Department). One week after our first showing, I sent our premiere print off to the first film festival, and the contest entry process started to grow from there . . . with one major problem, however: The festival contact information was almost impossible to find.

After extensive research, all I could come up with were names and addresses (and an occasional brief blurb) of intriguingly titled film events in far-off places, but with no hard facts as to their entry requirements, eligibility restrictions, awards, deadlines, fees, statistics, judging procedures, etc. That sort of vital information was practically nonexistent, unless you took the time and postage to write away to every contest you discovered an address for

Through several years of continuous address researching, blindly writing off for contest entry information and periodically submitting the film, *West Texas* won 48 international film awards, and a large file of information had been collected on about 180 international festivals—quite a few of which were not even open to *West Texas* for a variety of reasons (wrong gauge, length, category, the event turned out not to be a film festival, etc.).

The need was evident for an accurate, up-to-date, and detailed entry information source to the world's Contests, Festivals and Grants . . . Thus evolved the two editions of my previous book (GADNEY'S GUIDE TO INTERNATIONAL CONTESTS, FESTIVALS & GRANTS). Their first-of-a-kind success ultimately lead to this all new series of contest-grant guides.

ABOUT THE FINE ARTS & SCULPTURE BOOK

This book (devoted solely to the fields of FINE ARTS & SCULPTURE) is a single-source reference guide, providing you with vital entry information and statistics about a contest/grant before you even have to send away for the entry forms and shipping regulations (which you must always eventually do, as most require their own entry forms, and some have rather intricate shipping and customs requirements).

The 343 separate events listed in this volume were compiled through 3 years of active research on my earlier book, an additional year of research on this book, and thousands of questionnaires sent to worldwide art events (many requiring repeated mailings to obtain complete and up-to-date entry information). During this process, we have totally updated, revised, and expanded the scope of the original listings, added new competitions, and deleted a few which were too restricted or no longer in existence. (Commercial Art, Advertising, Architecture, Cartooning, Design, Illustration and Poster sections of art events have been included in a companion volume covering Design & Commercial Art contests and grants.)

The individual events have been further grouped into 33 special-interest subcategories (an increase in the number of subject categories over the earlier book, particularly in the areas of visual art scholarships, fellowships, and grants). These subcategories are further divided and cross-referenced in the SUBJECT/CATEGORY INDEX at the back of the book.

We have included two general types of events:

- Those AWARD EVENTS and SALES OUTLETS to which entrants may submit their works in order to receive SOMETHING OF VALUE in return, such as contests, festivals, competitions, salons, shows, exhibitions, markets, tradefairs, and various other award and sales programs primarily for new and unknown works.

- And BENEFIT PROGRAMS to which individuals or organizations may apply for some type of AID or SERVICE, such as grants, money and equipment loans, scholarships, fellowships, residencies, apprenticeships, internships, training programs, and so on.

Due to page length restrictions we have omitted those events that (1) are restricted to members of a specific organization, (unless you can join that organization upon entering the contest), or limited to residents of a small city or geographical area (usually of less than state size), or (2) are not open to general entry but whose participants are nominated or invited by the sponsors or national selecting organizations. Workshops, seminars, conferences, schools, service programs, and the like, have only been listed if they are free, have free benefits attached, or encompass a contest, festival, grant, scholarship, fellowship, residency, etc.

We have listed as much detailed information about each separate event as possible (that is, as much as could be culled from the materials provided us by the event—usually including current addresses, dates, deadlines, complete entry requirements, eligibility and fee information, awards available, judging aspects, catch clauses, purpose, theme, sponsors, average statistics, where held, and various historical aspects). All information was transcribed from the questionnaires and entry materials provided us and edited to fit the format of the book. (See HOW TO USE THE BOOK for description of format.)

The information listed is the most current we could obtain, and will normally be revised and updated every two or three years in this continuing reference series.

We have also included older events when there was no direct confirmation that the events had gone out of existence. Many events come and go in an on-again, off-again manner, depending on their finances, administration changes, and other factors . . . again, good reason to ALWAYS WRITE TO AN EVENT BEFORE ENTERING YOUR WORK. Most events require entry forms, which they provide. Many have special shipping regulations. And, as we have condensed and edited their rules and regulations, it is best to write for the complete versions (especially important in interpreting the meanings of occasional tricky "catch clauses" about the use and ownership of winning entries). Also remember to send along a self-addressed, stamped return envelope (SASE), particularly to smaller events operating on tight postage budgets.

It would be almost impossible to give an exact figure for the total amount of money offered through this book. Some events give cash, others give equipment (of varying value depending on how badly you need the equipment or how much you can sell it for), and others give trophies, cups, plaques, medals, certificates, etc. (all of great value to the winner, but of little real monetary worth). Grant sources, on the other hand, may offer millions of dollars in direct financial aid. Probably the safest thing to say about the total amount of money offered through this book is that it is well into the millions.

HOW TO USE THIS BOOK

In the TABLE OF CONTENTS you will find that this volume has been divided into a series of "special-interest" SUBCATEGORIES. Each contains all those events whose primary emphasis is within that particular subcategory. The listing is usually alphabetical—first those in the United States, followed by other countries in alphabetical order.

At the start of each subcategory is an italicized INTRODUCTORY SECTION giving (1) specific contents of that subcategory, (2) definitions, and (3) "also see" CROSS-REFERENCES to similar events in other subcategories in the book.

To find additional events accepting entries in your specific interest area (but which may be listed in other subcategories because their primary emphasis is stronger in those areas), use the SUBJECT/CATEGORY INDEX at the back of the book. This lists subjects of special interest by an identifying code number for each event. The code number is located in the box above each event.

To find a specific event, sponsor, or award by name, use the ALPHABETICAL EVENT/SPONSOR/AWARD INDEX at the back of the book (again listing entries by identifying code number). In this index, sponsors and events are usually listed by full names, abbreviations, and unique titles.

EACH EVENT consists of (1) a current address and telephone number; (2) entry month; (3) introductory paragraph, including entry restrictions, month/season held, date of establishment, former names, purpose, theme, motto, sponsors, average statistics, historical information, facilities and other aspects; (4) technical entry regulations and categories; (5) eligibility requirements; (6) awards; (7) judging aspects and catch clauses; (8) sales terms; (9) entry fees; (10) deadlines. All have a similar format designed for easy use, with the five most important aspects of each event noted in bold type:

1. Identifying Code Number (in box)
2. Name of event
3. Month of entry
4. Entrant restrictions
5. Type of event and subject-category

With these five main points in mind, a potential entrant can quickly skim through a series of events to find those of particular interest.

HOW TO ANALYZE AN EVENT

We have usually provided enough information about each event to help you in making various determinations before you send away for entry forms, shipping regulations, and additional instructions. These are some of the points you should consider in your analysis.

• **When is the event held?** The month/season held is listed in the first sentence.

• **When is the entry deadline?** Months of entry are designated by bold type immediately following the address and in the DEADLINES section at the end of each event listing, and are usually well in advance of the month held. However, as deadlines do vary, the event should always be contacted about the specific entry date for the year you are applying.

• **Do I qualify?** Entrant restrictions are listed in bold type in the first sentence, and may be further clarified in the ELIGIBILITY section.

• **Does my work qualify?** The type of event and specific subject categories are listed in bold type at the beginning of the second and subsequent paragraphs. Various technical entry requirements follow each.

• **How much does it cost?** Costs and hidden costs are found in the ENTRY FEE section. The reason most events charge entry fees is usually to pay for the awards, operating costs, judges, and attendance of well-known persons. Contests and festivals can be extremely expensive to operate, and the size and scope of the event usually dictates the fee structure. Amateur competitions can range from no entry fees to very nominal ones, while the fees for more professional contests are considerably higher.

• **What are the prizes?** Found in the AWARDS section are prizes varying from trophies, cups, plaques, and medallions (of personal value), to cash, trips, equipment, and services (of a more material value—meaning you may be able to resell them at a later date if you already have better equipment, cannot take the trip, or do not want the services). Exhibition, distribution, broadcast, sale, and publication may also be offered, but should always be analyzed in terms of their financial and legal implications (what you get for what you have to give in return, and how valuable your entry may become in the future).

• **What are the catch clauses?** A few events have tricky qualifying clauses, condensed in the JUDGING section. These may involve claims to use and ownership (sometimes of all entries, and on an extensive basis), or responsibility in the event of loss, damage, nonreturn, etc.

Occasionally the actual entry forms and regulations may be rather vague as to whether the sponsors just keep a copy of your winning entry or whether they receive full ownership of the work (and for what use). Possibly, in these instances, you should write to the sponsors for further clarification.

• **How is my work judged?** The number of judges, judging procedures, and criteria are listed in the JUDGING section. It is important to understand that during preliminary judging (sometimes performed by the event's staff and aides), many entries may be immediately disqualified because of failure to adhere to the various contest regulations, or eliminated because of technical flaws or oversights (good reason always to send away for, and to read carefully, the latest rules). This is especially true of large contests that thousands enter. Sponsors have to narrow the competition as rapidly and efficiently as possible, and the first to go are the rule breakers and sloppy entries.

A program of the event or listing of past winners may give you an overall feel for the event (if it is conservative or liberal, oriented in certain directions, etc.). There is the possibility of talking to past entrants and winners in order to get an idea of specific likes and dislikes of the event and its judges. Or if you know who the judges will be, you may be able to make an educated guess as to what they will choose. However, I have found that it is almost impossible to predict how judges will act on anything other than the widest of generalities. Judges change from year to year, the philosophy of the event may alter, and single-judge contests put you at the mercy of that particular year's judge. So, you can never really outguess the judges.

• **How old is the event?** Usually included in the first sentence is the founding date, the inference being that the older the event, the more stable and reputable it is.

• **How large is the event?** Average attendance, distribution, and sales figures can often be found in the first paragraph, indicating the potential promotional and sales values of participating in the event.

• **What is the duration of an event, and how long will it tie up my entry materials?** The number of days the event is usually held is found in the first paragraph; the entry and return-of-material dates are in the DEADLINES section.

• **What is the competition?** Average statistics on number of entries, entrants, countries competing, acceptances into final competition, and winners can be found in the first paragraph, giving some idea of possible competition in future events.

• **How legitimate is the event?** This can be determined to some extent by the names of familiar sponsors, cosponsors, financial supporters, and those organizations that officially recognize the event—again, all found in the opening paragraph, and giving some idea of reputability. Also important may be the purpose, theme, and motto.

These are just a few of the aspects to examine before writing away for further information, entry forms, the most current regulations . . . and before sending away your work.

YEARLY PLANNING GUIDE

This book can also serve as a planning guide for your contest entries throughout the year. By using the SUBJECT/CATEGORY INDEX, you can get an overall picture of the various world events accepting entries in your areas of interest. We would then suggest setting up a calendar, listing those events you wish to enter by (1) the date you should write away for entry forms and current rules (several months before the actual entry month), (2) the entry dates, and (3) the dates the event is held, which will give you some indication of when the sponsor will be announcing the winners and returning your materials.

HELPFUL HINTS ON HOW TO WIN

Here are a few recommendations to enhance your chances of winning:

• ANALYZE THE STATISTICS—Look at the average statistics (found in the first paragraph of an event listing) to determine the size of your competition. Remember, you should always calculate the number of awards/honors given against the number of entrants, and not just analyze on total entrants alone. Larger events with a greater number of entrants and more awards may in reality have a higher winner-ratio than smaller events with only one award. You may also stand a better chance of winning in newer events which have not yet built up their patronage.

• ANALYZE THE TYPE OF EVENT—Based on past winner/award listings, is the event consistently conservative or liberal in its selections (or does it change moods from one year to the next)? If a contest says it leans toward contemporary or experimental works, you should take this into account before entering. You may also wish to try and analyze how the judges will vote, again based on past records and who the current judges are. (See HOW TO ANALYZE AN EVENT for additional information.)

• PATRONIZE THE SPECIALIZED EVENTS—If you have a specialized entry, while it will normally qualify for more generalized contests, you might begin by concentrating on those events which have a special interest in, or specific subject categories for your particular entry. Because of their highly specialized nature, these contests may get fewer entries, and if your work fits their interests, you should stand a better chance of winning. You might also consider patronizing those events that have changing annual themes by designing your entry to fit that particular year's needs.

• FOLLOW THE RULES—The contest rules (obtained directly from the event) should be studied carefully, first to find hidden clauses, and second to ensure you will not be inadvertently excluded because you entered the wrong category, sent an incorrect entry fee or no return postage, entered with improper technical aspects, or not enough supplementary information, etc. So read the rules and follow them, and fill out the entry forms completely. Rule breakers usually are disqualified, sometimes even before the preliminary judging. Then, to further cut down the number of competitors, most judges go strictly by the regulations, automatically discarding those entries that in any way deviate from the rules.

• KEEP IT CLEAN—Keep it technically perfect. Again, judges will usually reject sloppy entries (sometimes these don't even reach the judges, but are weeded out by the contest staff). So send only clean entries in good condition. No dirty, smudged, or wet paintings or prints; chipped or broken sculpture. All of these reflect badly on your entry's artistic content. And if the sponsors tell you they want an entry mounted or framed, you had better follow their instructions. Also, it is best to send a duplicate rather than your original print work (unless they request the original, in which case you should study their rules carefully to see if you will ever get your original back).

• SEND IT AHEAD OF TIME—Send your materials well in advance of the entry deadlines. Last-minute entries may get abbreviated handling by judges who have already looked over the earlier entries and have made up their minds. They may not get listed in the contest programs, which have already gone to the printers—and if they are shown, they may be scheduled during the least desirable exhibition times. And of course, *late* entries are usually sent back unopened.

• SEND PUBLICITY AND INFORMATION MATERIALS—Send supporting materials unless positively prohibited. (Definitely send them when they are requested.) Every little bit helps: biographical, technical, and project background information; publicity and press materials; still photos, production philosophy, synopsis, translation, transcription (and advertising materials if appropriate). The judges may occasionally use some of these in making their final decisions, and the events may use the publicity in their programs, flyers, and press rooms. Remember to send along any special technical instructions or return shipping requests you feel are needed.

• USE PROPER SHIPPING—First a word about the U.S. and international mail systems (as opposed to international Air Freight; some foreign contests even prohibit the use of air freight, as the entries may become held up in customs). Provided your entries are properly packaged, sealed, marked, stamped, and insured, and have correctly filled-out customs stickers (information about all of this is available through the U.S. Post Office), they should be able to travel almost anywhere in the world with relative safety. (This is based on personal experience. *West Texas* was mailed to a large number of film festivals all over the world, and I never lost a print or received one back damaged in transit.)

Remember always to ship by air to overseas competitions (as boat mail may take as long as three months from the U.S. to Australia, for example). On domestic U.S. shipments, you can mail at various rates lower than First Class, if you take into account the time for possible delays. (Again, contact the post office for information about mailing costs and times.)

Of course, if you have a heavy international shipment (a large sculpture for example), you may be over the postal weight limitations, and have to ship by Air Freight. In this case, it may be best to contact a customs house broker/international freight forwarder about services and charges.

Short overseas messages will travel very rapidly by international telegram. And always remember to enclose sufficient return postage and a correctly sized self-addressed stamped return envelope (SASE) when requested. Finally, if your entry arrives with "Postage Due," it could be a negative factor in the contest staff preselection process.

A WORD ABOUT GRANTS

It would take an entire volume to discuss all the "ins" and "outs" of grant solicitation. However, we can touch on a few of the more important aspects.

• FIND OUT AS MUCH AS POSSIBLE about a potential grant source before investing the time in sending a proposal. Write to the granting organization for more information—and once you have this information, analyze it and focus your energies on the most likely prospects.

• WRITE AN INQUIRY LETTER—a brief letter of introduction, to see if they are interested in your project. Include a short description of the project and its unique aspects, background information about yourself and your sponsoring organization, the proposal budget, and ask them if they would be interested in further information. Keep your introductory letter brief, to the point, well written, easy to understand, and not exaggerated. If the foundation is interested, it will request what it needs, which may run anywhere from an expanded summary to a full-scale proposal and budget.

• GET AN ORGANIZATION TO SPONSOR YOU—Many foundations restrict their granting to only nonprofit, tax-exempt organizations, institutions, etc. However, this does not necessarily prohibit you from securing a grant from them. Simply get a nonprofit organization to sponsor you and your project, and have the organization apply for the grant in their name. Many organizations offer grant solicitations as one of their services, and this can have benefits for the sponsoring organizations: You give them credit and publicity through your finished project. They have a track-record as a successful fund raiser, which may help them in obtaining future grants. And they can even be paid through your budget for handling certain administrative and bookkeeping duties.

• GET SOME NAMES ON YOUR SIDE—well-known persons in the roles of advisors, technical consultants, etc. can help greatly toward building an impressive project package.

• TRY SPECIAL INTEREST GROUPS—If you have designed a project involving a special interest (Medical Graphics, for example), rather than only approaching sources that grant your medium (Art), you might consider going to those grant sources that fund the special interest instead (i.e., Medical Grants). Or you may find similar money sources through special-interest organizations, associations, institutions, and businesses. The public library is a good place to start your search.

• BUILD A TRACK RECORD—A series of smaller grants, scholarships, fellowships from local or regional sources can be extremely impressive on your presentation resume when you approach the larger granting organizations. And of course, prizes and honors awarded to you and your work will help to build you as a winning grant recipient with a previous track record. Remember that many times several grants can be awarded to the same project simultaneously. So apply to as many sources (those for which you qualify) as possible, and then keep on applying.

WHY ENTER CONTESTS

Finally, a word about the positive benefits of entering your work in contests, festivals, and competitions.

To start with, it is an extremely good way to test (and prove) the artistic and commercial value of your work before professional judges, critics, and the public. There is also the challenge of the competition—the excitement and glamour of knowing that your work is being seen in contests, festivals, salons, exhibitions, and publications around the world. Your entry competes with those of your peers —and if it reaches the finals and wins, there is the great personal satisfaction and certification of acceptance.

If you do win, you can win substantial cash prizes, trips, art items, equipment, services, exhibition, distribution, broadcast, publication, sales, trophies, and other awards. There can be useful free publicity for both you and your work, through (1) press information and literature released by the event, (2) the writings and reviews of others about your work, and (3) your own promotional materials designed around your winnings.

All of this can bring valuable international exposure through the print and broadcast media, and the resulting recognition and prestige can certainly help to sell both your award-winning work and yourself as an award-winning artist.

The end benefits can be sales, valuable contacts, jobs, contracts, increased fees, and the financing of other projects.

How does this translate into real terms . . . The 48 international film awards won by *West Texas* resulted directly in: (1) a large number of valuable art objects, trophies, and awards; (2) enough cash winnings to cover all the film festival entry fees, shipping, promotion, and other costs; (3) an enormous amount of free personal publicity; (4) the eventual sale and distribution of the film; (5) the writing and directing of a subsequent feature-length theatrical, *Moonchild;* (6) several paid speaking engagements; (7) a TV script assignment; (8) a stint as a film magazine contributing editor; and (9) eventually to writing this series of books on contests and grants . . . So, the entering of contests and the winning of awards in many ways can be quite profitable.

A FEW CLOSING THOUGHTS — While I have found the vast majority of events to be highly reputable and continually striving to improve their quality, there are still a few bad exceptions (lost entries, withheld awards, judging problems, etc.).

However, the interesting thing is that just as numbers and types of events change from year to year, so do most of these questionable conditions. Just when you hear someone complain about an unfair judging process, the next year the judges change, and that same person may come out a winner. Or the rules and administration change, and what was once a suspect practice disappears.

With this in mind, there has been no attempt on our part to editorialize about the occasional bad occurrences we hear of. This is strictly a reference guide (not a critical work). We list all those events which qualify, from the largest to the smallest, the oldest to the youngest, the well-known and the not so well-known. And we have tried to print enough information about each event to give you a firm basis upon which to decide whether or not to write for further information. (See HOW TO ANALYZE AN EVENT.)

It should also be stated that we do not endorse (or accept any responsibility for the conduct of) the events listed in this book.

Finally, no book of this type can ever be all-inclusive. That would be virtually impossible. Each year hundreds of new events start up, old ones lapse or go out of business, only to be replaced by similar events in a new form. As I have mentioned, there is constant growth and progression based on general changes in the art and media fields. However, considering the many individual events we have listed, each as thoroughly as possible within the edited format, and each updated and verified to the best of our knowledge based on entry materials and questionnaires provided us, we feel that we have brought you quite a comprehensive reference guide.

A special thank you to the American Library Association (the Reference and Adult Services Division, Reference Committee) for awarding the previous contest book an "OUTSTANDING REFERENCE SOURCE OF THE YEAR" . . . and to the many readers and reviewers of that book for their favorable response. These honors have been extremely gratifying.

And an additional thanks and grateful appreciation to the many events, sponsors, contributors, and correspondents who have so graciously provided us with the information included in this directory.

As a final reminder, please remember that to ensure you have the latest information, complete regulations, and proper entry forms, ALWAYS WRITE TO AN EVENT BEFORE ENTERING YOUR WORK

And please advise us of any new Contests and Grants you may know of, so that we may include them in our future editions.

Alan Gadney
Festival Publications
P.O. Box 10180
Glendale, California 91209 U.S.A.

FINE ARTS & SCULPTURE

AMATEUR, STUDENT, YOUTH

Drawing, Graphics, Painting, Prints, Sculpture, Visual Arts, Mixed Media and Collage, including FIGURATIVE and PORTFOLIOS. Amateur usually defined as made entirely for fun and pleasure, with no commercial purpose or profit in mind, by persons not engaged in art as their main source of income at the time of production; and which has not been sold, commissioned, sponsored, or subsidized. However, these definitions may vary. (Also see OTHER CATEGORIES.)

1

Anacortes Arts and Crafts Festival Nonprofessional Competition
Barbara Jackson, Director
414 Commercial Avenue
P. O. Box 6
Anacortes, Washington 98221 U.S.A.
Tel: (206) 293-6211

Entry July

State; **entry open to Anacortes-area amateurs;** annual in August; established 1961. Sponsored and supported by Anacortes Arts and Crafts Festival (nonprofit). Average statistics: 125 screened booths, 20,000 attendance. Also sponsor Skagit Artists Invitational. Second contact: Anacortes Chamber of Commerce, 14th and Commercial, Anacortes, Washington 98221; tel: (206) 293-2832.

DRAWING CONTEST: **Amateur Any Medium General,** framed under glass or plastic, ready for hanging; limit 2 per section. No class work, copies, kits. Also have crafts, photography sections.

PAINTING CONTEST: **Amateur Any Medium General,** framed, ready for hanging, dry; limit 2 per section. No class work, copies, kits.

PRINT CONTEST: **Amateur Any Type General.** Requirements, restrictions same as for Drawing.

SCULPTURE: **Amateur Any Medium General;** limit 2 per section. No class work, copies, kits.

ELIGIBILITY: Residents of Whatcom, Skagit, Snohomish, San Juan, Island counties.

AWARDS: $25 First, $15 Second, $5 Third Prize each to painting, drawing, prints, sculpture.

JUDGING: By local artists. Not responsible for loss or damage.

SALES TERMS: Work need not be for sale. 20% commission charge.

ENTRY FEE: $4 each section plus return postage.

DEADLINES: Entry, July. Event, August.

2

Arts NW Student Juried Fine Art Show

Diane Berge, President
1500 Western Avenue
Seattle, Washington 98101 U.S.A.
Tel: (206) 682-4435

Entry October

International; **entry open to U.S., Canadian, Mexican art students;** annual in December; established 1981. Purpose: to encourage development of visual artists through exhibition and sale of work. Sponsored by Arts NW (founded 1978). Held in Seattle for 1 month.

VISUAL ARTS CONTEST: By Student General (drawings, paintings, prints, sculpture, collage); limit 3 per entrant. Submit 35mm slides (1 for 2D, 4-5 for 3D) for judging. Competition includes photography.

AWARDS: $500 in Cash Prizes.

JUDGING: By panel of professionals. Based on merit. Sponsor temporarily keeps slides of accepted work for publicity; insures work during exhibit.

SALES TERMS: Work need not be for sale. 35% commission charge.

ENTRY FEE: $10.

DEADLINES: Entry, October. Judging, November. Event, December.

3

Four State Student Drawing Competition

Spokane Falls Community College (SFCC)
Patty Haag, Gallery Director
Visual Arts Department, Building 600
W3410 Fort George Wright Drive
Spokane, Washington 99204 U.S.A.
Tel: (509) 456-6100

Entry February

Regional; **entry open to Washington, Idaho, Montana, Oregon college students;** annual in March-April; established 1971. Purpose: to expose SFCC students to student work done in other locations. Sponsored by Visual Arts Department, SFCC Art Club. Average statistics: 100 entries, 50 finalists, 3 awards. Held at SFCC in Spokane for 10 days.

DRAWING CONTEST: By Student Any Medium General, on paper or board with paper content, any size, matted; limit 1 per entrant. No glass or plexiglass.

AWARDS: $150 First, $75 Second, $50 Third Prize.

JUDGING: By 1 academic. Sponsor may reproduce entries for publicity. Not responsible for loss or damage.

ENTRY FEE: None. No sales commission charge.

DEADLINES: Entry, February. Event, March-April. Materials returned, May.

4

Rockport National Amateur Festival

Rockport Chamber of Commerce
Sumner G. Ropper, Executive Director
P. O. Box 67
Rockport, Massachusetts 01966 U.S.A. Tel: (617) 546-6575

Entry September

International; **entry open to U.S., Canadian amateurs;** annual in October; established 1939. Purpose: to promote art, especially amateur. Sponsored and supported by Rockport Chamber of Commerce. Average statistics (all sections): 140 entries, 8000 attendance. Held at Rockport Art Association for 4 days. Have demonstrations by professionals.

DRAWING CONTEST: Amateur Charcoal, Pastel, Pen and Ink, Pencil General, 34x40 inches maximum including frame; limit 1 per entrant (all sections).

PAINTING CONTEST: Amateur, Casein, Oil, Watercolor General. Requirements same as for Drawing.

PRINT CONTEST: Amateur General. Requirements same as for Drawing.

SCULPTURE CONTEST: Amateur General. Requirements same as for Drawing.

AWARDS: Prizes and Certificates to best of show, first, second, third place, honorable mentions each medium (pastel, casein, pen and ink, charcoal, oil, watercolor). Prizes and Certificates in sculpture. $25 Popular Vote.

JUDGING: By professional artists. Not responsible for loss or damage.

ENTRY FEE: $3 plus $7.50 handling. No sales.

DEADLINES: Entry, September. Event, October.

5

Rocky Mountain School of Art Annual Scholarship Competition
Howard Hughes, Director of Admissions
1441 Ogden Street
Denver, Colorado 80218 U.S.A.
Tel: (303) 832-1557

Entry April

International; **entry open to graduating high school seniors;** annual in Spring; established 1963. Purpose: to recognize talented high school artists. Sponsored and supported by Rocky Mountain School of Art. Average statistics: 200 entries, 75 entrants, 3 semifinalists, 250 attendance. Held at Rocky Mountain School of Art in Denver for 2 weeks.

VISUAL ARTS CONTEST: By Student General, original, 22x30 inches maximum; 16x16 inches maximum for base of 3D; limit 3 per entrant.

AWARDS: 1 2-Year Fine Art Scholarship ($5560 value).

JUDGING: By 4 school administrators. Not responsible for loss or damage.

ENTRY FEE: None.

DEADLINES: Entry, April. Awards, event, Spring.

6

Scholastic Art Awards
Scholastic, Inc.
50 West 44th Street
New York, New York 10036 U.S.A.
Tel: (212) 944-7700, ext. 606

Entry January

International; **entry open to U.S., Canadian students under 20;** annual in January; established 1928. Purpose: to recognize and encourage student achievement in creative art. Sponsored and supported by Scholastic Inc., Armstrong World Industries, Eastman Kodak Company, Hallmark Cards Inc., Strathmore Paper Company. Average 200,000 entries.

DRAWING CONTEST: By Student Charcoal, Crayon, Ink, Pastel, Pencil General, original, 30x30 inches maximum including mounting or matting (reinforced) on white, covered with fixative or cellophane (pastel, crayon, charcoal). Divisions: grades 7-9, 10-12. No colored mats, frames, glass, copies from photographs, magazines, book illustrations. Competition includes crafts. Also have photography, writing sections.

PAINTING CONTEST: **By Student Acrylic General** (including all plastic paints), original, 36x36 inches maximum including mounting or matting (reinforced) on white. No colored mats, frames, glass, copies from photographs, magazines, book illustrations.

By Student Oil General, original, on stretched canvas, canvas board, or other prepared surfaces, 36x36 inches maximum. Other restrictions same as for Acrylic.

By Student Watercolor General, transparent or opaque (including tempera, gouache, casein) original, 30x30 inches maximum including mounting or matting (reinforced) on white. Other restrictions same as for Acrylic.

PRINT CONTEST: **By Student General,** any creative form. Requirements, restrictions same as for Painting (watercolor).

SCULPTURE CONTEST: **By Student General,** in round or relief, original, maximum 24 inches in any direction, 25 pounds. Competition includes crafts.

MIXED MEDIA CONTEST: **By Student General,** 2D, 30 inches maximum in any direction (collage limited to 1/4-inch above surface), mounted or matted (reinforced) on white. No colored mats, frames, glass, copies from photographs, magazines, book illustrations. Competition includes crafts.

ART PORTFOLIO CONTEST: **By Student General,** original, 24x31 inches maximum, hard covered, contents mounted or matted (reinforced) on white; limit 8 entries (3 must be drawings). Submit 5 photos or slides of 3D work. Other restrictions same as for Mixed Media.

ELIGIBILITY: Students in grades 7-12 (under age 20), enrolled in public or private schools; approved by school art department. Scholarship entrants must be in upper half of class graduating in January, June of award year; must meet entrance requirements of cooperating schools and colleges; must demonstrate financial need.

AWARDS: *Regional Honors:* Gold Achievement Keys, Certificates of Merit, Blue Ribbons. $100 Armstrong Award to sculpture (includes crafts). *National Honors:* Gold Medals to each medium in each section. 100 Scholastic Art Award Scholarships to top senior students. Art School Scholarships to outstanding portfolios. $100 Hallmark Honor Prize to best painting or drawing (each sponsored region). 5 $4000 Strathmore Scholarship Awards to senior portfolios. 95 National Awards to painting, 85 to drawing, 40 to print, 30 to sculpture, 30 to mixed media.

JUDGING: By educators and artists recommended by Advisory Committee of Art Educators. Juried on regional and national levels. Based on quality, school record. Sponsor may reproduce entries. Not responsible for loss or damage.

ENTRY FEE: None.

DEADLINES: Entry, January. Materials returned, September (portfolios, May; Hallmark Prize Winners, after 1 year).

7

Seventeen's Annual Art Contest
Seventeen Magazine
Murfy Alexander, Public Relations Director
Triangle Communications
850 Third Avenue
New York, New York 10022 U.S.A.
Tel: (212) 759-8100

Entry June

National; **entry open to U.S. teenagers age 13-20;** annual; established 1976. Sponsored by *Seventeen Magazine,* Triangle Communications. Average 500 entries. Held at New York offices for 6 months. Publish *Seventeen Magazine* (monthly). Also sponsor fiction, photography, cookery, sports contests.

VISUAL ARTS CONTEST: **By Youth Any Medium General,** original, 20x26 inches maximum, unframed, flat; limit 2 per entrant. Unpublished (except in school publications). No glass.

AWARDS: $500 First, $300 Second, $200 Third Place Prize. Winners illustrate prize-winning short stories in annual fiction contest.

JUDGING: By editorial staff. Based on skill, originality, suitability for publication in *Seventeen Magazine.* Sponsor owns awarded works, may publish in magazine. Not responsible for loss or damage.

ENTRY FEE: None. Entrant pays return postage.

DEADLINES: Entry, June. Awards, January.

8

Texas State Arts and Crafts Fair Young Artist Competition
Texas Arts and Crafts Foundation (TACF)
Audie Hamilton, Executive Director
P. O. Box 1527
Kerrville, Texas 78028 U.S.A.
Tel: (512) 896-5711

Entry November

State; **entry open to Texas residents under age 21;** annual in May-June; established 1972. Fair established as project of Texas Tourist Development Agency now administered by TACF. Purpose: to showcase talented young artists. Sponsored by TACF. Average statistics (all sections): 400 entrants, 245 finalists, 53 awards, 40,000 attendance. Held at Schreiner College campus for 2 weekends. Have State Fair events, food, lodging facilities. Tickets: $2-$4 fair admission. Also sponsor workshops.

VISUAL ARTS CONTEST: **By Youth General** (including graphics, painting, sculpture), original; limit 2 media. Submit 3 2x2-inch slides (each media) for entry review; resume; legal proof of age, residency. Entrant must attend sales display. No commercially produced entries. Competition includes photography, crafts. Also have art-craft fair sections.

AWARDS: 1 $500 college scholarship for following academic year to best young artist. 3 (1 to scholarship winner) free booth spaces at State Fair (includes overnight accommodations, meals at Schreiner College). 50 Excellence Certificates in State Fair sections.

JUDGING: Entry review by 3 jurors. Sponsor retains slides. Not responsible for loss or damage.

ENTRY FEE: None. Art Fair: $135 for 8x10-foot space.

DEADLINES: Entry, November. Notification, January. Event, May-June.

University of Wisconsin-Superior High School Art Scholarship Competition
Mel Olsen, Coordinator
University of Wisconsin-Superior
Visual Arts Department
Superior, Wisconsin 54880 U.S.A.
Tel: (715) 392-8101, ext. 391

Entry April

National; **entry open to U.S. graduating high school seniors;** annual; established 1974. Purpose: to recognize excellence in high school art; encourage talented individuals to pursue postsecondary education. Sponsored and supported by University of Wisconsin-Superior Foundation. Average statistics: 35 entries, 25 entrants, 4 awards. Exhibition held at Holden Fine Arts Center Galleries, Superior, Wisconsin for 2 weeks. Also sponsor University of Wisconsin-Superior On-Of Paper Exhibition, Visual Arts Graduate Assistantships.

VISUAL ARTS CONTEST: By Student All Media General, UPS or mailable size; limit 2 per entrant.

AWARDS: $500 First, $400 Second, $300 Third Scholarship Award.

JUDGING: By guest jurors holding masters of fine arts degrees.

ENTRY FEE: None. No sales commission charge.

DEADLINES: Entry, April.

10

Young Sculptor Awards Competition
National Sculpture Society
Claire A. Stein, Executive Director
15 East 26th Street
New York, New York 10010 U.S.A.
Tel: (212) 889-6960

Entry June

National; **entry open to U.S. residents under age 35;** annual in June. Purpose: to find young sculptors who demonstrate excellence in creating figurative sculpture. Sponsored by National Sculpture Society. Publish *National Sculpture Review.*

SCULPTURE CONTEST: By Young People Figurative; 5-10 per entrant. Submit brief biography with birthdate, 8x10-inch monochrome photographs of work for judging.

AWARDS: Possible $750 Prize. $500 John Gregory Memorial Prize to work showing originality, imagination. $300 Walter Lantz Prize to contemporary representational sculpture. Gloria Medal. Commendations. Winning entries published in *National Sculpture Review.*

JUDGING: By Education Committee Chair and 5 sculptors.

ENTRY FEE: Not specified. Entrant pays return postage.

DEADLINES: Entry, event, June.

Imperial Tobacco Portrait Award
National Portrait Gallery (London)
Jacquie Meredith, Competitions Officer
St. Martin's Place
London WC2H 0HE, ENGLAND
Tel: (01) 930-1552

Entry August

National; **entry open to U.K.;** annual in October-December; established 1980. Purpose: to encourage young British artists in portraiture. Sponsored and supported by Imperial Tobacco Limited. Recognized by National Portrait Gallery. Average statistics: 400 entries, 75 semifinalists, 8 awards, 66,000 attendance. Held at National Portrait Gallery in London for 3 months. Second contact: Heather Tilbury, Tilbury Sandford Brysson, 113 Gloucester Road, London SW7, England.

PAINTING CONTEST: **By Young Artist Acrylic, Oil, Tempera Portrait,** 12x15 inches (31x38cm) maximum, canvas on stretcher or board, framed, suitable for hanging; limit 1 per entrant. Completed in previous 16 months. Submit 35mm slide for entry review.

ELIGIBILITY: British subjects resident in U.K. ages 18 to 40 on January 1st in competition year.

AWARDS: £5000, Commemorative Medallion, £2000 Commission (painting to become part of National Portrait Gallery's permanent collection) to first place. £750, Medal to second. £250, Medal to third place. Up to 5 Special Commendations of £100 plus Commemorative Certificates.

JUDGING: Entry review by 1 judge, 2 of Gallery's senior curators. Awards judging by panel of 8 judges (artists, academics, Gallery Director, Chairman of Imperial Tobacco). Sponsor may withhold commission award; may reproduce entries for press, educational, reference purposes; retains slides for Gallery's archives; may require entries to be loaned for traveling exhibition. Copyright of commissioned work is property of National Portrait Gallery. Not responsible for loss or damage.

ENTRY FEE: None.

DEADLINES: Entry, August. Notification, September. Awards, October. Event, October-December.

ANIMAL, NATURE, WILDLIFE

Drawing, Painting, Prints, Sculpture, Mixed Media and Art Fairs, including ARKANSAS WILDLIFE, ENERGY-ENVIRONMENT, FOREST HERITAGE, INDIAN RELATED, and HARNESS RACING. (Also see OTHER CATEGORIES).

12

Arkansas Wildlife Federation (AWF) Art Exhibition

Lee Bowers, Secretary
505 Hudson Avenue
Pine Bluff, Arkansas 71603 U.S.A.

Entry June

National; **entry open to U.S.;** annual in Fall; established 1978. Purpose: to promote wildlife art, interest in Arkansas wildlife, natural resources. Sponsored by AWF, nonprofit organization dedicated to conservation of state, natural resources; Southeast Arkansas Art and Science Center (SEAASC). Supported by NEA, Arkansas Art Council. Average statistics (all sections): 151 entries, 90 entrants, 60 accepted works. Held at SEAASC, Pine Bluff for 5 weeks. Have painting workshop. Publish *Arkansas Out-of-Doors* (monthly). Second contact: 7509 Cantrell Road, Suite 210, Little Rock, Arkansas 72207.

DRAWING CONTEST: **Pen and Ink, Pencil Arkansas Wildlife,** original, never reproduced, 3x3 feet maximum, suitable for hanging; limit 3 per entrant (all sections). Submit 35mm slides for entry review. No unnatural scenes.

PAINTING CONTEST: Acrylic, Oil, Watercolor Arkansas Wildlife. No wet paintings. Other requirements, restrictions same as for Drawing.

MIXED MEDIA CONTEST: Arkansas Wildlife. No wet work. Other requirements, restrictions same as for Drawing.

AWARDS: (all sections): $750 Grand Purchase Award (becomes AWF Painting of the Year, reproduced for members), $250 Second, $150 Third, 4 $50 Honorable Mention Awards. Selected work may become part of 6-month traveling exhibition.

JUDGING: By 1 art professional. Sponsor may reproduce accepted entries for educational, publicity purposes. Not responsible for loss or damage.

SALES TERMS: Work may be for sale. All sales handled by SEAASC. 20% commission charge.

ENTRY FEE: $5 each plus return shipping.

DEADLINES: Entry, judging, June. Notifications, July. Event, August-September.

13

Ducks Unlimited National Wildlife Art Show

William A. Anderson, Jr., Director
P. O. Box 26130
City Center Square
Kansas City, Missouri 64196 U.S.A.
Tel: (816) 842-2300

Entry November

International; entry open to all; annual in March; established 1971. Purpose: to raise money for Ducks Unlimited. Sponsored by Ducks Unlimited. Average statistics (all sections): 1000 entries, 100 entrants. Held at Hilton Plaza Inn, Kansas City for 2 days. Have lodging, food, parking.

ART FAIR: All Media Wildlife Art; original, unlimited entry. Require donation of 1 work for judging and auction. Submit monochrome photograph (5x7 or 8x10 inches) and color slide of donated entry for entry review.

AWARDS: $500 Best of Show. $200 Judges' Order of Merit Awards.

JUDGING: Only donated entries are judged and auctioned. Sponsor may reproduce entries for publicity.

SALES TERMS: 50% commission charge on auctioned works. No commission charge on other sales.

ENTRY FEE: $150 (refundable) for 7x10-foot display rack or 3x8-foot table.

DEADLINES: Entry, November. Judging, event, March.

14

Energy Art Exhibition

Foothills Art Center
Marian J. Metsopoulos, Executive Director
809 15th Street
Golden, Colorado 80401 U.S.A.

Entry January

International; **entry open to U.S., Canada, Mexico;** annual in March-April; established 1982. Purpose: to encourage production or art reflecting positive aspect of energy and environment. Sponsored by and held at Foothills Art Center for 5 weeks. Supported by energy industry. Average statistics (all sections): 1000 entries, 150 finalists, 25 awards, 5000 attendance. Also sponsor North American Sculpture Exhibition, Rocky Mountain National Watermedia Exhibition.

DRAWING CONTEST: Energy Theme (including pastel) in permanent medium, original, 30x40 inches maximum (including frame), covered with glass or plexiglass, framed (wood or metal), wired, ready for hanging; limit 3 per entrant per section. Submit 2x2-inch 35mm slides (in cardboard or thin plastic mounts) for entry review. No copies from any other media, cooperative work. Competition includes photography (all sections).

PAINTING CONTEST: Oil, Water Media, Mixed Media Energy Theme. Requirements, restrictions same as for Drawing.

SCULPTURE CONTEST: Energy Theme, in permanent medium, original, maximum 4x4x4 feet (24x36 inches, bas relief), 500 pounds; limit 3 per entrant per section. Artist responsible for assembly. Submit 2x2-inch 35mm slides (in cardboard or thin plastic mounts) for entry review. No fiber or foam, copies from other media, or cooperative work.

AWARDS: (all sections): 25 Cash Awards totaling $15,000.

JUDGING: Entry review by 3, awards judging by 2 art professionals. Sponsor may photograph accepted work for catalog, calendar, publicity; keeps slides of accepted entries; insures work during exhibit only.

SALES TERMS: All work must be for sale. 30% commission charge.

ENTRY FEE: $10 per work.

DEADLINES: Entry, January. Acceptance, February. Awards, March. Event, March-April.

15

Harness Tracks of America Annual Art Competition and Auction

Stanley F. Bergstein, Executive Vice-President
35 Airport Road
Morristown, New Jersey 07960
U.S.A. Tel: (201) 285-9090

Entry August

International; entry open to all; annual in October; established 1976. Purpose: to encourage and create quality, professional art reflecting sport of harness racing. Sponsored and supported by Harness Tracks of America. Average statistics (all sections): 430 entries, 71 semifinalists, 600 attendance, $39,000 sales. Held in Lexington, Kentucky for 1 week during Grand Circuit Meeting at Red Mile. Publish *Horseman & Fair World, Harness Horse.* Second contact: Sara Short, United States Trotting Association, 750 Michigan Avenue, Columbus, Ohio 43215.

DRAWING CONTEST: Harness Racing, on paper, original, 36x48 inches maximum, framed; unlimited entry. Submit slides for entry review. No copies from photographs. Competition includes other unspecified visual arts media.

PAINTING CONTEST: Acrylic, Oil, Mixed Media Harness Racing, on canvas or panel.

Water Media Harness Racing, on paper. Requirements, restrictions same as for Drawing.

PRINT CONTEST: Harness Racing (including etchings), on paper. Requirements, restrictions same as for Drawing.

SCULPTURE CONTEST: Bronze, Plaster, Wood, Composition Harness

Racing. Requirements, restrictions same as for Drawing.

AWARDS: $1000 First, $500 Second, $300 Third, $200 Fourth Prize to works on canvas or panel. $750 First, $375 Second, $225 Third, $150 Fourth Prize each to works on paper, other media including sculpture. 2 Special Excellence Awards, each section.

JUDGING: By guest juror. Based on quality, technical accuracy, potential saleability, use for promotional purposes.

SALES TERMS: Works are auctioned. 30% commission charge.

ENTRY FEE: Not specified.

DEADLINES: Entry, August. Judging, event, October.

16

Kiamichi Owa-Chito Art Show
McCurtain County Art Club
Judie Miller, President
Route 1, Box 43-C
Idabel, Oklahoma 74745 U.S.A.
Tel: (405) 286-3921

Entry June

Regional; **entry open to Oklahoma, Texas, Arkansas, Louisiana;** annual in June. Sponsored by McCurtain County Art Club, Owa-Chito Committee. Supported by First State Bank of Idabel, Museum of Red River. Average statistics: 200 entries, 50 entrants, 25 awards. Held in Beaver's Bend State Park for 3 days. Have park facilities, Forest Heritage and Festival events. Second contact: Forest Heritage Center, P. O. Box 157, Broken Bow, Oklahoma 74728; tel: (405) 494-6497.

PAINTING CONTEST: Any Medium Forest Heritage, Indian-Related, original, 48x48 inches maximum, framed, ready for hanging; limit 5 per entrant. Completed in previous year. No copies; lewd, distasteful entries. Divisions: Adult, Student (McCurtain County Kindergarten-12th grade only).

AWARDS: $600 Purchase Award to best of show. $400 Purchase Award to Heritage of Forest. $300 to Western painting. $300 Purchase Award to Indian painting by Indian artist. $300 Purchase Award to Indian-oriented painting. Ribbons to all winners. Student division: First, Second, Third Place Ribbons.

JUDGING: By accredited judge. Not responsible for loss or damage.

SALES TERMS: All work must be for sale. 20% commission charge.

ENTRY FEE: $4 each work plus return postage.

DEADLINES: Entry, event, June.

ART HISTORY FELLOWSHIPS, INTERNSHIPS

Residence Fellowships and Internships primarily for STUDY, RESEARCH, and MUSEUM TRAINING in Art History. Includes AFRICAN, AMERICAN, EUROPEAN, SPANISH ART HISTORY. (Also see RESIDENCE GRANTS, SCHOLARSHIPS, FELLOWSHIPS.)

17

American Academy in Rome-NEH Fellowships
41 East 65th Street
New York, New York 10021 U.S.A.
Tel: (212) 535-4250

Entry June-November

National; **entry open to U.S.;** annual for academic year. Purpose: to promote study and practice of fine arts, archaeology, literature, history. Sponsored by and held at American Academy in Rome (founded 1894). Supported by NEH.

ART HISTORY RESIDENCE FELLOWSHIPS: Postdoctoral Study. Approximately 5 $7200 1-year fellowships (includes $450 monthly stipend, $1400 travel allowance, $400-$900 supply allowance, housing allowance to married fellows with children) to U.S. doctoral graduates for study of fine arts, archaeology, literature, history of classical and later periods. Competition includes classical studies, postclassical humanistic studies, modern Italian studies.

DEADLINES: Application, June-November.

18

Hirshhorn Museum and Sculpture Garden Summer Internships

Smithsonian Institution
Edward P. Lawson, Education Department
Washington, DC 20560 U.S.A.
Tel: (202) 357-1300

Entry February

International; entry open to all; annual in Summer. Museum opened in 1974 with focus on American and European painting, sculpture, and drawing of 19th and 20th centuries. Named after Joseph Hirshhorn, principal donator. Sponsored by Smithsonian Institution. Held at Hirshhorn Museum for 10 weeks. Have permanent collection of over 6500 works, loan exhibitions, research-educational facilities. Also sponsor scholarships, fellowships, internships in fields actively pursued by Smithsonian Institution.

ART HISTORY INTERNSHIPS: American-European Drawing-Painting-Sculpture Museum Training. 5 internships to undergraduate students completing junior or senior year by June with 12 semester hours of art history, for work on specific museum departmental projects and seminars on museum collection and organization. Academic credit may be arranged.

DEADLINES: Application, February. Event, Summer.

19

John Carter Brown Library Research Fellowships

The Librarian
Brown University
Providence, Rhode Island 02912
U.S.A.

Entry February

International; **entry open to U.S.;** annual. Named after John Carter Brown, who established early American history library in 1846. Sponsored and supported by John Carter Brown Library, Brown University. Have library facilities, bibliographical reference collections.

ART HISTORY RESIDENCE FELLOWSHIPS: Early American Prints Research. Unspecified number of $800 monthly stipends tenable for 1-6 months to pre-, postdoctoral scholars for research appropriate to resources of library. Submit curriculum vitae, project statement, 3 recommendation letters. Competition includes anthropology, archaeology, linguistics.

JUDGING: By John Carter Brown Faculty Liaison Committee. Based on scholarly qualifications, project merits, appropriateness to Library resources.

DEADLINES: Application, February. Notification, April. Awards, June-July.

20

Metropolitan Museum of Art Residence Fellowships
Fifth Avenue at 82nd Street
New York, New York 10028 U.S.A.
Tel: (212) 879-5500

Entry January

International; **entry open to doctoral, postdoctoral students;** annual for academic year. Sponsored by Metropolitan Museum of Art. Supported by museum, bequest from late curator-in-chief.

ART HISTORY RESIDENCE FELLOWSHIPS: Graduate, Professional, Postdoctoral Independent Study *(Chester Dale Fellowships).* $8000 maximum stipends plus $500 for related expenses per academic year to painter, sculptor, art historian, critic (preferably American citizen under age 40) to study fine arts of Western world at museum for 3 months to 1 year.

Graduate Research Project. *Andrew W. Mellon Fellowships:* $8000 maximum 1-year stipends plus $150 for related expenses per academic year to promising young scholar for research project related to museum collections; or to scholar serving as teacher-advisor for cataloging and refining museum collections with expertise. *J. Clawson Mills Scholarships:* $8000 maximum stipends plus $1500 for related expenses per academic year to scholar pursuing research project related to museum's collections.

MUSEUM CURATOR RESIDENCE FELLOWSHIPS: Doctoral-Postdoctoral Study in Europe *(Theodore Rousseau Fellowships).* $8000 maximum stipends plus $500 related expenses (amount varies depending on circumstances) to students of curatorship for related study in Europe. Submit application, resume, transcripts, 3 recommendation letters, project description.

DEADLINE: Entry, January. Fellowships for academic year.

21

Museum of African Art Academic Internships
Nancy Nooter, Internship Coordinator
318 A Street N.E.
Washington, DC 20002 U.S.A.

Entry continuous

International; entry open to all; annual for academic year. Museum established 1964 in Washington residence of Frederick Douglass, now expanded to include 9 townhouses. Purpose: to foster public understanding of Africa's rich creative heritage. Sponsored by and held at Smithsonian Institution Museum of African Art during academic semester or summer session. Have 8000-object permanent collection, photographic archives, library, loan exhibitions, publications, elementary and secondary educational materials and programs.

ART HISTORY INTERNSHIPS: African Art Museum Training. 6 maximum internships during academic semesters, 8 during summer sessions to candidates in junior or senior years or in graduate school with majors in art history, for museum work and related research. Competition includes anthropology, humanities.

DEADLINES: Application, six weeks before beginning of academic term. Event, academic year.

22

National Collection of Fine Arts (NCFA) Summer Internships
Smithsonian Institution
Patricia Chieffo
Committee on Professional Training Programs
8th and G Streets N.W.
Washington, DC 20560 U.S.A.

Entry January

International; **entry open to students;** annual in Summer. NCFA (founded 1937) is central depository for works of art under jurisdiction of Smithsonian. Formerly concerned with European and Oriental art, now directs attention to American art. Purpose: to foster appreciation of American art. Sponsored by Smithsonian Institution. Held at NCFA for 9 weeks. Have Renwick Gallery of crafts and design, Archives of American Art, library, conservation laboratory, photographic department. Also sponsor scholarships, fellowships, internships in fields actively pursued by Smithsonian.

ART HISTORY INTERNSHIPS: American Fine Art-Design Museum Training. 3 9-week internships to students completing junior or senior years or enrolled in graduate school with strong background in art history or studio art for work in 1 department of museum.

DEADLINES: Application, January. Event, Summer.

23

National Gallery of Art Center for Advanced Study in the Visual Arts Predoctoral Fellowship Program
Douglas Lewis
Washington, DC 20565 U.S.A.
Tel: (202) 737-4215

Entry November

International; **entry open to Ph.D. candidates;** annual. Purpose: to facilitate productive scholarly work in art history, architecture, Western urban form. Sponsored by National Gallery of Art. Also sponsor fellowships and grants.

ART HISTORY RESIDENCE FELLOWSHIPS: Research, Book, or Doctoral Dissertation Advancement-Completion. *David E. Finley Fellowship:* 1 $27,000 grant (disbursed in monthly payments amounting to $9000 per year for 3 years) to student for 2 years' European travel and research on advanced dissertation topic, plus period spent in research at National Gallery of Art. *Chester Dale Fellowship:* 4 $9000 1-year fellowships (disbursed in 9 monthly payments) to students for advancement of doctoral dissertation in U.S. and-or abroad. *Samuel H. Kress Fellowship:* 2 $18,000 2-year residencies (disbursed in 9 monthly payments each year) to students for curatorial research at National Gallery. Equal time may be devoted to dissertation work elsewhere in U.S. or abroad. *Robert H. and Clarice Smith Fellowship:* 1 $9000 1-year fellowship (disbursed in 9 monthly checks) to student for work on dissertation or book on Dutch or Flemish art. May work in U.S. or abroad. Candidates for all fellowships must submit statement of project, report of previous research, schedule of grant work, short biography, curriculum vitae with work samples accepted for publication, completed course transcripts, evidence of language examination passed, recommendation letter by chairman, 2 supporting letters from faculty.

ELIGIBILITY: Doctoral candidates who have completed course work and 1 year's research on proposed dissertation topic. Must be sponsored by Art History department.

DEADLINES: Application, November. Notification, May.

24

National Gallery of Art Center for Advanced Study in the Visual Arts Senior Fellow Program

Washington, DC 20565 U.S.A.
Tel: (202) 737-4215

Entry October

International; **entry open to Ph.D. or equivalent;** annual for up to full academic year. Purpose: to facilitate study of history, theory, criticism of art, architecture, urbanism. Sponsored by National Gallery of Art. Have collections, library, photographic archives, lectures, access to Library of Congress, specialized libraries, collections. Also sponsor Visiting Senior Fellowships, other fellowships and grants.

ART HISTORY RESIDENCE FELLOWSHIPS: Postdoctoral Study. *Senior Fellowships:* 1-year fellowships (2 years in special cases) including monthly stipend, materials, travel and housing allowances (support varies with individual need) to Ph.D. graduates for study of history, theory, criticism of visual arts (painting, sculpture, architecture, landscape architecture, urbanism, graphics, film, photography, decorative arts, industrial design, etc.). Submit financial statement. *Associate Fellowships:* 1-month to academic year fellowships to Ph.D. graduates who have obtained funding elsewhere. Qualifications same as for Senior Fellows.

ELIGIBILITY: Recent recipients of doctoral degree (or equivalent) or experienced scholars in visual arts; or scholars whose work examines physical objects, analyzes or criticizes physical form (i.e., archaeology, anthropology, history, urban geography).

JUDGING: By selection board of art history scholars.

DEADLINES: Application, October (March for Associate appointments less than 1 academic term). Fellowships for up to full academic year.

25

Smithsonian Institution Research Fellowships

Smithsonian Institution Office of Fellowships & Grants
Room 3300, L'Enfant Plaza
Washington, DC 20560 U.S.A.
Tel: (202) 287-3271

Entry January

International; entry open to all; annual for academic year. Purpose: to further research training of scholars in early stages of careers. Sponsored by and held at Smithsonian Institution for 6 months to 1 year. Have scholarships, fellowships, internships in sciences, arts, humanities, social sciences. Also sponsor Daniel & Florence Guggenheim Fellowship, Woodrow Wilson International Center for Scholars Residential Research Fellowships.

ART HISTORY RESIDENCE FELLOWSHIPS: Research Training *(Visiting Research Program).* Unspecified number of fellowships to help defray research-related and relocation expenses for research in field in which Smithsonian has particular strength for periods from 6 months to 1 year. **Predoctoral-Postdoctoral Fellowships:** Minimum $9000 predoctoral to candidates with completed course work and examinations, engaged in dissertation research; $16,000 postdoctoral to candidates within 5 years of completion of degree (5-year limitation may be waived, candidates with equivalent of doctorate may be considered). **Graduate Student Fellowships:** $105 per week for 10 weeks. Submit detailed proposal indicating why Smithsonian Institution is best place for study. Require residence at Smithsonian facilities. Competition includes natural history, science, environmental sciences, technology, American studies.

DEADLINES: Application, January. Fellowship for academic year.

26

Winterthur Program in Early American Culture Fellowships

Dr. Stephanie G. Wolf, Coordinator
University of Delaware
Newark, Delaware 19711 U.S.A.
Tel: (302) 738-2678

Entry January

International; **entry open to graduate or college seniors receiving undergraduate degree before program;** annual for 2-year program; established 1952. Purpose: to provide multidisciplinary approach to study of American decorative arts and material culture (including anthropology, art history, English, history, museum studies); encourage work in related areas. Sponsored by University of Delaware and the Winterthur Museum. Average statistics: 150 entrants, 20 semifinalists, 10 awards. Have mandatory summer program, field trips, museum training; optional courses and museum internships; museum, library, visiting scholars.

ART HISTORY RESIDENCE FELLOWSHIPS: **Early American Fine-Decorative Arts Graduate Study.** 5-10 fellowships, each including general stipend plus tuition fees and $500 travel allowance, for 2-year program (42 credit hours) at University of Delaware, leading to Master of Arts degree with concentration in American decorative arts, material culture. Submit college and Graduate Record Examination transcripts; 3 recommendation letters; education, experience, personal history, statement of purpose, background. Require acceptance to University of Delaware graduate division; interview (travel and accommodation paid by Winterthur Museum) for semifinalists. No language requirements.

ELIGIBILITY: College graduates at time program begins; minimum grade point average of 2.5 overall, 3.0 in major field; combined Graduate Record Examination score of 1050 in verbal, quantitative; undergraduate major in American studies, history, literature, art history, and-or sociology, anthropology, folklore, etc; demonstrated interest in program.

JUDGING: Entry review by University or museum staff, teachers.

ENTRY FEE: $20 graduate division application fee.

DEADLINES: Application, January. Interview (final screening), March. Scholarship for 2 academic years following.

27

U.S.-Spanish Joint Committee for Educational and Cultural Affairs Postdoctoral Research Grants

Joint Administrative Staff
Calle Cartagena, 83-85, 3
Madrid 28, SPAIN Tel: 255-0800, ext. 221

Entry February

National; **entry open to postdoctoral candidates;** annual in September; established 1976. Purpose: to enable students to do postdoctoral research in arts and sciences in Spain. Sponsored and supported by U.S.-Spanish Joint Committee for Educational and Cultural Affairs. Also sponsor Additional Artistic Studies Grants, Grants for the Dissemination of Spanish Culture in the U.S. Second contact: Council for International Exchange of Scholars, Suite 300, Eleven Dupont Circle, Washington, D.C. 20036; tel: (202) 833-4967.

ART HISTORY RESIDENCE FELLOWSHIPS: Postdoctoral Research in Spain. $1000-$1600 per month (depending on number of dependents) for 4-10 consecutive months, plus health and accident insurance, roundtrip travel expenses, 50% of first dependent's travel expenses, to students for pursuing postdoctoral degree.

ELIGIBILITY: Open to U.S. citizen with doctoral degree and some proficiency in Spanish language; in contact with Spanish university of choice or have received invitation to conduct research. No persons holding governmental positions, or associated with Sponsor.

DEADLINES: Application, February. Grants, September (10 months), February (4 months).

DRAWING

General Drawing in any medium. (Also see other DRAWING CATEGORIES.)

Appalachian National Drawing Competition
Appalachian State University Art Department
Willard Pilchard, Director
Boone, North Carolina 28608 U.S.A.
Tel: (704) 262-2220

Entry not specified

International; entry open to all; annual in Spring; established 1973. Purpose: to recognize drawing as fundamental and primary medium in art. Sponsored by Appalachian State University Foundation. Average statistics: 1000 entries, 3 countries, 5 awards. Held in Farthing Gallery for 3 weeks.

DRAWING CONTEST: General. Requirements, restrictions not specified.

AWARDS: $2000 in Purchase Awards.

JUDGING: By nationally known artists, critics.

DEADLINES: Entry not specified. Event, Spring.

Potsdam National Drawing Exhibition
State University of New York (SUNY)-Potsdam
Georgia Coopersmith, Gallery Director
Brainerd Art Gallery
College of Arts and Sciences
Potsdam, New York 13676 U.S.A.
Tel: (315) 268-2710

Entry February

National; **entry open to U.S.;** biennial (odd years) in March; established 1977. Alternates with Potsdam National Print Exhibition (even years). Sponsored by State University College of Arts and Sciences, Potsdam. Held at Brainerd Art Gallery for 4 weeks (may travel). Second contact: Arthur Sennet, Chair, Art Department, SUNY Potsdam, Potsdam, New

York 13676.

DRAWING CONTEST: Any Medium General, no size restrictions, matted or mounted on stiff board, covered with acetate or otherwise protected (no glass); limit 2 per entrant.

AWARDS: Purchase Awards.

JUDGING: By 1 juror. Sponsor insures during exhibition only; may reproduce accepted entries for catalog, publicity purposes.

SALES TERMS: 10% commission charge. Drawings not for sale should be marked.

ENTRY FEE: $10 plus postage.

DEADLINES: Entry, February. Event, March.

30

Cleveland (U.K.) International Drawing Biennale

Mike Hill, Organzier
P. O. Box 41
Middlesbrough, Cleveland TS1 2HE, ENGLAND Tel: 0642-248155, ext. 3375

Entry February

International; entry open to all; biennial in September-May; established 1973. Purpose: to promote good draughtsmanship, encourage creativity, re-establish importance of original drawing. Sponsored by Cleveland County Council, Arts Council of Great Britain, Northern Arts. Supported by Sotheby Parke Bernet. Average statistics: 3200 entries, 55 countries, 104 finalists, 10 awards. Held at various galleries throughout U.K. Second contact: Education Offices, Woodlands Road, Middlesbrough, Cleveland, England.

DRAWING CONTEST: General. Requirements, restrictions not specified.

AWARDS: £1000, 2 £750, 2 £500, 5 £300, and Purchase Prizes.

JUDGING: By 3 independent artists, critics, curators.

DEADLINES: Entry, February. Judging, May-June. Event, September-May.

DRAWING, PAINTING, MIXED MEDIA

Drawing, Painting, and Mixed Media including Charcoal, Ink, Pastel, Pencil, and Acrylic, Gouache, Oil, Watercolor. (Also see other DRAWING, PAINTING CATEGORIES.)

31

Brush and Palette Club National Art Exhibition

Marian Young, President
P. O. Box 338
Fruita, Colorado 81521 U.S.A.
Tel: (303) 858-3944

Entry June

International; entry open to all; annual in Summer; established 1946. Purpose: to give artists chance to exhibit, sell work, compete for prizes. Sponsored by Grand Junction Chamber of Commerce, Western Colorado Center for the Arts (WCCA). Average statistics: 500 entries, 250 entrants, 50 awards, 50-75 total sales. Held at WCCA for 3 weeks. Second contact: WCCA, 1803 North Seventh Street, Grand Junction, Colorado 81501.

DRAWING CONTEST: General (including charcoal, ink, pastel, pencil), original, 36x48 inches maximum including frame, wired for hanging; limit 2 per entrant (all sections). No class or supervised work. Divisions: Professional, Advanced, Amateur.

PAINTING CONTEST: Acrylic, Oil, Watercolor General. No wet paintings. Other requirements, restrictions, divisions same as for Drawing.

MIXED MEDIA CONTEST: General (including batik). No crafts, photographs. Other requirements, restrictions, divisions same as for Drawing.

AWARDS: $100 Grand Champion, $50 Reserve Champion Award (all sections). First, Second, Third, Popular Choice Awards, Honorable Mention, each division. Purchase Awards, Ribbons.

JUDGING: By 1-2 nationally recognized artists. Sponsor may photograph, reproduce entries for publicity. Not responsible for loss or damage.

SALES TERMS: All work must be for sale. 15% commission charge.

ENTRY FEE: $5 each (add $2 handling fee for shipped entries).

DEADLINES: Entry, June. Event, June-July.

32

California Survey of Watercolor and Drawing Competition

Humboldt Cultural Center
Jeffrey Hoffman, Gallery Manager
422 First Street
Eureka, California 95501 U.S.A.
Tel: (707) 442-2611

Entry February

State; **entry open to California;** annual in March; established 1981. Purpose: to survey California watercolor and drawing. Sponsored and supported by Humboldt Cultural Center, Humboldt Arts Council, Humboldt State University Art Department and Center Arts. Average statistics: 200 entries, 115 entrants, 60 finalists, 5 awards. Held at Humboldt Cultural Center in Eureka for 4 weeks. Also sponsor Made with Wood, Glass as Art (annual) competitions.

DRAWING CONTEST: General, original, unmatted, unframed. No photographs, prints. Competition includes watercolor.

PAINTING CONTEST: Watercolor General. Restrictions and requirements same as for Drawing.

AWARDS: 5 $200 Cash Prizes.

JUDGING: By competent artist. Sponsor may reproduce entries for publicity. Not responsible for loss or damage.

SALES TERMS: Work need not be for sale. 33-1/3% commission charge.

ENTRY FEE: $10 per work. Sponsor pays return postage.

DEADLINES: Entry, February. Event, March.

33

Greater Kingsport Competitive Art Show

First Eastern National Bank
Karen A. Sprinkle
P. O. Box 889
Kingsport, Tennessee 37662 U.S.A.
Tel: (615) 247-6111, ext. 378

Entry February

Regional; **entry open to Greater Kingsport Area artists over age 15;** annual in February; established 1964. Purpose: to recognize local artists; promote public relations. Sponsored by First Eastern National Bank (formerly National Bank of Sullivan

County), Kingsport Art Guild. Average statistics: 140 entries, 23 awards, 500 attendance. Held in Kingsport for 2 weeks.

DRAWING CONTEST: Charcoal, Ink, Pastel, Pencil General, original, 48x60 inches maximum including frame, framed, wired for hanging, titled; limit 1 per entrant (all sections). Completed in previous 2 years. No previous award winners.

PAINTING CONTEST: Acrylic, Oil, Watercolor General. No wet paintings. Other requirements, restrictions same as for Drawing.

MIXED MEDIA CONTEST: General. No wet work. Other requirements, restrictions same as for Drawing.

AWARDS: $200 to best of show. $100 First, $50 Second, $25 Third Prize each section. 9 $25 Awards of Excellence; $25 Popular Vote Award Ribbons (all sections).

JUDGING: By 1 local accredited judge. Sponsor may reject unsuitable entries. Not responsible for loss or damage.

SALES TERMS: Work may be priced for sale. No commission charge.

ENTRY FEE: $3 per work.

DEADLINES: Entry, event, February.

34

Puget Sound Area Painting Exhibition

Charles and Emma Frye Art Museum
Terry at Cherry
P. O. Box 3005
Seattle, Washington 98114 U.S.A.
Tel: (206) 622-9250

Entry February

Regional; **entry open to Puget Sound area;** annual in April; established 1959. Purpose: to encourage local artists. Sponsored and supported by Charles and Emma Frye Museum. Held at museum for 3 weeks. Publish *Frye Vues* (monthly).

DRAWING CONTEST: Pastel General, original, 10x12 to 42x42 inches, framed; limit 1 per entrant. Produced in previous 2 years. No graphics; previously exhibited entries. Competition includes painting.

PAINTING CONTEST: Any Medium General, dry. Restrictions, requirements same as for Drawing.

ELIGIBILITY: Open to Clallam, Grays Harbor, Island, Jefferson, King, Kitsap, Mason, Pierce, San Juan, Skagit, Snohomish, Thurston, Whatcom counties in Washington.

AWARDS: $1000 First Place Purchase Prize. $350 Second, $250 Third Place Cash Awards. Paintings not for sale ineligible for Purchase Prize.

JUDGING: By competent artist. Sponsor insures entries while in museum. Not responsible for loss or damage.

SALES TERMS: Work need not be for sale. 20% commission charge.

ENTRY FEE: None. Entrant Pays return postage.

DEADLINES: Entry, February. Event, April.

35

Inveresk International Artists in Watercolor Competition

Inveresk Paper Company Ltd.
E. D. Rex
Gower Richards Promotions
96 High Street
Billericay, Essex CM12 9BT,
ENGLAND Tel: Billericay 59952-3

Entry May

International; entry open to all; biennial in August-September (odd years); established 1973. Sponsored by Inveresk Paper Company Ltd. Held in Mall Galleries, London for 2 weeks. Second contact: 62 Ozonia Avenue, Wickford, Essex, England; tel: Wickford 3812.

DRAWING CONTEST: **Pastel General,** on T.H. Sanders or Bockingford paper or board, no size restrictions. Submit 35mm slide for entry review. Divisions: U.S., Canada, U.K. and Ireland, Other Countries, Junior.

PAINTING CONTEST: **Acrylic, Gouache, Watercolor General.** Requirements and divisions same as for Drawing.

AWARDS (all sections): Over £ 7000 in Prizes including continental holidays for U.K. entrants, Cash Prizes to overseas entrants. Merchandise Prizes. All finalists exhibited.

JUDGING: By 3 art professionals. Sponsor may reproduce entries in publications, calendar. Not responsible for loss or damage.

ENTRY FEE: 80p each work.

DEADLINES: Entry, May (slides) July (works). Event, August-September.

DRAWING, PAINTING, PRINTS

Drawing, Painting, Prints including Pastel, Acrylic, Oil, Watercolor. (Also see other DRAWING, PAINTING, PRINT CATEGORIES.)

36

Artists' Days at Vizcaya International Competition

Vizcaya Museum & Gardens
Rick Vahan, Public Information
3251 South Miami Avenue
Miami, Florida 33129 U.S.A.

Entry February

International; entry open to all; annual in February; established 1958. Purpose: to promote annual revival of life, costumes, music of Villa Vizcaya (Italian Renaissance palace). Sponsored by The Renaissance Guild. 220 maximum participants. Held at Vizcaya Museum, Miami for 3 days. Tickets: $3.50. Also sponsor Renaissance Festival (annual). Second contact: Renaissance Guild, Chris Laham; tel: (305) 758-8458.

DRAWING CONTEST: **General, Vizcaya Villa-Grounds;** limit 1 per entrant (first day), 3 per entrant (second day). Artists admitted free to grounds for 2 weekends prior to competition to create work. Submit 2 slides of work for entry review (booth space). No dealers. Categories: General, Vizcaya Villa-Grounds. Competition includes photography, other 2D media.

PAINTING CONTEST: **Acrylic, Oil, Watercolor General, Vizcaya Villa-Grounds.** Requirements, restrictions, categories same as for Drawing.

PRINT CONTEST: **General, Vizcaya Villa-Grounds.** No commercially reproduced prints. Requirements, restrictions, categories same as for Drawing.

AWARDS (all sections): $500 First, $300 Second, $100 Third Prize to best in show (first day). $500 First (purchase prize) plus $100 Founders Prize, Plaque; $125 Second, $75 Third Prize to art depicting Villa Vizcaya, grounds (second day). Honorable Mention Ribbons.

JUDGING: By 3 art critics.

ENTRY FEE: $85 for space (optional). $2.50 (competition only). No sales commission charge.

DEADLINES: Entry, event, February.

37

Kansas National Small Painting, Drawing and Print Exhibition
Fort Hays State University Art Department
Zoran Stevanov, Exhibition Chair
600 Park Street
Hays, Kansas 67601 U.S.A.
Tel: (913) 628-4247

Entry December

National; **entry open to U.S.;** annual in February-March; established 1974. Purpose: to provide exhibition on contemporary visual arts. Sponsored and supported by Fort Hays State University Art Department. Average statistics: 550 entries, 200 entrants, 75 finalists, 15 awards, $300 average sales per entrant. Held at Visual Arts Center Art Gallery, Rarick Hall Campus, Fort Hays State University for 6 weeks.

DRAWING CONTEST: General (including charcoal, pastel, pencil), on paper or paper substance, maximum 84 inches total length and width, 40 pounds, (including crate), mounted or matted with heavy backboarding, covered with clear acetate (including mat), no glass, unframed, fixative recommended on soft media; limit 2 per entrant. Submit 2x2-inch slides for entry review.

PAINTING CONTEST: General, maximum 84 inches total length and width, 40 pounds (including crate), framed; limit 2 per entrant. Submit 2x2-inch slides for entry review.

PRINT CONTEST: General (including monotypes, hand-colored, color photocopy), on paper or paper substance. Requirements same as for Drawing.

AWARDS: $400 Top Award. $350, $300, $250 Purchase Awards. $200 Art Department Purchase Award. 5 $100-$200 Cash Awards.

JUDGING: Entry review, awards judging by museum curator. Sponsor may reproduce entries for catalog, publicity. Not responsible for loss or damage.

SALES TERMS: 20% commission charge.

ENTRY FEE: $10 per entrant.

DEADLINES: Entry, December. Materials, January. Event, February-April.

38

Mid America Biennial Art Exhibition
Owensboro Museum of Fine Art (OMFA)
Jane Wilson, Registrar
901 Frederica Street
Owensboro, Kentucky 42301 U.S.A.
Tel: (502) 685-3181

Entry March

National; **entry open to U.S.;** biennial in Spring; established 1979. Formerly called MID AMERICA ART EXHIBITION. Purpose: to provide national art showcase in Middle America; acquire significant permanent collection by contemporary artists. Sponsored by OMFA. Supported by OMFA, private and corporate donations. Held at OMFA for 8 weeks.

DRAWING CONTEST: General, original, framed, covered by glass or plexiglass if on paper; limit 2 per entrant. Completed in previous 3 years.

PAINTING CONTEST: General. Requirements, restrictions same as for Drawing.

PRINT CONTEST: General. Requirements, restrictions same as for Drawing.

AWARDS: Average $16,500 in Cash and Purchase Awards. $5000 to best painting.

JUDGING: By nationally prominent judge. Not responsible for loss or damage.

SALES TERMS: All work must be for sale. 30% commission charge (excluding purchase awards).

ENTRY FEE: $15 1 entry, $20 2 entries plus return shipping.

DEADLINES: Entry, judging, March. Event, April-May.

39

North Kitsap Annual Open Art Show

North Kitsap Arts and Crafts Committee
Anne Thomas, Art Chair
1240 N.W. Comyn Road
Poulsbo, Washington 98370 U.S.A.
Tel: (206) 779-5243

Entry May

International; entry open to all; annual in May; established 1959. Purpose: to promote community arts, support local art scholarships. Sponsored by North Kitsap Arts and Crafts Committee. Supported by art patrons. Average statistics (all sections): 300 entries, 150 entrants, 5000 attendance, $4000 total sales. Held at North Kitsap Middle School, Poulsbo for 2 days. Have children's art tours, summer art classes. Second contact: Karen Small, Chair, 20867 Pugh Road, Poulsbo, Washington 98370.

DRAWING CONTEST: General, original, framed, ready for hanging, dry; limit 2 per entrant. Completed in previous 2 years. Divisions: Professional, Nonprofessional, Senior High School, Junior High School. Also have crafts show (by invitation) and juried photography show.

PAINTING CONTEST: General. Requirements, restrictions, divisions same as for Drawing.

PRINT CONTEST: General. Requirements, restrictions, divisions same as for Drawing.

AWARDS (all sections): $200 Award to best of show. $200 First, $150 Second, $100 Third Prize to professional. $125 First, $75 Second, $50 Third Prize to nonprofessional. $35 First, $25 Second, $15 Third Prize to senior high school. $20 First, $15 Second, $10 Third Prize to junior high school. $25 Viewer's Choice Award.

JUDGING: By 3 professional artists. May refuse inappropriate work. Not responsible for loss or damage.

SALES TERMS: Work need not be for sale. 20% commission charge.

ENTRY FEE: $3 professional; $1.50 nonprofessional; 50 senior, junior high school.

DEADLINES: Entry, event, May.

40

Parkersburg Art Center (PAC) Print, Painting, and Drawing Exhibition

William Simonett, Exhibit Coordinator
220 Eighth Street
P. O. Box 131

Parkersburg, West Virginia 26101
U.S.A. Tel: (304) 485-3859

Entry May

International; entry open to all; annual in June; established 1980. Purpose: to provide opportunities for sales and public forum for young artists. Sponsored by and held at PAC for 3 weeks. Supported by West Virginia Arts and Humanities Division, Department of Culture and History, NEA. Also sponsor photography exhibit, film festival.

DRAWING CONTEST: **General,** original, framed, ready for hanging; limit 2 per entrant (all sections). Produced in previous 3 years. No frames in poor condition, improper wiring.

PAINTING CONTEST: **General.** Requirements same as for Drawing.

PRINT CONTEST: **General.** Requirements same as for Drawing.

AWARDS: $900 in Cash Awards (all sections).

JUDGING: By 3 judges. Not responsible for loss or damage.

SALES TERMS: Work may be for sale. 30% commission charge.

ENTRY FEE: $5 plus return postage.

DEADLINES: Entry, May. Event, June. Materials returned, July.

41

Salmagundi Club Open Juried Nonmember Exhibition
Annette Lombard, Exhibition Chair
47 Fifth Avenue
New York, New York 10003 U.S.A.
Tel: (212) 255-7740

Entry April

National; **entry open to U.S.;** annual in May; established 1978. Sponsored and supported by Salmagundi Club (founded 1870), oldest professional art club in U.S. Average 175 entrants. Held at Salmagundi Club in New York City for 2 weeks. Have library, billiard room, 2 galleries, entertainment, exhibitions, lectures, demonstrations, classes.

DRAWING CONTEST: **General** (including pastel), 40x40 inches maximum including frame, framed, wired, ready for hanging; limit 1 per entrant. Submit 35mm color slides (residents outside 30-mile radius of New York City) for entry review.

PAINTING CONTEST: **Acrylic, Oil, Watercolor General.** Requirements, restrictions same as for Drawing.

PRINT CONTEST: **General.** Requirements, restrictions same as for Drawing.

AWARDS: Oil: $500 Emile Gruppe Award, $200, $100. Watercolor: 3 $100 Awards. Acrylic: $150, 2 $100 Awards, Bronze Medallion. Pastels: $100, $50, Pastel Society Brass Plaque. Drawings: 2 $50 Awards. Graphics: $100 Washington Square Award. $150 Philip Isenberg Award. Other Cash Awards, Club Awards, Merit Certificates. Salmagundi Club Awards.

JUDGING: By 7 artists. Not responsible for loss or damage.

SALES TERMS: Works need not be for sale. 20% commission charge.

ENTRY FEE: $12.

DEADLINES: Entry, April. Event, judging, May.

42

Santa Rosa Annual Statewide Art Show

Santa Rosa Art Guild (SRAG)
Betty Aust, Treasurer
3481 Guerneville Road
Santa Rosa, California 95401 U.S.A.

Entry July

State; **open to California artists over 18;** annual in August; established 1964. Sponsored by SRAG. Supported by SRAG, businesses, individuals. Average statistics: 650 entries, 200 entrants, $1250 total awards, 2000 attendance, $8000 in total sales. Held at Santa Rosa Veterans Memorial Building for 3-4 days. Second contact: Marion M. Barthel, 3134 Montgomery Drive, Santa Rosa, California 95405.

DRAWING CONTEST: **Pastel General,** original, 46x46 inches maximum including frame, under glass, ready for hanging; limit 8 per entrant (all sections). Completed in previous 2 years. Require hand-delivery. No obscene entries, work done under supervision, work partially or totally prepared by commercial printing methods. Also have graphics section.

PAINTING CONTEST: **Oil, Watercolor** (Traditional, Modern), original, watercolor under glass. Requirements and restrictions same as for Drawing. Categories: Oil, Watercolor (Modern, Traditional).

PRINT CONTEST: **General.** Restrictions and requirements same as for Drawing.

AWARDS: $150 Best of Show (all sections). $100 First, $50 Second, $25 Third, 2 $10 Honorable Mentions, each section and category.

JUDGING: By 3-4 judges. Not responsible for loss or damage.

SALES TERMS: Work need not be for sale. 25% commission charge.

ENTRY FEE: $4 each item.

DEADLINES: Entry, July. Event, awards, August.

43

Suntan Art Center Open Juried Show

Joella Hall
3300 Pass-a-Grille Way
St. Petersburg Beach, Florida 33706
U.S.A. Tel: (813) 343-4843

Entry September

Regional; **entry open to Tampa Bay Area;** annual in September; established 1980. Purpose: to promote art in community. Sponsored by and held at Suntan Art Center in St. Petersburg Beach for 3 weeks. Supported by St. Petersburg Beach Chamber of Commerce. Average statistics (all sections): 187 entries, 100 entrants, 3 awards, 500 attendance. Also sponsor art classes, workshops. Second contact: Joella Hall, 7954 9th Avenue South, St. Petersburg, Florida 33707.

DRAWING CONTEST: **General,** original, 44x44 inches maximum including frame, ready for hanging; limit 2 per entrant (all sections). Require hand-delivery. No previous award winners.

PAINTING CONTEST: **General.** Requirements same as for Drawing.

PRINT CONTEST: **General.** Requirements same as for Drawing.

AWARDS: $300 First, $200 Second, $100 Third Place Prize (all sections).

JUDGING: By 3 judges.

SALES TERMS: All work must be for sale. 20% commission charge.

ENTRY FEE: $10 per entrant.

DEADLINES: Entry, event, September. Materials returned, October.

44

White Lake Water Festival Art Exhibition
Elizabethtown-White Lake Chamber of Commerce
Elaine Lomax, Executive Secretary
Courthouse Drive
P. O. Box 306
Elizabethtown, North Carolina 28337
U.S.A. Tel: (919) 862-4368

Entry May

State; **entry open to North Carolina;** annual in May; established 1979. Purpose: to promote White Lake as a resort with water activities. Sponsored by The Water Festival, Elizabethtown-White Lake Chamber of Commerce, Bladen County Arts Council, Southeastern Arts Council, North Carolina Arts Council. Supported by local businesses. Held at Goldston Beach, White Lake for 3 days. Have craft show, golf tournament, dances, parades, performing arts, races, fireworks, shows. Also sponsor Water Festival Open Photography Competition and Exhibition. Second contact: Jane King, Director, Route 1, Box 334-C, Bladenboro, North Carolina 28320.

DRAWING CONTEST: Any Medium General, original, 60x60 inches maximum, framed or matted, ready for hanging; limit 3 per entrant (2 for Student). Require hand-delivery. Divisions: Adult, Student.

PAINTING CONTEST: Any Medium General. Requirements, restrictions, divisions same as for Drawing.

PRINT CONTEST: Any Type General. Requirements, restrictions, divisions same as for Drawing.

ELIGIBILITY: Age 19 or older residing in North Carolina. Student division: age 13-18 attending public or private school in North Carolina.

AWARDS: $600 in Cash Awards at judge's discretion.

JUDGING: By 1 artist (usually from North Carolina). Not responsible for loss or damage.

ENTRY FEE: $5. $2.50 (student). No sales commission charge.

DEADLINES: Entry, event, May.

DRAWING, PAINTING, PRINTS, COLLAGE, MIXED MEDIA

Drawing, Painting, Prints, Collage, Mixed Media including Crayon, Ink, Pastel, Pencil, and Acrylic, Oil, Watercolor. (Also see other DRAWING, PAINTING, PRINT CATEGORIES.)

45

Alice Lloyd College (ALC) Works on Paper Art Exhibition
Wendell Barry Stevens, Art Department Chair
Pippa Passas, Kentucky 41844
U.S.A. Tel: (606) 368-2101

Entry February

International; **entry open to U.S., Canada, Mexico, Puerto Rico;** annual in March-April; established 1980. Purpose: to provide international artists with exhibition opportunities; include quality art exhibits in academic program. Sponsored by ALC Art Department. Supported by ALC, local businesses. Average statistics: 200-1000 entries, 250-300 entrants, 6 awards, 150 attendance. Held at Red Bud Gallery, ALC, Pippa Passas for 1 month. Also sponsor ALC Traveling Exhibition service, children's free art classes.

DRAWING CONTEST: Any Medium General (including pastel), 48x48 inches maximum including mat, unframed, protected by acetate; limit 3 per entrant (all sections). Produced in previous 2 years. Submit mounted 2x2-inch 35mm slides for entry review. Entrants may participate in traveling exhibition (duration 1 year).

PAINTING CONTEST: Acrylic, Oil, Watercolor, Mixed Media General. Requirements same as for Drawing.

PRINT CONTEST: General. Requirements same as for Drawing.

COLLAGE CONTEST: General. Requirements same as for Drawing.

AWARDS: Purchase Prizes.

JUDGING: Entry review by 1 art professor. Sponsor may reproduce entries for publicity. Not responsible for loss or damage. No sales commission charge.

DEADLINES: Entry, February. Materials, March. Event, March-April.

46

American Annual at Newport Exhibition

Art Association of Newport (AAN)
Stephanie Shoemaker, Administrative Assistant
76 Bellevue Avenue
Newport, Rhode Island 02840 U.S.A.
Tel: (401) 847-0179

Entry July

National; **entry open to U.S.;** annual in Fall; established 1911. Average statistics: 500 entries, 177 entrants, 12 awards. Held at AAN Newport for 1 month. Have 4 galleries in historic Victorian building.

DRAWING CONTEST: General, (including pastel), 72x72 inches maximum including frame, ready to hang; limit 3 per entrant (all sections). Completed in previous 2 years. Submit slides for entry review. Competition includes photography sections.

PAINTING CONTEST: General, original. Requirements same as for Drawing.

PRINT CONTEST: General, original. Requirements same as for Drawing.

MIXED MEDIA: General. Requirements same as for Drawing.

AWARDS: $2500 in Cash Awards.

JUDGING: Entry review by 3 jurors. Awards judging by 1 professional. Sponsor insures work during exhibit only; not responsible for loss or damage while in transit.

SALES TERMS: %25 commission charge.

ENTRY FEE: $15 per entrant plus return postage.

DEADLINES: Entry, July. Acceptance, August. Materials, judging, September. Event, September-October.

47

Chautauqua National Exhibition of American Art

Chautauqua Art Association Galleries
Millie Giles, Director
Box 1365
Chautauqua, New York 14722
U.S.A. Tel: (716) 357-2771

Entry April

National; **entry open to U.S. residents age 18 and over;** annual in June-July; established 1957. Formerly called THE NATIONAL JURY SHOW to 1979. Purpose: to present artwork to summer audiences of Chautauqua Institution, provide exhibition opportunities for artists. Sponsored by Chautauqua Institution. Recognized by Gallery Association of New York State, Chautauqua County Art Association. Average statistics (all sections): 2500 entries, 1200 entrants, 76 finalists, 19 awards, 20,000 attendance, $1300 sales. Held at Chautauqua Institution for 3 weeks. Have 4 galleries, art lectures, film series. Also sponsor National Exhibition of American Art Sculpture Invitational. Second contact: P. O. Box 12916, N.T. Station, Denton, Texas 76203.

DRAWING CONTEST: General, original, maximum 60x72 inches, 100 pounds; framed, ready for hanging; limit 2 per entrant. Completed in previous 2 years. Submit 2 35mm slides (cardboard or thin plastic mounts) for entry review. Competition includes graphics, photography.

PAINTING CONTEST: General (including acrylic, oil, watercolor). Requirements, restrictions same as for Drawing.

PRINT CONTEST: General. Requirements, restrictions same as for Drawing.

MIXED MEDIA CONTEST: General. Requirements, restrictions same as for Drawing.

AWARDS: Over $4000 in Cash and Purchase Awards.

JUDGING: Entry review by notable artworld personage. Awards judging by 2 professionals. Sponsor may reproduce entries for publicity purposes. Not responsible for loss or damage.

SALES TERMS: Works need not be for sale. 25% commission charge.

ENTRY FEE: 1 entry $6, 2 entries $10 plus postage.

DEADLINES: Entry, notification, April. Event, June-July.

48

Dogwood Festival International Art Show

Atlanta Playhouse Theatre Ltd.
Sloan Borochoff
3450 Old Plantation Road N.W.
Atlanta, Georgia 30327 U.S.A.

Entry February

International; entry open to all; annual in March-April; established 1973. Purpose: to show international artists' works. Sponsored by Atlanta Womens Chamber of Commerce. Held at Georgia Tech Student Center Art Gallery for 3 weeks. Second contact: Becky Kirkland, 4724 Dudley Lane N.W., Atlanta, Georgia 30327.

DRAWING CONTEST: General. Submit 3 slides for entry review. Competition includes photography, textiles.

PAINTING CONTEST: General. Submit 3 slides for entry review.

PRINT CONTEST: General. Submit 3 slides for entry review.

COLLAGE CONTEST: General. Submit 3 slides for entry review.

AWARDS: Merit Awards. First, Second, Third Places. Purchase Prize for Georgia Tech Art Gallery.

JUDGING: By 1 qualified judge. Sponsor insures during exhibition only.

ENTRY FEE: $10.50 plus return shipping. No sales commission charge.

DEADLINES: Entry, February. Event, March-April. Awards, April.

49

San Jose Art League 2-Dimensional Art Regional Exhibition
482 South Second Street
San Jose, California 95113 U.S.A.
Tel: (408) 294-4545

Entry October

State; **entry open to California residents over age 18;** annual in October-November; established 1970. Formerly called ART REGIONAL to 1976. Purpose: to give recognition to emerging artists. Sponsored by San Jose Art League (nonprofit). Supported by Art League, Santa Clara Music and Arts Foundation, City of San Jose, Fine Arts Commission. Average statistics (all sections): 300 entries, 100 entrants, $1000 in awards. Held at Art League Galleries for 4 weeks. Also sponsor 3-D Regional, monthly Art Festival.

DRAWING CONTEST: **General** (including crayon, ink, pencil), original, 50 inches maximum width including frame, ready for hanging; unlimited entry. Require hand-delivery. No class work.

PAINTING CONTEST: **Acrylic, Oil, Watercolor, Mixed Media General,** dry. Requirements, restrictions same as for Drawing.

PRINT CONTEST: **General,** (including aquatints, etchings, lithographs, serigraphs). Requirements, restrictions same as for Drawing.

COLLAGE CONTEST: **General** (including fabric, paper). Requirements, restrictions same as for Drawing.

AWARDS: $1000 in Cash Awards (all sections).

JUDGING: By museum director. Not responsible for loss or damage.

SALES TERMS: Work need not be for sale. 25% commission charge.

ENTRY FEE: $5 each work (set equals 1).

DEADLINES: Entry, October. Event, October-November.

50

University of Wisconsin-Superior On-Of Paper Exhibition
University of Wisconsin-Superior Art Department
Patricia Spencer
Holden Fine Arts Center
Superior, Wisconsin 54880 U.S.A.
Tel: (715) 392-8101, ext. 391

Entry March

Regional; **entry open to over age 18 residing in Minnesota, Wisconsin, Iowa, North Dakota, South Dakota, Illinois, Nebraska, Michigan;** annual in Spring; established 1980. Purpose: to exhibit works, cross disciplines. Sponsored and supported by University of Wisconsin-Superior Art Department. Recognized by Arrowhead Regional Arts Commission, Minnesota Arts Board. Average statistics: 300 entries, 150 entrants, 2 awards. Held at Kruk Gallery (Holden Fine Arts Center) in Superior for 1 month. Have gallery, lecture-performance halls, art studios. Also sponsor University of Wisconsin-Superior Visual Arts Graduate Assistantships, High School Art Scholarship Competition ($300-$500 for study at University of Wisconsin-Superior).

DRAWING CONTEST: **Any Medium General** (including pastel), on paper, maximum 20x24 inches (if display under glass desired, 8x10, 11x14, 16x20, or 20x24 inches), framed, ready for hanging; limit 5 per entrant (includes all sections). Produced in previous 2 years. Competition includes photography, other works on-of paper.

PAINTING CONTEST: **Any Medium General,** on paper. Requirements, restrictions same as for Drawing.

PRINT CONTEST: **Any Type General,** on paper. Requirements, restrictions same as for Drawing.

COLLAGE CONTEST: **Any Medium General,** on paper. Requirements, restrictions same as for Drawing.

AWARDS: 2 $100 Merit Awards (all sections).

JUDGING: Entry review and awards judging by 1 art professional. Sponsor may photograph entries for publicity; insures during exhibition; not responsible for in-transit loss or damage.

ENTRY FEE: $5 each plus return postage and insurance. No sales commission charge.

DEADLINES: Entry, March. Notification, April. Event, April-May.

DRAWING, PAINTING, PRINTS, SCULPTURE

Drawing, Painting, Prints, and Sculpture in various media, including ABSTRACT, REPRESENTATIONAL. (Also see other DRAWING, PAINTING, PRINT, SCULPTURE CATEGORIES.)

51

Academic Artists Association National Exhibition of Contemporary Realism in Art

Marion Knight, Secretary
22 Pomeroy Street
Wilbraham, Massachusetts 01095
U.S.A.

Entry September

National; **entry open to U.S.;** annual in October-November; established 1949. Purpose: to encourage realistic art forms. Sponsored by Academic Artists Association. Average statistics (all sections): 300 entries and entrants. Held at Greek Cultural Center in Springfield for 3 weeks. Also sponsor annual Academic Artists Association Member Exhibition.

DRAWING CONTEST: **Representational,** all classic media including pastel, 40x40 inches maximum (excluding frame), suitable frame, under glass or plexiglass (works on paper), ready for hanging; limit 1 per entrant. Produced recently. Submit 1 35mm color slide for entry review (optional). No photographs, or entries previously shown in Springfield or adjacent area. Also have graphics section.

PAINTING CONTEST: **Oil, Watercolor, Representational.** Requirements, restrictions same as for Drawing.

PRINT CONTEST: **Representational,** all classic media. Restrictions, requirements same as for Drawing.

SCULPTURE CONTEST: **Representational,** all classic media, 250 pounds maximum (per work); limit 2 per entrant. Produced recently. Submit 5x7- or 8x10-inch photographs (2 views) for entry review. Require complete description. Not previously shown in Springfield or adjacent area. Also have graphics section.

AWARDS: 2 Gold Medals, $100 Grumbacher Awards (watercolor, oil). 2 $100 Associate Members Cash Awards (sculpture). 3 $100 (watercolor, oil), 2 $50 (pastel, sculpture) Academic Artists Association Awards. $150, $50, $25 Cash Awards (watercolor). 3 $50, 1 $25 Cash Awards (pastel). $100 Cash Award (sculpture). All sections: 1 $100, 3 $50, 1 $25 General Cash Awards, Medals of Honor.

JUDGING: By 3 nationally known artists, council panel (preliminary). Not responsible for loss or damage.

SALES TERMS: Work need not be for sale. 20% commission charge.

ENTRY FEE: $15. $4 handling fee and return postage for shipped entries.

DEADLINES: Entry, September. Judging, October. Event, October-November.

52

Alameda County Fair Exhibition of Fine Arts

Alameda County Agricultural Fair Association
Lee R. Hall, Secretary-Manager
4501 Pleasanton Avenue
P. O. Box 579
Pleasanton, California 94566 U.S.A.
Tel: (415) 846-2881

Entry June

International; entry open to all; annual in June-July; established 1912. Purpose: to promote exhibiting in public shows; encourage aspiring artists. Motto: "Family fun for everyone." Sponsored by Alameda County Agricultural Fair Association. Recognized by California Fairs & Expositions. Average statistics (all sections): 400 entrants, 400,000 attendance. Held in Alameda, Contra Costa counties for 15 days. Tickets: free (fairgrounds admission, $2.50).

DRAWING CONTEST: **Pastel General,** original, 11x14 to 52x52 inches (including frame), framed, under glass, ready for hanging; limit 2 per entrant (all sections). Require hand-delivery. No copies, crated or supervised work. Categories: General, Out-of-County California Resident. Competition in Out-of-County category includes prints. Also have photography section.

PAINTING CONTEST: **Acrylic, Oil, Watercolor General.** Requirements, restrictions same as for Drawing. No heavy or ornate frames, wet paintings. Categories: Landscape-Marine, Portrait-Still Life (Acrylic-Oil, Watercolor); Abstract-Nonobjective (Oil or Watercolor); Out-of-County California Resident (Oil, Watercolor). Also have photography section.

PRINT CONTEST: **General.** Requirements, restrictions, categories same as for Drawing.

SCULPTURE CONTEST: **General.** Requirements, restrictions, categories same as for Drawing.

AWARDS: $100 First, $70 Second, $55 Third Place Premiums to best landscape or marine (oil and acrylic, watercolor), still life or portrait (oil and acrylic, watercolor), pastel, print, abstract or nonobjective oil or watercolor, sculpture, out-of county California resident (oil, watercolor, pastel or print, sculpture). Up to $400 Purchase Awards each for permanent collection. Popular Vote Ribbons to best each category. Honorable Mention Ribbons.

JUDGING: By jury. May reclassify, disqualify entries; withhold awards. Limit 1 cash award per entrant. Fair display at judges' discretion based on space availability. Sponsor may photograph for publicity; not responsible for loss or damage.

SALES TERMS: Work need not be for sale. 10% commission charge.

ENTRY FEE: $2 per work plus return postage.

DEADLINES: Entry, judging, June. Event, June-July.

53

Alaska State Fair Art Competition

Sara Jansen, Assistant Manager
Mile 40 Glenn Highway
P. O. Box 1128
Palmer, Alaska 99645 U.S.A.
Tel: (907) 745-4827

Entry August

International; entry open to all; annual in August-September; established 1936. Purpose: to promote agriculture, home arts; provide family entertainment setting for Alaskans. Sponsored by Alaskan State Fair (formerly Mantanuska Valley Fair Association). Recognized by IAFE, WFA, IFA. Average statistics (all sections): 7000 entries, 3500 awards, 250,000 attendance. Held at Alaskan State Fairgrounds, Palmer for 11 days. Tickets: $5 fair admission (children, senior citizens free).

DRAWING CONTEST: **General,** 4 feet maximum framed width; matted, under transparent protection, ready for hanging; limit 1 per category (maximum 3 entries all sections). Produced in previous 2 years. No copies, kits, molds. Divisions: Junior, Adult. Junior categories: age 0-5, 6-8, 9-11, 12-14, 15-17, 18-20. Adult categories: Landscapes (Black and White, Color), Still Life (Black and White, Color), Animal Studies, Portraits, Abstracts, Seascapes. Competition includes all media (Abstract, Seascape categories). Also have crafts, photography sections.

PAINTING CONTEST: **Acrylic, Oil, Watercolor General.** Restrictions, requirements same as for Drawing. Divisions: Junior, Adult. Adult categories: Landscapes (Acrylic, Oil, Watercolor), Still Life (Acrylic, Oil, Watercolor), Animal studies, Portraits, Abstracts, Seascapes. Competition includes all media (Abstract, Seascape categories).

PRINT CONTEST: **Any Type General.** Requirements, restrictions, divisions same as for Drawing.

SCULPTURE CONTEST: **Any Medium Abstract,** representational, 4 feet maximum width. Other requirements, restrictions, divisions same as for Drawing.

AWARDS: Junior Division: $10 First, $8 Second, $6 Third Prize (each category). Purple Rosette to outstanding work (all sections). Adult Division: $15 First, $12 Second, $10 Third (each category, all sections). Purple Rosette to outstanding work (all sections).

JUDGING: By 4 judges. Based on composition, imagination, reaction to subject, color, depth, craftsmanship, presentation (matting, framing), overall appearance. Sponsor may withhold awards. Not responsible for loss or damage.

ENTRY FEE: None. Entrant pays return postage.

DEADLINES: Entry, judging, August. Notification, Event, August-September.

54

Arkansas Annual Art Exhibition

Southeast Arkansas Art and Science Center (SEAASC)
Ellen Stern, Registrar
Civic Center
200 East 8th Avenue
Pine Bluff, Arkansas 71601 U.S.A.
Tel: (501) 536-3375

Entry October

International; entry open to all; annual in December-January; established 1968. Formerly called ARKANSAS ARTISTS EXHIBITION to 1979. Purpose: to provide professional, nonprofessional artists opportunity to exhibit in museum setting, gain recognition. Sponsored by and held at SEAASC for 6 weeks. Supported by SEAASC, Simmons First National Bank (SFNB), Arkansas Arts Council, NEA. Average statistics: 325 entries, 150 entrants, 70 finalists, 8 awards.

DRAWING CONTEST: Any Medium General, original, maximum 5x5 feet, 100 pounds, framed, ready for hanging; limit 3 per entrant (all sections). Completed in previous 2 years. Submit 35mm slides for entry review.

PAINTING CONTEST: Any Medium General. No wet work. Other requirements, restrictions same as for Drawing.

PRINT CONTEST: Any Type General. Requirements, restrictions same as for Drawing.

SCULPTURE CONTEST: Any Medium General, original, maximum 5x5x5 feet, 100 pounds; limit 3 per entrant (all sections). Completed in previous 2 years. Submit 4 slides (of front, back, both profiles) per work for entry review.

AWARDS: (all sections): $750 SFNB Grand Purchase Award. $750 in additional purchase awards. Grumbachers Medallion.

JUDGING: Entry review and awards judging by 1 art professional. Sponsor may reproduce accepted entries for educational, publicity purposes. Not responsible for loss or damage.

SALES TERMS: Work may be priced for sale. 20% commission charge.

ENTRY FEE: $5 per work. Entrant pays postage.

DEADLINES: Entry, notification, October. Acceptance, November. Event, December-January. Materials returned, February.

55

Coca-Cola Bottling Company (CCBC) of Elizabethtown Art Show

Jan Schmidt, Chair
1201 North Dixie Highway
P. O. Box 647
Elizabethtown, Kentucky 42701
U.S.A. Tel: (502) 737-4000, ext. 222

Entry April

National; **entry open to U.S.;** annual in May; established 1972. Purpose: to encourage, promote visual arts; educate, entertain. Sponsored and supported by CCBC of Elizabethtown Art Show, Inc., nonprofit, charitable organization. Average statistics (all sections): 600 entries (200 accepted), 500 entrants, 17 awards, 7000 attendance, $9000 in total sales. Held in Elizabethtown for 3 weeks. Have demonstrations, 3-week traveling exhibit, children's workshops, tours.

DRAWING CONTEST: Any Medium General, original, matted and framed, ready for hanging; limit 2 (Adult), 1 (Young People) per entrant (all sections). Completed in previous 3 years. No work made from, based on kits. Divisions: Adult, Young People (High School, Junior High, Elementary and under). Competition includes photography, crafts.

PAINTING CONTEST: Any Medium General. Watercolors suitably matted. Other requirements, restrictions same as for Drawing.

PRINT CONTEST: General. No photomechanically reproduced prints. Other requirements, restrictions same as for Drawing.

SCULPTURE CONTEST: Any Medium General, original. No work assembled from purchased parts. Other requirements, restrictions same as for Drawing.

AWARDS: All media: First, Second, Third Place Juror Awards; Purchase Awards ($3000 at artists' price); Special Merit Awards (approximately 25 for special touring exhibit); First, Second, Third Place Public Vote Awards. Ribbons to Purchase, Special Merit Awards. Young People: First, Second, Third Place, Honorable Mention Ribbons, each division.

JUDGING: By 1 renowned juror (Adult), special judge (Young People).

SALES TERMS: 20% commission charge (except on Purchase Awards).

ENTRY FEE: $7 per work ($3 Young People) plus $4 handling fee. Entrant pays postage.

DEADLINES: Entry, April. Event, May.

56

Electrum Juried Art Show

Helena Arts Council
Nadine M. Shafer, Director
P. O. Box 1231
Helena, Montana 59624 U.S.A.
Tel: (406) 442-6400

Entry September

International; **Entry open to U.S., Canada;** annual in October; established 1972. Purpose: to recognize man's search for beauty in the arts. Sponsored by Helena Arts Council (nonprofit organization). Average statistics (all sections): 400 entries, 250 entrants, 2 countries, 175 finalists, 45 awards, 5000 attendance. Held at Helena Civic Center as part of 3-day art festival. Have Marketplace for display of work ($40 for 8-foot space), performances, demonstrations, lectures. Also sponsor Electrum Medallion Design Competition. Second contact: Sally Starnes, Electrum, 814 Gilbert, Helena, Montana 59601; tel: (406) 442-9666.

DRAWING CONTEST: Charcoal-Pastel, Pen and Ink, Pencil, Mixed Media General, reasonable size, ready for hanging or display; limit 4 per entrant (all sections). Completed in previous year. Competition includes calligraphy, graphic design. Also have photography, crafts sections.

PAINTING CONTEST: Acrylic, Oil, Watercolor, Mixed Media General. Requirements, restrictions same as for Drawing.

PRINT CONTEST: Etchings, Engravings, Linoleum, Bloin, Lithographs, Serigraphs, Woodcuts General. Requirements, restrictions same as for Drawing.

SCULPTURE CONTEST: Clay-Porcelain, Metal, Plastic, Wax, Wood, Mixed Media General. Requirements, restrictions same as for Drawing.

AWARDS (all sections): $600 in Cash Awards. Electrum Medallion and Cash Award to best of show. Electrum Honorarium.

JUDGING: By 3 judges. May reproduce works for publicity, publications. Not responsible for loss or damage.

SALES TERMS: Work need not be for sale. 20% commission charge (none on Marketplace sales).

ENTRY FEE: $4 per work. Sponsor pays return postage of award winners.

DEADLINES: Entry, September. Judging, event, October.

57

Fairfield Art Show Oak Room Exhibition
Fairfield Chamber of Commerce
Harold B. Harris, Executive Director
1597 Post Road
Fairfield, Connecticut 06430 U.S.A.
Tel: (203) 255-1011

Entry June

International; entry open to all; annual in June; established 1963. Sponsored by Fairfield Chamber of Commerce. Held at Fairfield University for 4 days. Also sponsor Sidewalk Arts and Crafts Show and Sale.

DRAWING CONTEST: **Pastel General,** original, 50x50 inches maximum (including frame), framed, clear glass preferred, ready for hanging; limit 4 per entrant. Require hand-delivery. Also have photography and other fine arts sections.

PAINTING CONTEST: **Acrylic, Casein, Oil, Watercolor General.** Requirements, restrictions same as for Drawing.

PRINT CONTEST: **General.** Requirements, restrictions same as for Drawing.

SCULPTURE CONTEST: **General,** original, 200 pounds maximum; limit 4 per entrant. Require hand-delivery.

AWARDS: Over $3000 total cash prizes including $500 to best of show; $200 and Medallion to best oil, acrylic, watercolor, casein, pastel, print (includes graphics), sculpture; Purchase Awards for Fairfield Art Collection.

JUDGING: By 3 jurors. Not responsible for loss or damage.

SALES TERMS: All work must be for sale. 25% commission charge.

ENTRY FEE: $10 first, $7.50 each additional entry. (Sidewalk Show, $20 for 2-day space fee.)

DEADLINES: Entry, event, June.

58

LaGrange National Competition
Chattahoochee Valley Art Association (CVAA)
William B. Gay, Director
112 Hines Street
P. O. Box 921
LaGrange, Georgia 30241 U.S.A.
Tel: (404) 882-3267

Entry December

National; **entry open to U.S.;** annual in March-April; established 1962. Formerly called CALLAWAY GARDENS ART FESTIVAL to 1975. Purpose: to provide showplace for established and new artists in all media. Sponsored by CVAA, LaGrange College. Supported by Callaway Foundation, local businesses. Average statistics (all sections): 3000 entries (90-175 accepted), 900 entrants, $9000 in awards, 10,000 attendance. Held at CVAA Gallery for 1 month. Have special outdoor space for sculpture. Publish *CVAA Newsletter* (monthly). Also sponsor Affair on the Square (May sidewalk art show), Harvest Heyday Arts and Crafts Show (October). Second contact: John Lawrence, LaGrange College, LaGrange, Georgia 30240.

DRAWING CONTEST: **Any Medium General,** matted or mounted with firm backing (no frame, glass, or plexiglass); limit 3 per entrant (all sections). Recent work only. Submit 35mm slides for entry review. Competition includes photography.

PAINTING CONTEST: Any Medium General, 10 feet maximum, wired for hanging (watercolors suitably framed); limit 3 per entrant. Other requirements same as for Drawing.

PRINT CONTEST: General. Requirements, restrictions same as for Drawing.

SCULPTURE CONTEST: Any Medium General, 800 pounds maximum; limit 3 per entrant. Other requirements same as for Drawing.

AWARDS: $5000-$9000 in Purchase Awards; 10 Merit Awards (all media).

JUDGING: Entry review, final selection by 1 judge. Sponsor keeps slides for catalog, publicity; insures accepted entries during exhibition only; not responsible for in-transit loss or damage.

SALES TERMS: 20% commission charge (except Purchase Awards).

ENTRY FEE: $9 per work. Entrant pays shipping.

DEADLINES: Entry, December. Judging, February. Notification, March. Event, March-April.

59

Mondak Historical and Arts Society Annual Art Show

J. K. Ralston Museum and Art Center
Anne Schneider, Director
P. O. Box 50
221 Fifth Street SW
Sidney, Montana 59270 U.S.A.
Tel: (406) 482-3500

Entry September

National; **entry open to U.S. artists age 14 and over;** annual in Fall; established 1975. Purpose: to give exposure, recognition to contemporary artists. Sponsored and supported by Mondak Historical and Arts Society; J. K. Ralston Museum and Art Center. Recognized by Art Museum Association. Average statistics: 44 entries, 25 entrants, 6 awards, 200 attendance. Held at Art Center for 4 weeks.

DRAWING CONTEST: General, original, 4x6 feet maximum, ready for hanging; limit 3 per entrant (includes all 2D work). Completed in previous 3 years.

PAINTING CONTEST: General. Requirements, restrictions same as for Drawing.

PRINT CONTEST: General. Requirements, restrictions same as for Drawing.

SCULPTURE CONTEST: General, original; 4x6x2 feet, 100 pounds maximum; limit 3 per entrant. Completed in previous 3 years. Competition includes ceramics, fabrics.

AWARDS: $250 in Cash and Purchase Awards. First, Second, Third Place Prizes each to 2D, 3D work.

JUDGING: By 3 judges each year. Based on originality, design, creativity, craftsmanship. Not responsible for loss or damage.

SALES TERMS: Work need not be for sale. 25% commission charge.

ENTRY FEE: $5 plus return shipping.

DEADLINES: Entry, September. Event, October-November.

60

National Academy of Design Annual Exhibition
1083 Fifth Avenue
New York, New York 10028 U.S.A.
Tel: (212) 369-4880

Entry January

International; entry open to all; annual in February-March; established 1826. Purpose: to encourage fine arts, introduce emerging artists in America. Sponsored by National Academy of Design. Held at National Academy Galleries in New York for 1 month. Also sponsor Edwin Austin Abbey Memorial Scholarship for Mural Painting.

DRAWING CONTEST: **Any Medium General** (including pastel), 28x48 (LxW) inches maximum, matted, framed, under glass or plexiglass; limit 1 per entrant.

PAINTING CONTEST: **Oil General** (including acrylic or casein on canvas and-or varnished) 84x50 (LxW) inches, framed, cardboard backed; limit 1 per entrant.
Watercolor General (including acrylic, casein, tempera, watercolor) on paper, width 42 inches maximum, framed, under glass or plexiglass, unvarnished, cardboard backed; limit 1 per entrant.

PRINT CONTEST: **Any Type General.** Requirements, restrictions same as for Drawing.

SCULPTURE CONTEST: **General,** 300 pounds maximum, enclosed in glass or plexiglass case (small sculpture); limit 1 per entrant.

AWARDS: Over $40,000 in Cash Prizes, Medals, Purchases.

JUDGING: By jury of fellow artists. Sponsor may reproduce entries for catalog, publicity. Not responsible for loss or damage.

SALES TERMS: Work need not be for sale. 20% commission charge.

ENTRY FEE: None. Entrant pays return postage.

DEADLINES: Entry, January. Event, February-March.

61

Quinebaug Valley Council for the Arts and Humanities (QVCAH) All Arts Festival
Mark Winetrout, Executive Director
111 Main Street
Southbridge, Massachusetts 01550
U.S.A. Tel: (617) 764-3341,
764-7613

Entry April-May

International; entry open to all; annual in June; established 1978. Purpose: to encourage appreciation of and participation in arts, crafts. Sponsored by QVCAH, local businesses. Average statistics (all sections): 1000 entries, 100 entrants, 5000 attendance. Held at QVCAH Cultural Center, Southbridge, for 2 days (fair), 1 month (juried exhibit). Fair has performing arts programs, demonstrations.

DRAWING CONTEST: **General,** original, 4x5 feet maximum, framed, ready for hanging. Require hand-delivery. Also have photography and crafts sections.

PAINTING CONTEST: **General.** Requirements, restrictions same as for Drawing.

PRINT CONTEST: **General.** Requirements, restrictions same as for Drawing.

SCULPTURE CONTEST: **General,** original, 4x5 feet maximum. Submit pedestals for display. Require hand-delivery.

ART FAIR: Visual Arts. Submit 3-10 slides or prints of work and display for entry review. Entrants provide and attend sales displays. No dealers. Divisions: Adult, Youth. Also have photography, crafts sections.

AWARDS: Exhibit: $600 Cash Awards to best of show (all sections). Fair: Cash, Gift Certificates, each division. Popular Vote Award (all sections).

JUDGING: By art professionals. Not responsible for loss or damage.

ENTRY FEE: $8 each (exhibit); $15 Adult, $3 Youth (fair). No sales commission charge.

DEADLINES: Entry, April (fair), May (exhibit). Events, June.

62

San Mateo County Fair International Visual Arts Competition

San Mateo County Fair Arts Committee
Lois Kelley, Administrator
171 Flying Cloud Isle
Foster City, California 94404 U.S.A.
Tel: (415) 349-2787

Entry August

International; entry open to all; annual in September; established 1934. Sponsored by San Mateo County Fair Arts Committee. Held at County Fairgrounds for 19 days; 200,000 attendance. Also sponsor scholarship competitions of $1760 to San Francisco Academy of Art College and $625 to Instituto Allende in Guanajuato, Mexico.

DRAWING CONTEST: General (including pastel on paper), size to fit through Art Room double doors, requiring no more than 2 persons to lift, wired, ready for hanging. Also have photography, video, crafts, writing, dance sections.

PAINTING CONTEST: General. No wet entries. Other requirements, restrictions same as for Drawing.

Water Media General (gouache, tempera, watercolor) on paper. Requirements, restrictions same as for Drawing.

PRINT CONTEST: General, on paper. Requirements, restrictions same as for Drawing.

SCULPTURE CONTEST: General (including mobiles). Requirements, restrictions same as for Drawing.

AWARD: Painting: $300 Marian W. Stinton Memorial Award to artist under age 30. $200 and First Place Trophy. $50 Second, $25 Third Prize. Entries on paper (including drawing, print, all water media): $100 and First Place Trophy. $50 Second, $25 Third Prize. Sculpture: $100 and First Place Trophy. $50 Second, $25 Third Prize. All sections: $100 and First Place Trophy to best floral interpretation. $35 Merchandise Certificates Second Place Prize. $25 Third Prize. Other Special Subject Awards.

JUDGING: Entry review and awards judging by art expert. Not responsible for loss or damage.

SALES TERMS: 20% commission charge (tax-exempt donation).

ENTRY FEE: $6 per work plus $3 handling charge.

DEADLINES: Entry, August. Notification, event, September.

63

Shreveport Art Guild National Exhibition

Friends of the Meadows Museum of Art
2911 Centenary Boulevard
Shreveport, Louisiana 71104 U.S.A.

Entry September

International; entry open to all; annual in January-February; established 1924. Sponsored by Shreveport Art Guild, Friends of Meadows Museum of Art (founded 1975). Held at Meadows Museum for 1 month.

DRAWING CONTEST: **Any Medium General,** original, matted and-or framed, ready for hanging; unlimited entry. Completed in previous 2 years. Submit 1-3 2x2-inch color slides per work for entry review. No supervised work. Competition includes crafts.

PAINTING CONTEST: **Any Medium General,** original, framed, ready for hanging; unlimited entry. Other requirements, restrictions same as for Drawing.

PRINT CONTEST: **Any Type General.** Requirements, restrictions same as for Drawing.

SCULPTURE CONTEST: **Any Medium General,** original; unlimited entry. Other requirements, restrictions same as for Drawing.

AWARDS: (all sections): $1000 to best of show. $500 Second Place. $1000 in Merit Awards.

JUDGING: Entry review and awards judging by art professional. Sponsor may reproduce accepted entries for catalog, publicity. Review slides not returned. Not responsible for loss or damage.

SALES TERMS: 10% commission charge.

ENTRY FEE: $10 first 3 works, $1 each additional.

DEADLINES: Entry, September. Event, January-February.

64

Sister Kenny Institute (SKI) International Art Show by Disabled Artists

Mary Ellefson, Assistant Coordinator
Room 2728
800 East 28th Street at Chicago Avenue
Minneapolis, Minnesota 55407
U.S.A. Tel: (612) 874-4577, 874-4482

Entry January

International; **entry open to disabled artists;** annual in April-May; established 1964. Purpose: to increase public awareness of abilities of disabled artists; give disabled artists chance to gain recognition, sell art. Sponsored and supported by SKI, Abbott-Northwestern Sister Kenny Auxiliary. Average statistics (all sections): 450 entries, 150 entrants, 15 countries, 18 awards, 2000 attendance, $15,000 total sales. Held at SKI for 2 weeks.

DRAWING CONTEST: **General,** original; limit 4 per entrant. Submit brief (up to 75 words) biographical sketch, photograph. No glass mountings through mail. Competition for some awards includes photography.

PAINTING CONTEST: **Acrylic, Oil, Watercolor, General.** Requirements, restrictions same as for Drawing.

PRINT CONTEST: **General,** original, hand printed from hand etched, drawn, carved, or engraved plates, stones, or blocks. Other requirements, restrictions same as for Drawing.

SCULPTURE CONTEST: General, original, model or 1 of first 10 castings, replicas or reproductions made from original. Other requirements, restrictions same as for Drawing.

AWARDS: 6 Special Awards totaling over $1000 (all sections). First, Second, Third Place Ribbons, Honorable Mention Award, each section. Purchase Prizes. Sponsor may purchase entries for permanent collection, national touring exhibition.

JUDGING: By 4-6 local professional art critics. Sponsor may photograph entries for publicity, education, public relations.

SALES TERMS: 20% commission charge.

ENTRY FEE: None. Entrant pays postage.

DEADLINES: Entry, January. Event, April-May.

65

Springville Museum of Art
National April Salon
Vern G. Swanson, Director
126 East 400 South
P. O. Box 258
Springville, Utah 84663 U.S.A.
Tel: (801) 489-9434

Entry February

National; **entry open to U.S.;** annual in April; established 1937. Purpose: to allow art to build character, improve people's lives. Motto: "As the sun colors flowers, so art colors life." Sponsored by City of Springville, Springville Museum Association. Supported by state, private donations. Average statistics (all sections): 420 entries, 200 entrants, 35,000 attendance, $8000 total sales. Held at Springville Museum of Art for 2 weeks. Also sponsor art classes, lectures, workshops, concerts, docent and intern training programs.

DRAWING CONTEST: Representational, original, framed, ready for hanging (prefer plexiglass); limit 3 per entrant (all sections). Completed in previous 3 years. Submit slides (6 maximum) for entry review. No abstract, nonobjective entries. Competition includes photography.

PAINTING CONTEST: Representational, original, framed, ready for hanging (prefer plexiglass over work on paper). Other requirements, restrictions same as for Drawing.

PRINT CONTEST: Representational. Requirements, restrictions same as for Drawing.

SCULPTURE CONTEST: Representational, original; limit 3 per entrant. Other requirements, restrictions same as for Drawing.

AWARDS: (all sections): 5-10 Gold, 10-20 Silver Medals. Purchase Awards.

JUDGING: By artists, professors, critics, collectors, dealers. Sponsor insures entries during exhibit only; not responsible for glass breakage.

SALES TERMS: 25% commission charge.

ENTRY FEE: $4 per work.

DEADLINES: Entry, February. Judging, March. Event, March-May.

66

Texas Fine Arts Association
National Exhibition
Beverly Petty, Assistant to Director
3809 West 35th Street
P. O. Box 5023

Austin, Texas 78763 U.S.A.
Tel: (512) 453-5312

Entry January

National; **entry open to U. S.;** annual in April-May. Purpose: to honor excellent work by visual artists throughout U. S. Sponsored by Texas Fine Arts Association (founded 1911). Held at Laguna Gloria Art Museum, Austin for 1 month, followed by statewide touring exhibition of selected works.

DRAWING CONTEST: Any Medium General (including pastel), original, 50x50 inches maximum including frame, under plexiglass, ready for hanging. Submit 35mm slides of work for entry review (no glass, thicker than standard cardboard mounts). Competition includes photography.

PAINTING CONTEST: Any Medium General, original, 50x50 inches maximum including frame, ready for hanging. Watercolor, fragile media under plexiglass. Submit 35mm slides of work for entry review.

PRINT CONTEST: Any Medium General. Requirements, restrictions same as for Drawing.

SCULPTURE CONTEST: Any Medium General, 65 inches maximum including base. Submit minimum 2 35mm slides (different angles) of each work for entry review.

AWARDS: $500 to best of show. Additional $1000 Cash Prizes. $3500 Purchase Awards. Approximately 50 works selected for statewide tour.

JUDGING: By art professional. Sponsor may reproduce for exhibition catalog, promotion.

SALES TERMS: 30% commission charge.

ENTRY FEE: $10 per work plus return postage.

DEADLINES: Entry, January. Works due, March. Event, April-May.

67

Monte-Carlo International Grand Prix of Contemporary Art
Monaco National Museum
Annette Bordeau, Secretary General
17 Avenue Princesse Grace
Monte-Carlo, MONACO
PRINCIPALITY Tel: (93) 30-91-26

Entry January

International; entry open to all; annual in Winter; established 1967. Purpose; to discover, encourage, make known work with potential. Sponsored and supported by Sovereign Prince and Princess of Monaco. Average statistics (all sections): 400 entries, 50 countries. Held at Congress Centre Auditorium of Monte-Carlo, Monaco for several weeks. Also sponsor social, educational, artistic, scientific events year-round. Second contact: Dr. Helene Day, Consul of Monaco in New England, 251 Payson Road, Belmont, Massachusetts 02178; tel: (617) 489-1240.

DRAWING CONTEST: Any Medium General, 41x24cm to 300x300cm, framed or unframed, ready for hanging. Submit 6 slides maximum for entry review.

PAINTING CONTEST: Any Medium General. Requirements, restrictions same as for Drawing.

PRINT CONTEST: Any Type General. Requirements, restrictions same as for Drawing.

SCULPTURE CONTEST: Any Medium General. Requirements, restrictions same as for Drawing.

AWARDS: 10,000F Grand Prix De

S.A.S. Le Prince Rainier III Medal, Diploma. 3 5000F, 1 2000F Diplomas. 5000F Prix de la Ville de Monaco Diploma to work with subject of Principality of Monaco or Mediterranean landscape. 5000F Diplomas to sculpture, figurative work. Prix d'Art Sacre Diploma, Medal to sacred art. 2 Diplomas and Volumes of Art Awards. Honorable Mentions.

JUDGING: Entry review by selection committee. Awards judging by jury. Not responsible for loss or damage.

ENTRY FEE: 100F per work. No sales commission charge.

DEADLINES: Entry, August. Judging, event, late Winter.

DRAWING, PAINTING, PRINTS, SCULPTURE (Regional-State)

Limited to specific Region, State. Drawing, Painting, Prints, Sculpture, Collage, Mixed Media, including ARIZONA, CALIFORNIA, COLORADO, INDIANA, MICHIGAN, NEW YORK, OHIO, PENNSYLVANIA, TENNESSEE, WISCONSIN REGION, SOUTHEAST, ONTARIO. (Also see other DRAWING, PAINTING, PRINT, SCULPTURE CATEGORIES.)

68

Baycrafters Annual Juried Art Show
Sally Price
28795 Lake Road
Huntington Metropark
Bay Village, Ohio 44140 U.S.A.
Tel: (216) 871-6543

Entry August

Regional; **entry open to Ohio residents age 18 and over;** annual in August-September; established 1963. Sponsored by Baycrafters (founded 1948), arts and crafts organization. Held at Baycrafters Gallery House in Bay Village for 2 weeks. Have shops, art classes, scholarships, touring exhibition, Picture Rental Gallery. Also sponsor Renaissance Fair, Octoberfair, Higbee Show, Emerald Necklace Art Competition.

DRAWING CONTEST: General, original; framed, backed, ready for hanging; limit 3 per entrant (includes prints). Completed in previous 2 years. Competition includes photography, crafts.

PAINTING CONTEST: General, original, 5x5 feet maximum, framed, backed, ready for hanging; limit 3 per entrant. Completed in previous 2 years.

PRINT CONTEST: General. Requirements same as for Drawing.

SCULPTURE CONTEST: General, original; limit 6 per entrant. Completed in previous 2 years.

AWARDS: (all sections): $350 to best in show. $300 First, $200 Second, $150 Third Prize. Purchase Awards.

JUDGING: Not specified.

SALES TERMS: Work need not be for sale. 25% commission charge.

ENTRY FEE: $5.

DEADLINES: Entry, August. Event, August-September.

69

Beloit and Vicinity Exhibition
Wright Art Center
Marylou S. Williams, Director
Beloit College

Beloit, Wisconsin 53511 U.S.A.
Tel: (608) 365-3391

Entry January

Regional; **entry open to Wisconsin and neighboring states;** annual in March-April; established 1957. Purpose: to provide exposure to regional artists, encourage purchase of their work. Sponsored by Art League of Beloit, Wright Art Center, Beloit College. Supported by area corporate and private donors. Average statistics (all sections): 200 entries, 6-8 awards, 900 attendance. Held at Wright Art Center, Beloit College for 3 weeks. Also sponsor workshops, lectures, classes, exhibitions.

DRAWING CONTEST: General, suitably presented for displaying; original, works on paper framed under glass, wired for hanging; limit 1 per entrant (all sections). Completed after May previous 2 years and not exhibited in Beloit vicinity. Submit slide for entry review. No work done under supervision. Also have photography and crafts sections.

PAINTING CONTEST: Any Medium General. Requirements, restrictions same as for Drawing.

PRINT CONTEST: General. Requirements, restrictions same as for Drawing.

SCULPTURE CONTEST: Any Medium General, 8 feet any dimension maximum, presented for displaying; original; limit 1 per entrant. Completed after May previous 2 years and not exhibited in Beloit vicinity. Submit slides for entry review. No work done under supervision.

AWARDS: $2000 in Cash Prizes. Beloit College Collection Purchase Award.

JUDGING: Entry review by jury. Awards judging by 1 juror. Sponsor insures during exhibition only. Not responsible for loss or damage.

SALES TERMS: Work need not be for sale. 25% commission charge.

ENTRY FEE: $8.

DEADLINES: Entry, January. Judging, February. Event, March-April.

70

Berks Art Alliance Regional Juried Show
Lynda Potter, Chair
Box 153, Rd #1
Birdsboro, Pennsylvania 19508
U.S.A.

Entry October

State; **entry open to residents within 50 miles of Reading;** annual in November; established 1976. Purpose: to provide opportunity for local artists to enter juried show. Sponsored and supported by Berks Art Alliance, Reading Public Museum. Average statistics (all sections): 350 entries, 180 entrants, 8 awards, $200 sales per entrant. Held at Reading Public Museum for 1 month. Second contact: Berks Art Alliance, Trent & Belmont Avenues, Wyomissing, Pennsylvania 19610.

DRAWING CONTEST: General (including pastel), original, 60 inches maximum, framed, ready for hanging; limit 2 per entrant (all sections). No wet work; copies from photographs.

PAINTING CONTEST: Acrylic, Oil, Tempera, Watercolor, Mixed Media General. No wet paintings. Other requirements, restrictions same as for Drawing.

PRINT CONTEST: General. Requirements, restrictions same as for Drawing.

SCULPTURE CONTEST: General. Requirements, restrictions same as for Drawing.

AWARDS: 1 $350, 3 $300 Purchase Awards. 3 $100 Merit Awards. $100, $50 Gift Certificates. 2 $50 Framing Awards. (Amounts vary each year.)

JUDGING: By 3 artists. Sponsor may photograph work for publicity. Sponsor insures entries against fire only.

SALES TERMS: Work need not be for sale. 10% commission charge.

ENTRY FEE: $5 per work.

DEADLINES: Entry, judging, October. Event, November.

71

Burbank Fine Arts Federation Multimedia Juried Show
Creative Arts Center
Betsy Lueke, Director
1100 West Clark Avenue
P. O. Box 6459
Burbank, California 91510 U.S.A.
Tel: (213) 847-8763

Entry September

Regional; **entry open to Southern California;** annual in September; established 1975. Purpose: to present quality exhibition of contemporary, traditional art to general public; offer exposure, awards to Southern California artists. Sponsored by Fine Arts Federation of Burbank (FAFB). Supported by FAFB, local businesses. Average statistics (all sections): 150 entries (85 accepted), 75 entrants, 15 finalists, 5 awards, 5000 attendance. Held at Creative Arts Center for 2-1/2 weeks. Have gallery, classes, seminars, workshops. Also sponsor monthly art shows, annual membership show.

DRAWING CONTEST: General, original, 48 inches diameter maximum, mounted under glass, framed, ready for hanging; limit 2 per entrant (all sections). Recently produced. Require hand-delivery. No copies or class work. Categories: Traditional, Contemporary. Competition includes monochrome and color photography.

PAINTING CONTEST: Any Medium General. Requirements, restrictions, categories same as for Drawing. No wet or supervised work.

PRINT CONTEST: General. Requirements, restrictions, categories same as for Drawing.

SCULPTURE CONTEST: General, original, 40 inches in diameter maximum; limit 2 per entrant (all sections). Recently produced. Require hand-delivery. No cooperative or supervised work. Categories: Tradition, Contemporary.

AWARDS: $2000 in Cash and Purchase Awards (all sections).

JUDGING: By 1-3 renowned art authorities. Sponsor may photograph accepted entries for publicity. Not responsible for loss or damage.

SALES TERMS: Work must be for sale to be eligible for purchase awards. 15% commission charge.

ENTRY FEE: $5 per work.

DEADLINES: Entry, event, September.

72

Central South Art Exhibition
Tennessee Art League
3011 Poston Avenue
Nashville, Tennessee 37203 U.S.A.

Entry May

Regional; **entry open to Southeastern U.S. age 16 and over;** annual in June; established 1963. Sponsored by Tennessee Art League. Held at Parthenon Galleries, Centennial Park in Nashville for 1 month. Also sponsor Parthenon monthly 1-person shows. Second contact: Wesley Paine, Director, The Parthenon, Centennial Park, Nashville, Tennessee 37201; tel: (615) 259-6358.

DRAWING CONTEST: General (including pastel), original, 60 inches maximum any direction, framed, under glass or plexiglass (if shipped), ready for hanging; limit 5 per entrant (all sections). Completed in previous 2 years. No photography, craftwork.

PAINTING CONTEST: General. Requirements, restrictions same as for Drawing.

PRINT CONTEST: General. Requirements, restrictions same as for Drawing.

SCULPTURE CONTEST: General, 300 pounds maximum; limit 5 per entrant (all sections). Completed in previous 2 years.

ELIGIBILITY: Residents age 16 and over living in Tennessee, Missouri, Arkansas, Mississippi, Alabama, Georgia, South Carolina, North Carolina, Virginia, Kentucky, other states within 300-mile radius of Nashville.

AWARDS: 1 $500, 3 $250, 5 $100, 1 $75, 7 $50, 3 $25 Cash Awards. $1000 in purchases, Pickering Galleries, Inc. Purchase of 1 or more works, Metropolitan Board of Parks and Recreation.

JUDGING: By 1 artist. Not responsible for loss or damage.

SALES TERMS: Work need not be for sale. 20% commission charge by Parthenon Galleries.

ENTRY FEE: $5 per work plus return postage.

DEADLINES: Entry, judging, May. Event, June.

73

Gilpin County Arts Association Annual Exhibition

Kay Russell, Secretary
Box 98
Central City, Colorado 80427 U.S.A.
Tel: (303) 582-5952

Entry April

State; **entry open to Colorado;** annual in June-September; established 1947. Purpose: to promote and show work of Colorado artists. Sponsored by Gilpin County Arts Association. Supported by Association membership, entry fees, sales commissions. Average statistics (all sections): 1000 entries, 350 entrants, 200 finalists, $1500 awards, 30,000 attendance, $40,000 total sales. Held at Gilpin County Arts Association Gallery for 3 months. Have bin sale.

DRAWING CONTEST: General (including charcoal, ink, pastel, pencil), 5x5 feet maximum, framed, ready for hanging; limit 3 per entrant. Require hand-delivery. Competition includes photography, crafts.

PAINTING CONTEST: General (including acrylic, oil, watercolor). Requirements same as for Drawing.

PRINT CONTEST: General (including etchings, intaglios). Requirements same as for Drawing.

SCULPTURE CONTEST: General (including clay, metal, stone, wood), maximum 5x5 feet, 300 pounds; limit 3 per entrant. Require hand-delivery.

AWARDS: $1500 in Cash Awards. Accepted entrants may submit up to 15 items without charge for nonjuried bin sale.

JUDGING: By 1 academic. Sponsor

may reproduce entries for publicity. Not responsible for loss or damage.

SALES TERMS: All entries must be for sale. 35% commission charge (includes bin sale).

ENTRY FEE: $6 per item.

DEADLINES: Entry, April. Event, June-September.

74

Hartland Art Show
Hartland Art Council
Sandy Scherba
P. O. Box 126
Hartland, Michigan 48029 U.S.A.
Tel: (313) 632-5200

Entry June

State; **entry open to Michigan;** annual in June; established 1967. Purpose: to provide Michigan artists opportunity to display, sell work. Sponsored by Hartland Art Council. Supported by Hartland Foundation. Average statistics (all sections): 700 entries, 350 entrants, 175 finalists, 20 awards, 2000 attendance. Held at Hartland High School for 1 week.

DRAWING CONTEST: General (including crayon, graphite, pastel, pen and ink, pencil), original, framed, ready for hanging (metal frames must have hangers); unlimited entry. Competition includes photography, crafts.

PAINTING CONTEST: Acrylic, Oil, Watercolor, Mixed Media General. Requirements same as for Drawing.

PRINT CONTEST: General (including aquatint and other intaglio processes, linoleum prints, lithographs, silkscreens). Requirements same as for Drawing.

SCULPTURE CONTEST: General, original; unlimited entry.

AWARDS (all sections): $2000 in Purchase and Cash Awards. Excellence Awards. Sponsor may display award-winning entries in private gallery.

JUDGING: By 2 art professors or museum curators. Not responsible for loss or damage.

ENTRY FEE: $8 per work. No sales commission charge.

DEADLINES: Entry, event, June.

75

Ink and Clay Exhibition
California State Polytechnic University (Cal Poly) Art Department
Diane Divelbess, Coordinator
3801 West Temple Avenue
Pomona, California 91768 U.S.A.
Tel: (714) 598-4567

Entry October, December

State;**entry open to California;** annual in January; established 1972. Purpose: to provide university with exhibition of outstanding contemporary art. Sponsored by Cal Poly, Pomona Art Department, Library. Average statistics (all sections): 200 entries, 150 entrants, 7 awards, 1500 attendance. Held at University Library Gallery for 3 weeks. Second contact: Madelyn Mellon, University Library, Cal Poly, Pomona, CA 91768.

DRAWING CONTEST: Ink General; 90 inches maximum, framed or under protective covering, ready for hanging; limit 2 per entrant.

PRINT CONTEST: Any Type General, in ink. Requirements, restrictions same as for Drawing.

SCULPTURE CONTEST: Clay General (may be combined with other materials), maximum 90 inches, 300 pounds; limit 2 per entrant. Entrants more than 100 miles from Cal Poly submit slides for entry review.

AWARDS: $1500 in Purchase Prizes for James Jones Collection at Cal Poly.

JUDGING: By 1 ink, 1 clay specialist. Not responsible for loss or damage.

SALES TERMS: Work need not be for sale. 20% commission charge.

ENTRY FEE: $8 plus return postage.

DEADLINES: Entry, October (slides), December (works). Judging, event, January.

76

Michigan State Fair Fine Arts Exhibit

Community Arts Section
Leona J. Dudzinski, Supervisor
1120 West State Fair Avenue
Detroit, Michigan 48203 U.S.A.
Tel: (313) 368-1000, ext. 112

Entry August

State; **entry open to Michigan adults;** annual in August-September; established 1965. Nation's oldest state fair (founded 1849). Sponsored by Department of Natural Resources. Average statistics (all sections): 7000 entries, 1300 entrants. Held at Michigan State Fairgrounds for 11 days.

DRAWING CONTEST: Ink, Pastel, Pencil, Mixed Media General, dimensions unspecified, framed under glass or plexiglass, suitable for hanging; limit 2 per entrant. Require hand-delivery. Divisions: Professional, Amateur. Competition includes photography. Also have crafts, cooking sections.

PAINTING CONTEST: Acrylic, Oil, Tempera, Watercolor, Collage, Mixed Media General, dimensions unspecified, framed under glass or plexiglass (watercolor only), suitable for hanging. Other restrictions, divisions same as for Drawing.

PRINT CONTEST: Etchings, Intaglios, Lithographs, Serigraphs, Woodcuts General. Restrictions, requirements, divisions same as for Drawing.

SCULPTURE CONTEST: General, made of durable materials. Restrictions, requirements, divisions same as for Drawing.

AWARDS: Professional: $400 Best of Show (all sections); $200 First, $125 Second, $50 Third Prizes to paintings. $125 First, $75 Second, $25 Third Prizes (includes prints, drawings). $200 First, $125 Second, $50 Third Prizes to sculptures. Honorable Mentions. Amateur: $100 Best of Show (all sections); $40 First, $30 Second, $20 Third Prizes to paintings. $40 First, $30 Second, $20 Third Prizes (includes prints, drawings). $40 First, $30 Second, $20 Third Prizes to sculptures. Honorable Mentions. $100 Lewis Artist Supply Gift Certificate to People's Choice Award winner (all media).

JUDGING: By 2 professionals. Sponsor may photograph entries for catalog, promotion; keeps unclaimed works; may withhold awards. Not responsible for loss or damage.

ENTRY FEE: $5 Professional, $3 Amateur. No commission charge.

DEADLINES: Entry, August. Judging, event, August-September.

77

Santa Clara County Fair Art Exhibit

William R. Smethers,
Secretary-Manager
344 Tully Road
San Jose, California 95111 U.S.A.
Tel: (408) 295-3050

Entry July

Regional; **entry open to Santa Clara County;** annual in August. Held at Statehouse Art Building for 11 days.

DRAWING CONTEST: General (including pastel), Original, original, 80 inches maximum horizontally including frame, mounted under glass, ready for hanging; unlimited entry. Require hand-delivery. Competition includes photography. Also have crafts sections.

PAINTING CONTEST: Acrylic (Oil Technique), Oil, Mixed Media General, maximum 80 inches horizontally including frame, ready for hanging; unlimited entry. Require hand-delivery. No wet work or items projecting more than 3 inches from back side.

Watercolor General (acrylic in watercolor technique, casein, gouache, tempera, watercolor). Requirements, restrictions same as for Drawing.

PRINT CONTEST: Creative General (including etchings, intaglios, lithographs, serigraphs). Requirements, restrictions same as for Drawing. Competition includes drawing, photography.

SCULPTURE CONTEST: Any Medium General (except plaster, other perishable entries), includes bas-relief projecting more than 3 inches, original, 200 pounds maximum; unlimited entry. Require hand-delivery.

AWARDS: $100 First, $50 Second Prize; Third, Fourth, Fifth Place Ribbons, each section. $25 and Bronze Medal Special Award (all sections).

JUDGING: By 3 judges. Sponsor may withhold awards. Not responsible for loss or damage.

ENTRY FEE: $3 (up to 3 works). $3 per additional 3 works.

DEADLINES: Entry, July. Event, August.

78

Southern California Exposition Art in All Media Exhibition

Lolly Stuckenschneider, Exhibit Supervisor
Entry Office, Fairgrounds
Del Mar, California 92014 U.S.A.

Entry May

State; **entry open to Southern California;** annual in June-July; established 1890. Oldest art exhibition in San Diego County. Purpose: to present finest exhibition of art and craft. Sponsored by Southern California Exposition. Average statistics: 2300 entries, 1400 entrants, 600 finalists, 100,000 attendance, $8000 total sales. Held at Turf Club Gallery, Southern California Exposition, Del Mar for 3 weeks.

DRAWING CONTEST: Any Medium General, 6 feet maximum any dimension including frame, under glass or plexiglass; limit 3 per section. Recent work, suitable for family viewing. No copies, works produced under supervision, electrical entries. Also have crafts.

PAINTING CONTEST: Acrylic, Oil, Watercolor, Other Media General. No wet entries. Requirements, restrictions same as for Drawing.

PRINT CONTEST: Any Type General. No photographs. Requirements, restrictions same as for Drawing.

SCULPTURE CONTEST: Any Medium General, maximum 6x8 feet, 250 pounds any component; limit 3 per section. Recent work, suitable for family viewing. No copies, work produced under supervision, electrical entries. Categories: Metal, Other (including ceramics, stone, marble, wood).

ELIGIBILITY: Residents of San Diego, Imperial, Orange, Riverside, Los Angeles, San Bernardino, Ventura, Santa Barbara counties.

AWARDS: Painting: $250 Best of Show. $100 First, $50 Second, $25 Third Prize to each medium. Drawings, Prints: $250 Best of Show. $100 First, $50 Second, $25 Third Prize to each. Sculpture: $250 Best of Show. 2 $100 First, 2 $50 Second, 2 $25 Third Prizes.

JUDGING: By 3 judges each for painting, drawing-prints, sculpture. Sponsor may reproduce entries for publicity. Not responsible for loss or damage.

SALES TERMS: Work need not be for sale. 25% commission charge.

ENTRY FEE: $4 each work.

DEADLINES: Entry, notification, May. Event, June-July.

Tennessee Annual All-State Artists Exhibition
Watkins Institute
Sixth Avenue at Church Street
Nashville, Tennessee 37219 U.S.A.

Entry October

State; **entry open to Tennessee;** annual in November. Purpose: to advance and preserve Tennessee art; establish a permanent collection. Sponsored by First American National Bank, Watkins Institute Art Department. Held at Parthenon Galleries, Centennial Park in Nashville for 3 weeks.

DRAWING CONTEST: **Pastel General,** original, 6 feet maximum any direction, framed, ready for hanging. Completed in previous 3 years.

PAINTING CONTEST: **Acrylic, Oil, Watercolor, Mixed Media General.** Requirements same as for Drawing.

PRINT CONTEST: **General.** Requirements same as for Drawing.

SCULPTURE CONTEST: **General,** original, 6 feet maximum any direction. Completed in previous 3 years.

AWARDS: 3 $1000 Purchase Prizes (1 to oil, acrylic or mixed media; 1 to sculpture; 1 to watercolor). $250 Purchase Prizes, prints, pastels. Second and Third Awards, all sections.

JUDGING: By 1 art professional. All entries must be eligible for Purchase Awards. Not responsible for loss or damage.

SALES TERMS: Works need not be for sale. 20% commission charge.

ENTRY FEE: $5 per item plus return postage.

DEADLINES: Entry, October. Event, November.

80

Vahki Juried Arts and Crafts Competition
City of Mesa Cultural Activities Department
Gerry Hulcher, Superintendent
155 North Center Street
P. O. Box 1466
Mesa, Arizona 85201 U.S.A.
Tel: (602) 834-2198

Entry May

State; **entry open to Arizona;** annual in June; established 1979. Named after Vahki phase of Hohokam people (300 BC-100 AD), period noted for introduction of new cultural traits into Gila River Basin. Purpose: to provide Arizona artists opportunity to exhibit, sell work. Sponsored and supported by City of Mesa Cultural Activities Department; held in their Gallery for 3 weeks. Have workshops, lectures, panel discussions.

DRAWING CONTEST: General, original, framed and-or mounted under glass or acrylic, ready for hanging; limit 4 per entrant. Completed in previous 2 years. Submit slides for entry review. No entries previously entered in any Arizona juried show. Competition includes photography, crafts.

PAINTING CONTEST: General, original, framed, watercolors mounted under glass or acrylic. Other requirements, restrictions same as for Drawing.

PRINT CONTEST: General. Requirements, restrictions same as for Drawing.

SCULPTURE CONTEST: General, original, fully assembled; limit 4 per entrant (sets may be classified as 1 entry). Other requirements, restrictions same as for Drawing.

AWARDS: $500 in Cash Awards (all sections).

JUDGING: By 3 professional artists. Not responsible for loss or damage.

SALES TERMS: Entries may be for sale. 15% commission charge.

ENTRY FEE: $5 per work.

DEADLINES: Entry, judging, May. Event, June.

81

Wabash Valley Exhibition

Sheldon Swope Art Gallery
25 South Seventh Street
Terre Haute, Indiana 47807 U.S.A.
Tel: (812) 238-1676

Entry February

Regional; **entry open to Terre Haute area residents;** annual in March-April; established 1943. Sponsored by Sheldon Swope Art Gallery. Recognized by American Association of Museums. Held at Sheldon Swope Art Gallery for 1 month.

DRAWING CONTEST: General, original, 5x5 feet maximum, matted, framed, covered with glass; limit 3 per entrant. Completed in previous 3 years. Collaborative work acceptable. Competition for some awards includes photography.

PAINTING CONTEST: General, original, 5x5 feet maximum; watercolors matted, covered with glass. Other requirements, restrictions same as for Drawing.

PRINT CONTEST: General. Requirements, restrictions same as for Drawing.

SCULPTURE CONTEST: General, original, 5 feet per side maximum. Other requirements, restrictions same as for Drawing.

AWARDS: Gallery Acquisition Awards: $1000 Swope Art Gallery Award of Excellence; $500, $300, $250 Cash Prizes (all sections); $750 Swope Art Gallery Sculpture Award; $150 Print Award. 17 $100-$350 Purchase Prizes (all sections); $100 Watercolor Purchase Prize. 8 $25-$100 Merit Awards (all sections).

JUDGING: By 1 judge. Not responsible for loss or damage.

SALES TERMS: Work may be for sale. 20% commission charge.

ENTRY FEE: $5, 1 entry; $9, 2; $12, 3.

DEADLINES: Entry, judging, February. Awards, March. Event, March-April.

82

Western New York Exhibition
Albright-Knox Art Gallery (AKAG)
Serena Rattazzi, Public Relations Coordinator
1285 Elmwood Avenue
Buffalo, New York 14222 U.S.A.
Tel: (716) 882-8700

Entry January

Regional; **entry open to senior high school and older Western New York State residents;** biennial (even years) in March-April; established 1934. Purpose: to give regional artists opportunity to show work to public. Sponsored by AKAG. Supported by local corporations, businesses. Average statistics (all sections): 755 entries, 400 entrants, 125 acceptances, 22 awards. Held at AKAG in Buffalo for 4 weeks. Also sponsor Film-Video Exhibitions.

DRAWING CONTEST: General (including pastel), original, any dimension, framed, mounted, covered with plexiglass or glass; limit 2 per entrant (all sections). Completed in previous 3 years. Competition for some awards includes constructions, photography.

PAINTING CONTEST: General, original, any dimension, suitably framed to protect surface; limit 2 per entrant (all sections). Completed in previous 3 years.

PRINT CONTEST: General. Requirements, restrictions same as for Drawing.

SCULPTURE CONTEST: General, original, any dimension; limit 2 per entrant. Completed in previous 3 years.

ELIGIBILITY: Senior high school or older students or residents of Western New York State counties: Allegany, Cattaraugus, Chautauqua, Erie, Genesee, Niagara, Orleans, Wyoming.

AWARDS: 16 $50-$500 Cash Awards (all sections). Special Awards: $200 to acrylic; $150, $100 to drawing; $150 to sculpture; $100 to watercolor; $100 to print; $50 to painting.

JUDGING: By 1 nationally known artist or museum professional. Sponsor may photograph entries for catalog, publicity purposes; insures work during exhibition only.

ENTRY FEE: $10. Work need not be for sale. No commission charge.

DEADLINES: Entry, January. Judging, February. Event, awards, March-April.

83

Artforms Open Juried Exhibit
Kitchener-Waterloo Art Gallery
Brad Blain, Director
101 Queen Street North
Kitchener, Ontario N2H 6P7
CANADA Tel: (519) 579-5860

Entry March

Regional; **entry open to Central Ontario;** annual in April-May; established 1973. Purpose: to provide region's artists exhibition opportunity. Sponsored by and held at Kitchener-Waterloo Gallery for 4 weeks. Supported by Ontario Arts Council, Ontario Ministry of Culture and Recreation. Average statistics (all sections): 250 entries, 150 entrants, 60 finalists.

DRAWING CONTEST: General, framed, ready for hanging; limit 2 per entrant. Require hand-delivery. No work done under supervision.

PAINTING CONTEST: General. Requirements, restrictions same as for Drawing.

PRINT CONTEST: General. Requirements, restrictions same as for Drawing.

SCULPTURE CONTEST: General, portable by 2 people; limit 2 per entrant. Require hand-delivery. No work done under supervision.

ELIGIBILITY: Artists residing in Brant, Dufferin, Huron, Oxford, Perth, Waterloo, Wellington, Wentworth counties.

AWARDS: Cash awards. $20 per item selected for show.

JUDGING: By 3 local art professionals. Sponsor insures entries on premises.

ENTRY FEE: $1 per item.

DEADLINES: Entry, March. Event, April-May.

DRAWING, PAINTING, PRINTS, SCULPTURE, COLLAGE, MIXED MEDIA

Drawing, Painting, Prints, Sculpture, Collage and Mixed Media. (Also see other DRAWING, PAINTING, PRINT, SCULPTURE CATEGORIES.)

84

AAO Gallery International All on Paper Exhibition

Associated Art Organizations (AAO) of Western New York
Jeanette Blair, President
698 Main Street
Buffalo, New York 14202 U.S.A.
Tel: (716) 856-6530

Entry June

International; entry open to all; annual in September-October; established 1979. Became international 1982. Purpose: to give local artists, gallery visitors opportunity to view international art work on paper. Motto: "All on paper." Sponsored by AAO of Western New York. Supported by the artists. Average statistics: 500 entrants, 6 countries, 58 finalists, 9 awards, 400 attendance. Held at AAO Gallery, Buffalo for 4 weeks.

DRAWING CONTEST: General on Paper, dimensions not specified, matted or mounted with sturdy backing, covered by acetate; limit 2 per entrant (all sections). Submit 2x2-inch cardboard-mounted slides for entry review.

PAINTING CONTEST: General on Paper. Requirements, restrictions same as for Drawing.

PRINT CONTEST: General on Paper. Requirements, restrictions same as for Drawing.

SCULPTURE CONTEST: Paper General, requirements not specified; limit 2 per entrant (all sections). Submit 2x2-inch cardboard-mounted slides for entry review.

COLLAGE CONTEST: General on Paper. Requirements, restrictions same as for Drawing.

MIXED MEDIA CONTEST: Gen-

eral on Paper. Requirements, restrictions same as for Drawing.

AWARDS: (all sections): $500 to best of show. 8 $250 Awards of Distinction.

JUDGING: Entry review and awards judging by 1 art professional. Sponsor may eliminate work which differs from slide entry; may photograph entries for publicity. Not responsible for loss or damage.

SALES TERMS: Work need not be for sale. 25% commission charge.

ENTRY FEE: $10.

DEADLINES: Entry, June. Acceptance, July. Judging, August. Event, September-October.

85

Art Association of Newport (AAN) American Exhibition
Stephanie Shoemaker
76 Bellevue Avenue
Newport, Rhode Island 02840 U.S.A.
Tel: (401) 847-0179

Entry April

National; **entry open to U.S.;** annual (sculpture biennial, odd years) in June; established 1911. Purpose: to show contemporary U.S. art. Sponsored by AAN. Held in Newport for 1 month. Have monthly exhibits.

DRAWING CONTEST: General (including pastel), 72x72 inches maximum, framed, ready for hanging. Completed in previous 2 years. Submit slides for entry review. Also have photography section (biennial, even years).

PAINTING CONTEST: Acrylic, Oil, Watercolor General. Requirements, restrictions same as for Drawing.

PRINT CONTEST: General, original. Requirements, restrictions same as for Drawing.

SCULPTURE CONTEST: General, 72x72x72 inches, 50 pounds maximum. Other requirements, restrictions same as for Drawing.

MIXED MEDIA CONTEST: General. Requirements, restrictions same as for Drawing, Sculpture.

AWARDS: $200 AAN Prize; 2 $150 Prizes (includes all sections). $250 Prize to drawing. 2 $200, $100 Prizes to paintings. $200 and Grumbacher Bronze Medallion to prints. $250 First, $150 Second, $100 Third Prizes to sculptures.

JUDGING: By 3 judges. Not responsible for loss or damage. May withhold awards.

SALES TERMS: 25% commission charge.

ENTRY FEE: $17 plus shipping and handling.

DEADLINES: Entry, April. Event, awards, June.

86

Burleson Annual Open Juried Art Exhibition
Burleson Area Chamber of Commerce
Irene Davis, Exhibition Chair
34 Caddo Peak
Joshua, Texas 76058 U.S.A.

Entry March

National; **entry open to age 18 and over;** annual in May; established 1980. Sponsored by Burleson Area Chamber of Commerce. Average statistics: 221 entries, 37 finalists, 10 awards, $2000 total sales. Held at Burleson Community Center, for 10 days.

DRAWING CONTEST: General (including pastel), original, 40 inches maximum including frame, wired, ready for hanging, under 1/16 or heavier plexiglass; limit 3 per entrant. Submit 1-3 slides of each work for entry review.

PAINTING CONTEST: Acrylic, Oil, Watercolor General. Requirements, restrictions same as for Drawing.

PRINT CONTEST: General. Requirements, restrictions same as for Drawing.

SCULPTURE CONTEST: General, original, portable by one person; limit 3 per entrant. Submit 1-3 slides of each work for entry review.

MIXED MEDIA CONTEST: General, original. Requirements, restrictions same as for Drawing.

AWARDS: $500 Lone Star Award. $300 Chamber of Commerce Award. $200 Good Life, Ambassador Awards. 2 $150 Special Merits. 5 $100 Merits.

JUDGING: Entry review and awards judging by art expert. Not responsible for loss or damage.

SALES TERMS: Work need not be for sale. 25% commission charge. Auction held on opening night for entries selected by sponsor who retains all money above minimum auction price set by artist. No commission charge.

ENTRY FEE: $7 per work plus return postage.

DEADLINES: Entry, March. Acceptance, April. Event, May.

87

Cooperstown Art Association (CAA) Art Exhibition

Olga Welsh, Director
28 Pioneer Street
Cooperstown, New York 13326
U.S.A. Tel: (607) 547-9777

Entry June

National; **entry open to U.S.;** annual in July-August; established 1928. Purpose: to foster interest in fine and applied arts. Sponsored and supported by CAA. Average statistics (all sections): 500 entries, 200 finalists, 5000 attendance, $10,000 sales. Held at CAA Galleries, Cooperstown for 4 weeks. Tickets: 50¢ (children under 12 free). Also sponsor education art classes, demonstrations by artists. Second contact: 22 Main Street, Cooperstown, New York 13326.

DRAWING CONTEST: General, original, maximum 60 inches horizontal dimension, 40 pounds; framed, ready for hanging; limit 1 per entrant. Recently produced.

PAINTING CONTEST: General; watercolors framed under glass, plexiglass, acetate. Other requirements, restrictions same as for Drawing.

PRINT CONTEST: General; framed under glass. Other requirements, restrictions same as for Drawing.

SCULPTURE CONTEST: General, maximum 48 inches in greatest lateral direction, 200 pounds; limit 1 per entrant.

MIXED MEDIA CONTEST: General. Requirements, restrictions same as for Drawing, Sculpture.

AWARDS: $7275 in Awards.

JUDGING: Entry review by 3 judges. Awards judging by juror.

Sponsor may photograph works for publicity. Not responsible for loss or damage.

SALES TERMS: Work need not be for sale. 20% commission charge.

ENTRY FEE: $10.

DEADLINES: Entry, June. Judging, event, July-August.

88

La Junta Fine Arts League National Art Show

Mignon Hively, Founder
P. O. Box 55
La Junta, Colorado 81050 U.S.A.
Tel: (303) 384-7035, 384-2682

Entry April

International; entry open to all; annual in May; established 1968. Formerly called FINE ARTS LEAGUE NATIONAL SPRING SHOW. Purpose: to afford artists opportunity to compete; encourage self-evaluation; promote public appreciation of fine arts. Sponsored and supported by La Junta Fine Arts League (founded 1967). Recognized by Colorado Artist Association. Average statistics (all sections): 450 entries, 225 entrants, 3000 attendance, $5000 total sales, $100 average sale per entrant. Held at Koshare Kiva, La Junta for 1 week. Have annual member show, one-person shows, workshops. Second contact: Koshare Kiva, 115 West 18th, La Junta, Colorado 81051; tel: (303) 384-2768, 384-9696.

DRAWING CONTEST: **Charcoal, Ink, Pastel, Pencil General,** original, maximum 36x48 inches, 50 pounds; matted, mounted; limit 2 per entrant (all sections). Submit resume of art career for publicity, files. Divisions: Professional, Nonprofessional. Competition includes photography.

PAINTING CONTEST: **Oil, Watercolor General** (including acrylic in oil medium, other media in watercolor technique). No wet paintings. Other requirements, divisions same as for Drawing.

PRINT CONTEST: **General.** Requirements, restrictions, divisions same as for Drawing.

SCULPTURE CONTEST: **General,** castings, carvings, original, maximum 36x48 inches, 50 pounds; limit 2 per entrant (all sections). No crafts. Other requirements, divisions same as for Drawing.

MIXED MEDIA CONTEST: **General,** including collage. Requirements, restrictions, divisions same as for Drawing, Sculpture.

AWARDS: (all sections): $100 Best of Show. $50 best professional. $25 best nonprofessional. $25 Jurors' Choice Award. Purchase Awards. Ribbons.

JUDGING: By 2 professionals. Not responsible for loss or damage.

SALES TERMS: All work must be for sale. 15% commission charge.

ENTRY FEE: $6 plus $1 handling fee and return postage (if sold, return postage refunded).

DEADLINES: Entry, April. Event, May.

New Jersey Painters and Sculptors Society National Exhibition

Helen B. Price, Secretary
61 Tweed Boulevard
Grandview, New York 10960 U.S.A.
Tel: (914) 359-3765

Entry March

National; **entry open to U.S.;** annual in Spring; established 1942. Sponsored by Painters and Sculptors Society of New Jersey (national, nonprofit organization). Average statistics (all sections): 160 entries, 39 awards, 8 total sales. Held at Bergen Community Museum, Paramus, New Jersey for 4 weeks. Second contact: Susan B. Liss, 59 Oxford Place, Glen Rock, New Jersey 07452; tel: (201) 652-6638.

DRAWING CONTEST: Pastel General, original, 44x50 inches maximum including frame, wired, ready for hanging; limit 1 per entrant (all sections). Completed in previous 2 years.

PAINTING CONTEST: Casein, Oil, Polymer, Tempera, Watercolor General. Requirements, restrictions same as for Drawing.

PRINT CONTEST: General. Requirements, restrictions same as for Drawing.

SCULPTURE CONTEST: General, including constructions and reliefs, original; works over 25 pounds must be free-standing, attached to base (artist supplies pedestal); limit 1 per entrant (all sections). Completed in previous 2 years. Submit advance data on weight, dimensions of heavy, oversized sculpture.

MIXED MEDIA CONTEST: General. Requirements, restrictions same as for Drawing, Sculpture.

AWARDS: (all sections): Over $1200 in cash, medals, merchandise.

JUDGING: Entry review by society members (3 in painting, 2 sculpture). Awards judging by members (2 in painting, 1 sculpture). Not responsible for loss or damage.

SALES TERMS: 15% commission charge.

ENTRY FEE: $10 plus return postage.

DEADLINES: Entry, March (shipped), April (hand-delivered). Event, April-May.

90

Ridge Art Association Annual Fine Arts Competition
210 Cypress Gardens Boulevard
Winter Haven, Florida 33880 U.S.A.
Tel: (813) 294-3551, ext. 279

Entry January

National; **entry open to U.S.;** annual in January-February; established 1961. Sponsored by and held at Ridge Art Association, Winter Haven for 2 weeks. Also sponsor gallery shows, annual outdoor sidewalk show.

DRAWING CONTEST: General, original, 72 inches wide maximum, framed, ready for hanging; limit 3 per entrant. Completed in previous 2 years. No commercial work. Competition includes photography.

PAINTING CONTEST: Acrylic, Oil, Watercolor General. Requirements same as for Drawing. No wet paint or frames.

PRINT CONTEST: General. Requirements same as for Drawing.

SCULPTURE CONTEST: General, original, 72 inches wide maximum, prepared for exhibition; limit 3 per entrant. Completed in previous 2 years. No commercial work.

MIXED MEDIA CONTEST: General. Requirements same as for Drawing.

AWARDS (all sections): $1000 to best of show. $500 First, $300 Second, $200 Third Place. 3 $100 Merit Awards.

JUDGING: By 1 art professional. Sponsor may withhold awards, reproduce entries for publicity. Not responsible for loss or damage.

SALES TERMS: 33-1/3% commission charge.

ENTRY FEE: $20.

DEADLINES: Entry, judging, January. Event, January-February.

91

Summit Art Center Juried Show
Perijane Zarembok
68 Elm Street
Summit, New Jersey 07901 U.S.A.
Tel: (201) 273-9121

Entry January

International; entry open to all; annual in January-February. Sponsored by Summit Art Center. Average statistics (all sections): 400 entries, 125 finalists, 6 awards. Held for 1 month. Have monthly art exhibition, classes.

DRAWING CONTEST: **General,** any medium on paper, 50x70 inches maximum, framed, ready for hanging; limit 1 per entrant (all sections).

PAINTING CONTEST: **General.** Requirements, restrictions same as for Drawing. Competition includes graphics.

PRINT CONTEST: **Any Type General** (including silkscreen). Requirements, restrictions same as for Drawing.

SCULPTURE CONTEST: **Clay, Glass, Metal, Paper, General** (or of material whose content is at least 50% of one of the foregoing), maximum 7 feet high, 12 square feet floor space, 75 pounds. Require preassembly, ready for display. Entrant provides base.

MIXED MEDIA CONTEST: **General,** or of material whose content is at least 50% composed of clay, glass, metal, or paper. Requirements, restrictions same as for Sculpture.

AWARDS: 6 $200 Cash Prizes.

JUDGING: Sponsor insures for $500 maximum.

SALES TERMS: 30% commission charge on sales.

ENTRY FEE: $8 plus return postage.

DEADLINES: Entry, judging, January. Event, January-February.

92

Tahoe Ehrman Mansion Art Show and Crafts Fair
North Tahoe Fine Arts Council
Eileen Janowitz-Ward, Coordinator
P. O. Box 249
Tahoe Vista, California 95732 U.S.A.
Tel: (916) 546-5562

Entry August

International; entry open to all; annual in August; established 1967. Purpose: to provide high-quality fine arts show. Sponsored by North Tahoe Fine Arts Council, Lake Tahoe State Parks Advisory Committee. Average $5000 total sales (all sections). Held at Ehrman Mansion (west shore of Lake Tahoe, Sugar Pine Point Park) for 1 week. Have reception, music. Publish *Arti-facts* (semimonthly). Also sponsor Outdoor Arts and Crafts Fair ($15 handling fee, $75 for 10x15-foot space for 1 week, no commission charge).

DRAWING CONTEST: **Pastel General,** original, maximum 48-inch width, ready for hanging; limit 2 (Adult), 1 (Children-High School) per entrant (all sections). Divisions: Adult, Children-High School. Competition includes crafts, photography.

PAINTING CONTEST: **Acrylic, Oil, Watercolor General** (including sand painting). Requirements, restrictions same as for Drawing.

PRINT CONTEST: **General** (including etchings and serigraphs). Requirements, restrictions same as for Drawing.

SCULPTURE CONTEST: **Clay, Metal, Wood, Mixed Media General,** maximum 3 feet, 100 pounds. Other requirements (except framing), restrictions same as for Drawing.

COLLAGE CONTEST: **General.** Requirements, restrictions same as for Drawing.

AWARDS: Cash Awards, first place each division.

JUDGING: By 3 art professionals.

SALES TERMS: 20% commission charge.

ENTRY FEE: $6 each entry Adult, free Children-High School.

DEADLINES: Entry, judging, event, August.

DRAWING, PAINTING, PRINTS, SCULPTURE, COLLAGE, MIXED MEDIA (Regional-State)

Limited to specific Region, State. Drawing, Painting, Prints, Sculpture, Collage, Mixed Media, Mosaic, Illuminated Art, Visual Art, and Art Fairs, including CALIFORNIA, CONNECTICUT, INDIANA, MICHIGAN, NEW YORK, OHIO, OREGON, PENNSYLVANIA, SOUTH CAROLINA, VIRGINIA, WEST VIRGINIA. (Also see other DRAWING, PAINTING, PRINT, SCULPTURE CATEGORIES.)

93

All Oregon Art Exhibition
Oregon State Fair
Lyn and Steven Nance-Sasser, Directors
State Fairgrounds
2330 17th Street N.E.
Salem, Oregon 97310 U.S.A.
Tel: (503) 378-3247

Entry July

State; **entry open to Oregon;** annual in August-September. Sponsored and supported by Oregon State Fair (founded 1866), Oregon Arts Commission, NEA. Average statistics (all sections): 300 entries, 100 finalists, $3500 in awards, 500,000 attendance. Held at Oregon State Fairgrounds, Salem for 11 days. Tickets: $3. Have art gallery, 2 $300 Honoraria for site-related projects. Also sponsor Oregon Salon of Photography, International Exhibition of Photography.

DRAWING CONTEST: **General,** original, 84x108 inches maximum, works on paper under glass or acrylic, ready for hanging; limit 1 per entrant (all sections). Completed in previous 2 years. Submit 3 slides of work (in plastic sheet) for entry review. Require hand-delivery of accepted works. No work from models or kits, supervised work. Divisions: Professional, Amateur, Student (Junior-Senior High School), Young Art (age 12 and under). Competition includes photography, crafts, environmental-conceptual work.

PAINTING CONTEST: **General.** Requirements, restrictions same as for Drawing.

PRINT CONTEST: General. Requirements, restrictions same as for Drawing.

SCULPTURE CONTEST: General. No excessive weight. Other requirements, restrictions same as for Drawing.

MIXED MEDIA CONTEST: General. Requirements, restrictions same as for Drawing, Sculpture.

AWARDS: Professional: 5 $300, 5 $200, 5 $100 Awards. Amateur: 5 $100, 5 $50, 6 $25 Awards; 2 Special Projects up to $300.

JUDGING: Entry review, awards judging by 3 judges. Not responsible for loss or damage.

ENTRY FEE: Amateur, $2.50. Students, $1. Professional, Young, free.

DEADLINES: Entry, July. Judging, August. Event, August-September.

94

California Exposition and State Fair Art Show

Peter Scott, Chief of Exhibits
Art Department, Building 7,
Exposition Center
1600 Exposition Blvd., P.O. Box 15649
Sacramento, California 95813 U.S.A.
Tel: (916) 924-2015

Entry June

State; **entry open to California;** annual in August-September. Originally agricultural fair; now includes industry, culture, science and arts. Sponsored by California State Fair, California State General Fund. Average statistics (all sections): 2000 entries, 1200 entrants, $15,000 in awards, 755,000 attendance. Held at California State Fairground in Sacramento for 18 days. Tickets: $4.

DRAWING CONTEST: General, framed, under glass or plastic, ready for hanging; limit 2 per entrant (all sections). Also have photography, crafts, agricultural sections.

PAINTING CONTEST: Acrylic, Oil, Gouache, Tempera, Watercolor, General, framed (non-opaque watercolor under glass or plastic); limit 2 per entrant (all sections). Categories: Acrylic, Oil, Gouache-Tempera-Watercolor.

PRINT CONTEST: Any Type General. Requirements, restrictions same as for Drawing.

SCULPTURE CONTEST: General, equipped for hanging or based for structural support and presentation; limit 2 per entrant (all sections). Submit minimum of 2 8x10-inch photographs or slides plus description for entry review.

ILLUMINATED ART CONTEST: Electronic-Incandescent General, framed, ready for hanging; limit 2 per entrant (all sections). No candlelight.

MIXED MEDIA CONTEST: General, framed, ready for hanging; limit 2 per entrant (all sections).

VISUAL ARTS CONTEST: All Media American West, California Agriculture, framed, ready for hanging; limit 2 entries (all sections). Categories: American West, California Agriculture.

AWARDS: $300 and State Fair Plaque First, $200 and State Fair Ribbon Second, $150 and Ribbon Third, $100 and Ribbon Fourth, $50 and Ribbon Fifth Place Awards. Maximum 15 Honorable Mentions to each drawing, painting (each category), prints, sculpture, illuminated art, mixed media, visual arts (each category). $100 and Wine Goblet to best of show (includes all sections). Honorable Mention Ribbons.

JUDGING: By 3 art professionals. May withhold awards or duplicate award in case of tie. Not responsible for loss or damage.

SALES TERMS: Work need not be for sale. No commission charge.

ENTRY FEE: $5 per work each category-section. Entrant pays return postage.

DEADLINES: Entry, June. Judging, July. Event, August-September.

95

Connecticut Women Artists Annual Exhibition
Jean Dalton, President
202 Shallowbrook Lane
Glastonbury, Connecticut 06033
U.S.A. Tel: (203) 646-1990

Entry September

State; **entry open to Connecticut women;** annual in September; established 1929. Purpose: to provide forum where women artists may exhibit their proficiency and creativity to public. Sponsored by Connecticut Women Artists, Inc. (formerly Connecticut Society of Women Painters). Average 450 entries (all sections). Held at Slade Ely House in New Haven for a month. Second contact: Jean Mazo, 3 Old Field Road, West Hartford, Connecticut 06117.

DRAWING CONTEST: **By Women General** (including pastel) original, framed; limit 2 per entrant. Recently produced. No works previously exhibited in exhibition area.

PAINTING CONTEST: **By Women Acrylic, Oil, Watercolor General.** Requirements, restrictions same as for Drawing.

PRINT CONTEST: **By Women General.** Requirements, restrictions same as for Drawing.

SCULPTURE CONTEST: **By Women General.** Requirements, restrictions same as for Drawing.

COLLAGE CONTEST: **By women General.** Requirements, restrictions same as for Drawing.

AWARDS: $300, $200, 2 $100 Connecticut Women Artists Awards. 2 $50 Awards. $50, 3 $25 Gift Certificates. $25 Award to watercolor. One-Woman Show to outstanding member entrant.

JUDGING: Entry review and awards judging by 1 juror. Not responsible for loss or damage.

SALES TERMS: Entries must be for sale (except portraits). No commission charge.

ENTRY FEE: $6 first, $4 second entry.

DEADLINES: Entry, event, September.

96

Falkirk Annual Juried Art Exhibition
San Rafael Recreation Department
Consuelo Underwood, Director
1408 Mission Avenue
San Rafael, California 94901 U.S.A.
Tel: (415) 456-1112

Entry February

Local; **entry open to Marin County, California;** annual in March-May; established 1974. Average statistics: 300 entries, 1000 attendance. Sponsored by San Rafael Recreation Department. Held at Falkirk Community Cultural Center in San Rafael for 6 weeks.

DRAWING CONTEST: **Any Me-**

dium General, 42-inch maximum width including frame, wired, ready for hanging; limit 2 per entrant (only one accepted). Completed in previous year.

PAINTING CONTEST: Any Medium General. Requirements same as for Drawing. No wet entries.

PRINT CONTEST: Any Type General. Requirements, restrictions same as for Drawing.

SCULPTURE CONTEST: General, portable by one person up steep stairway; limit 2 per entrant (only one accepted).

ASSEMBLAGE-COLLAGE CONTEST: General. Requirements, restrictions same as for Drawing. No wet entries.

AWARDS: $250 Purchase Award. $150 Best in Show. 2 $75 Merit Awards. Honorable Mentions.

JUDGING: Entry review and awards judging by 1 art expert. Insure accepted works only.

SALES TERMS: 30% commission charge.

ENTRY FEE: $3 per work.

DEADLINES: Entry, February. Acceptance, March. Event, March-May.

97

Irene Leache Memorial Art Exhibition
Chrysler Museum
Mowbray Arch at Olney Road
Norfolk, Virginia 23510 U.S.A.
Tel: (804) 622-1211

Entry January

Regional; **entry open to Virginia residents or former residents age 18 and over;** biennial in May-June; established 1930. Sponsored by Irene Leache Memorial. Held at Chrysler Museum in Norfolk for 6 weeks. Second contact: Box 6087, Milan Station, Norfolk, Virginia 23508.

DRAWING CONTEST: General, original, 8 inches to 8 feet any dimension including frame, under glass or plexiglass; limit 3 per entrant. Completed in previous 2 years. Submit 1 slide of each work for entry review. No pastels; entries requiring special handling, lighting, installation.

PAINTING CONTEST: General. Requirements, restrictions same as for Drawing.

PRINT CONTEST: General. Requirements, restrictions same as for Drawing.

SCULPTURE CONTEST: Small Works, maximum 4 feet any dimension; limit 3 per entrant. Completed in previous 2 years. Submit 1-3 slides of each work for entry review. No entries requiring special handling, lighting, or installation.

COLLAGE CONTEST: General. Requirements, restrictions same as for Drawing.

AWARDS: Certificates of Distinction with $200 Cash Prizes.

JUDGING: Entry review and awards judging by art expert. May withhold awards. Sponsor insures while in possession.

ENTRY FEE: None. No sales commission charge.

DEADLINES: Entry, January (slides), April (works). Judging, April. Event, May-June.

98

Mid-Michigan Art Exhibition

The Midland Art Council of the
Midland Center for the Arts
Toni Pott & Linda Wingfield, Chairs
1801 West St. Andrews Street
Midland, Michigan 48640 U.S.A.
Tel: (517) 631-3250

Entry January

State; **entry open to Michigan residents age 18 and over;** annual in January-February; established 1959. Sponsored and supported by Midland Art Council of the Midland Center for the Arts, Michigan Foundation of Arts. Average statistics (all sections): 750 entries, 250 entrants, 2000 attendance. Held at Midland Center for the Arts for 1 month.

DRAWING CONTEST: **General,** original, dimensions not specified, framed, ready for hanging; limit 3 per entrant. Produced in previous 2 years. Require hand-delivery. No works done under supervision. Competition for some awards includes crafts, photography.

PAINTING CONTEST: **General.** Requirements, restrictions same as for Drawing.

PRINT CONTEST: **General.** Requirements, restrictions same as for Drawing.

SCULPTURE CONTEST: **General,** original, dimensions not specified; limit 3 per entrant. Produced in previous 2 years. Require hand-delivery, assembly by artist. No work done under supervision. Competition for some awards includes crafts, photography.

MIXED MEDIA CONTEST: **General.** Requirements, restrictions same as for Drawing.

AWARDS (includes all sections): $750 First, $500 Second, $300 Third Prize. Up to $400 in Honorable Mentions. Viewer's Choice Award.

JUDGING: By 1 curator. Not responsible for loss or damage. Sponsor may withdraw entry from exhibition.

ENTRY FEE: $15. No sales commission charge.

DEADLINES: Entry, January. Event, January-February.

99

Mid-States Art Exhibition

Evansville Museum of Arts and
Science Art Committee
411 S. E. Riverside Drive
Evansville, Indiana 47713 U.S.A.
Tel: (812) 425-2406

Entry September

Regional; **entry open to Indiana and within 200 miles of Evansville;** annual in November-December; established 1947. Alternates with Mid-States Craft Exhibition (annual in Winter). Purpose: to provide artists with opportunity to exhibit and sell work, earn awards. Sponsored by Evansville Museum of Arts and Science. Supported by business and private donations. Average statistics (all sections): 440 entries, 95 exhibitors, 13 awards, 10,000 attendance. Held at Evansville Museum of Arts and Science for 5 weeks. Have juror lecture, traveling show. Also sponsor artist-in-residence program, workshops, classes, programs, traveling exhibition.

DRAWING CONTEST: **General** (including charcoal, pencil) original, maximum 96 inches any dimension, 150 pounds; framed (unframed works on paper must be matted, covered with acetate); limit 1 per entrant (all sections). Completed in previous 3 years. No entries requiring artist supervision for moving, assembly.

PAINTING CONTEST: General (including acrylic, gouache, oil, watercolor). No unframed work. Other requirements, restrictions same as for Drawing.

PRINT CONTEST: General (including etchings, intaglios, lithographs, serigraphs). No photographs. Other requirements, restrictions same as for Drawing.

SCULPTURE CONTEST: General (including bronze, steel, wood), original, maximum 96 inches any dimension, 150 pounds; limit 1 per entrant. Completed in previous 3 years. Large works weatherproofed for outdoor display.

COLLAGE CONTEST: General (including assemblage). Requirements, restrictions same as for Drawing.

AWARDS: All sections: $3000 Museum Guild Purchase Award. $1500 Laketon Asphalt Purchase Award. 2 $500, 2 $250 Purchase Awards. 4 $100 Merit Awards. Prints, drawing, watercolor: $200, 2 $100 Purchase Awards.

JUDGING: By out-of-area juror. Sponsor insures during exhibition only. Not responsible for in-transit damage, unclaimed work.

SALES TERMS: Work need not be for sale. 20% commission charge.

ENTRY FEE: $8.

DEADLINES: Entry, September. Judging, November-December.

100

San Bernardino County Museum Association Traditional Artists Exhibition

Fine Arts Institute
Dorothy Hanna, President
2024 Orange Tree Lane
Redlands, California 92373 U.S.A.
Tel: (714) 792-1334, 815-4825

Entry October

State; **entry open to California;** annual in November; established 1966. Purpose: to exhibit excellent, original art in traditional media. Sponsored and supported by San Bernardino County Museum Association. Held at Fine Arts Institute, San Bernardino for 24 days. Second contact: Elizabeth Hopkins, Exhibition Chair, 620 Via Vista, Redlands, California 92373.

DRAWING CONTEST: Representational, original, 46 inches maximum length (including frame), under glass, ready for hanging; limit 3 per entrant (all sections). Recently executed. Require hand-delivery.

PAINTING CONTEST: Acrylic, Oil, Watercolor Representational, watercolors under glass. Other requirements, restrictions same as for Drawing. No wet paint or frames.

PRINT CONTEST: Representational. Requirements same as for Drawing.

SCULPTURE CONTEST: Representational, original, 46 inches maximum dimension, easily transportable by 2 adults; limit 3 per entrant. Recently executed. Require hand-delivery.

MIXED MEDIA CONTEST: Representational. Requirements same as for Drawing and Painting.

AWARDS (includes all sections): $500 First, $300 Second, $200 Third Prize. 3 $500 Purchase Awards. $50 Merit Award. Grumbacher Silver Medallion for paintings. Certificates of Excellence.

JUDGING: By 2 art professionals. Not responsible for loss or damage.

SALES TERMS: Work need not be for sale. 25% commission charge.

ENTRY FEE: $5 per item.

DEADLINES: Entry, October. Event, November.

101

San Diego Art Institute (SDAI) Annual Exhibition
Shirley Viennese, Gallery Director
1449 El Prado
Balboa Park
San Diego, California 92101 U.S.A.
Tel: (714) 234-5946

Entry September

Local; **entry open to San Diego County;** annual in October-November; established 1953. Began as Fiesta, photography added 1978. Purpose: to stimulate excellence in work by local artists; provide exhibition; promote understanding, appreciation. Sponsored by SDAI (founded 1941). Supported by private donations. Average statistics: 960 entries, 550 entrants, 22 awards, 450 attendance, $1934 total sales. Held at SDAI Gallery for 4-5 weeks. Have concerts. Publish *San Diego Art Institute Journal* (monthly). Also sponsor monthly juried membership shows, concerts; continuous Little Gallery exhibition; art classes, workshops, lectures, panel discussions.

DRAWING CONTEST: General, original; 8x6 feet maximum, framed, ready for hanging; limit 3 per entrant (all sections). Produced in previous 2 years. Require hand-delivery. No wet or unsafe work; previously exhibited in any California juried show. Competition includes photography, related media.

PAINTING CONTEST: General (including acrylic, oil, watercolor). Watercolors must be under protective coating (glass, plexiglass, plastic spray coat). Other requirements, restrictions same as for Drawing (not in competition with other media).

PRINT CONTEST: General. Requirements, restrictions same as for Drawing.

SCULPTURE CONTEST: Any Medium General, original; 8-84 inches high, 5 feet long, 150 pounds; limit 3 per entrant. Require hand-delivery. No wet or unsafe work, previously exhibited in any California juried show.

MIXED MEDIA CONTEST: Assemblage, Collage, Experimental. No crafts, electrical work. Other requirements, restrictions same as for Drawing, Sculpture.

AWARDS: $1750 in Cash Awards. $350 to best in show. $200 First, $100 Second, $50 Third Prize each to best paintings, graphics (drawing or print), sculptures, mixed media. 9 $25 Honorable Mentions.

JUDGING: By 1-2 prominent artists. Sponsor insures accepted entries during exhibition.

SALES TERMS: All work must be for sale. 30% commission charge.

ENTRY FEE: $6 per item.

DEADLINES: Entry, judging, September. Awards, October. Event, October-November.

102

South Carolina State Fair Fine Arts Juried Show
South Carolina State Fair
Meg McLean, Superintendent of Fine Arts
505 Winston Road
Columbia, South Carolina 29209
U.S.A. Tel: (803) 776-4698

Entry October

State; **entry open to South Carolina;** annual in October; event over 25 years old. Purpose: to exhibit fine art from professionals, amateurs, children. Sponsored by The State Fair Association. Held at Fairgrounds Cantey Building, Columbia for 10 days. Tickets: $2 fair admission.

DRAWING CONTEST: **General** (including pastel), 11x54 inches maximum framed size, ready for hanging; limit 1 per entrant (all sections). Divisions: Professional, Amateur. Competition for some awards includes photography, crafts, commercial art.

PAINTING CONTEST: **Acrylic, Encaustic, Oil, Tempera, Watercolor General.** Requirements, restrictions, divisions same as for Drawing. Categories: Acrylic, Encaustic, Oil, Tempera, Watercolor.

PRINT CONTEST: **General.** Requirements, restrictions, divisions same as for Drawing.

SCULPTURE CONTEST: **General,** 150 pounds maximum, permanent materials, ready for hanging (hanging sculptures); limit 1 per entrant. Divisions: Professional, Amateur.

COLLAGE-MIXED MEDIA CONTEST: **General.** Requirements, restrictions, divisions same as for Drawing, Sculpture.

AWARDS: $1000 State Fair Purchase Award, $500 State Record Merit Award (all sections). Professional: $100 First, $50 Second, $25 Third Place Prize (each category and sections); $350 Pioneer Purchase Award to rural life theme; $50 Pioneer Merit Award (all sections); $50 Richtex Merit Award to best sculpture in ceramic medium. Amateur: $50 First, $25 Second, $10 Third Place Prize (each category and sections); $250 Pioneer Purchase Award to rural life theme; $50 Pioneer Merit Award (all sections); $50 Trenholm Artist Guild Award to realism in oil, mixed-media, watercolor, prints, drawing.

JUDGING: By 3 local professional artists for entry review (each section), 1 out-of-state awards judge. Sponsor may photograph winners for publicity.

ENTRY FEE: None. Entrant pays postage. No sales commission charge.

DEADLINES: Entry, event, October.

103

Three Rivers Arts Festival

Carnegie Institute
John Jay, Executive Director
4400 Forbes Avenue
Pittsburgh, Pennsylvania 15213
U.S.A. Tel: (412) 687-7014

Entry March

Regional; **entry open to age 18 and over in Pennsylvania, Ohio, West Virginia, western New York;** annual in June; established 1960. Purpose: to offer best of visual, performing arts in parklike setting. Sponsored by Carnegie Institute. Supported by businesses, city-county government, Art Institute of Pittsburgh, Pittsburgh History and Landmarks Foundation. Recognized by NEA as exemplary arts festival. Average statistics (all events, sections): 1500 entrants, 300 artist market participants, 300,000 attendance, 200 performances. Have musical, dance, theatrical performances; environmental projects; sky sculpture; food; children's activities. Held at Gateway Center, Pittsburgh, and Point State Park for 10 days.

DRAWING CONTEST: **General,** original, 48x84 inches maximum framed size, suitable for outdoor hanging; limit 3 per entrant per maximum 2 sections. Submit 2x2 35mm slides of each entry for entry review. No commercial, molded, kit-assembled entries. Competition includes photography, videography.

PAINTING CONTEST: General. Requirements, restrictions same as for Drawing.

PRINT CONTEST: General, hand-pulled. Other requirements, restrictions same as for Drawing.

SCULPTURE CONTEST: General. Original; limit 3 per category. Submit 3 2x2-inch 35mm slides (1 close-up) of each entry. Categories: Outdoor, Indoor. No commercial, molded, kit-assembled entries.

COLLAGE CONTEST: General. Requirements, restrictions same as for Drawing.

ART FAIR: Drawings, Paintings, Prints, Sculpture, Collage. Submit 5 2x2-inch 35mm slides of 5 representative works for entry review, publicity information; picture of display unit. Entrants provide and attend sales displays; limit 1 5-day period per entrant. No agents, dealers, commercial entries.

AWARDS: Cash totaling $4200 (all events, media). (Also have 4 $125 awards for fair displays of 2D and 3D works.)

JUDGING: Entry review by art professionals. Awards judging by 1 specialist for 2D, 2 for 3D (1 each for small indoor, large outdoor). Not responsible for loss or damage of art fair entries; sponsor insures contest entries.

SALES TERMS: All work (both events) must be for sale. 25% commission charge (contest); no commission charge (fair).

ENTRY FEE: $13 screening-jury fee (both events). $125 for 8x8-foot, 5-day outdoor boothspace (fair).

DEADLINES: Entry, March. Notification, April. Events, judging, June.

104

Toledo Area Artists' Exhibition

Toledo Museum of Art
Robert Phillips, Curator of Contemporary Art
P. O. Box 1013
Toledo, Ohio 43697 U.S.A. Tel: (419) 255-8000

Entry April

Regional; **entry open to 17 counties in Northwest Ohio and Southeast Michigan;** annual in June-July; established 1918. Sponsored and supported by Toledo Museum of Art, Toledo Federation of Art Societies. Held at Toledo Museum of Art for 1 month. Second contact: Toledo Federation of Art Societies, 2445 Monroe Street, Toledo, Ohio 43610.

DRAWING CONTEST: General, original, framed under glass or plexiglass; limit 3 per entrant (all sections), set counts as 1 entry. Completed in previous 2 years. No copies or student work. Competition includes photography.

PAINTING CONTEST: Gouache, Oil, Synthetic, Watercolor, Mixed Media General, original, framed. No wet paint.

PRINT CONTEST: General. Requirements, restrictions same as for Drawing.

SCULPTURE CONTEST: General. Requirements (except framing), restrictions same as for Drawing.

MOSAIC CONTEST: Tile General, fired. Other requirements (except framing), restrictions same as for Drawing.

AWARDS: $500 to best of Show. 5 $250 First, 5 $175 Second, 5 $100 Third Awards. $100 Molly Morpeth Canaday Award for outstanding painting. Roulet Medal for best painting, graphic, or sculpture. Purchase Awards.

JUDGING: Cash awards by 3 art professionals. Purchase awards by Toledo Museum of Art. Sponsor may copy for catalog, publicity. Not responsible for loss or damage.

ENTRY FEE: $10 plus $7.50 return postage.

DEADLINES: Entry, notification, April. Event, June-July. Materials returned, August.

DRAWING, PAINTING, SCULPTURE

Drawing, Graphics, Painting, Sculpture, Mixed Media, including REPRESENTATIONAL. (Also see other DRAWING, PAINTING, SCULPTURE CATEGORIES.)

105

Allied Artists of America (AAA) Annual Open Exhibition
Marion Roller, Corresponding Secretary
1 West 67th Street
New York, New York 10023 U.S.A.

Entry October

International; **entry open to U.S., Canada, South America;** annual in December-January; established 1914. Purpose: to provide exhibit space for, further cause of contemporary American artists. Sponsored by AAA (nonprofit corporation). Supported by AAA, art manufacturers. Average statistics (all sections): 250 entries, 42 awards, 800 attendance. Held at National Arts Club, New York for 1 month. Have demonstrations, films, lectures. Also sponsor art scholarships. Second contact: Reta Soloway, President, 145 Lexington Avenue, Franklin Square, New York, New York 11010; tel: (516) 439-4369.

DRAWING CONTEST: Pastel General, 44x44 inches maximum (including frame), under glass or plexiglass, framed, ready for hanging; limit 1 per entrant (all sections). Submit 1 35mm cardboard-mounted color slide for entry review.

PAINTING CONTEST: Oil General (including varnished acrylic, casein, and tempera framed like oils). Requirements, restrictions same as for Drawing (no glass).

Watercolor General (including all water media). Requirements, restrictions same as for Drawing.

SCULPTURE CONTEST: Any Medium General, in the round, maximum 24x34x80 inches, 300 pounds; limit 1 maximum per entrant. Request 2-3 35mm cardboard-mounted color slides for entry review.

AWARDS: $600 AAA Gold, $400 Silver Medals (oil, watercolor, sculpture). *Oil:* $300 Lowe Award to contemporary oil painting. $250 Grand Central Art Galleries Award to traditional realism. $250 Grumbacher Gold Medal. $200 Advancement of Art Award. $150 Lehrer Memorial Award to traditional landscape. $100 Salmagundi Club Award. 1 $300, 2 $200, 1 $150, 2 $100 additional awards. *Watercolor* (including pastel): $500 DeMaree Award. $500 Stacks Award to Southern artist. $100 National Arts Club Award. $100 Grumbacher Silver Medal. $100 Pastel Society Award. . $200, $150, 4 $100 additional awards.

Sculpture: $500 Hexter Award. $500 AAA Award. $250 Montana Memorial Award to traditional. $150 Sculptor's Supplies-Porton Award to wood or stone work. $150 Armour Memorial Award (female figure). $100 Richard Memorial Award to religious sculpture. $100 Roman Bronze Works Award. $350, 2 $200 additional awards.

JUDGING: Entry review and awards judging by 2 different panels of 3 jurors each section. Sponsor may photograph accepted entries for catalog. Not responsible for loss or damage.

SALES TERMS: Entries may be for sale. 20% commission charge.

ENTRY FEE: $10 plus shipping charges.

DEADLINES: Entry, October. Awards, December. Event, December-January.

106

Hudson Valley Art Association (HVAA) Annual Exhibition
Joan Rudman, Publicity Chair
274 Quarry Road
Stamford, Connecticut 06903 U.S.A.
Tel: (203) 322-1448

Entry April

National; **entry open to U.S. artists over age 21;** annual in May; established 1928. Purpose: to preserve, perpetuate, promote American tradition of traditional representative art. Sponsored by HVAA (nonprofit organization founded 1928 by Hudson Valley Region artists). Supported by private donations, membership fees. Recognized by Council of American Artists Societies. Average statistics: 500 entries, 340 finalists, 42 awards, 3260 attendance. Held at Westchester County Center Exhibition Galleries in White Plains, New York for 1 week. Have reception, demonstrations, art appreciation tour. Also sponsor Scholarship Fund. Second contact: Rayma Spaulding, 15 Minivale Road, Stamford, Connecticut 06907; tel: (203) 322-1110.

DRAWING CONTEST: Pastel Representational, original, realistic, maximum 60 inches width (including frame), wired, ready for hanging; limit 1 per entrant (all sections). No crates, oval frames.

GRAPHICS CONTEST: Representational, framed under glass or rigid plastic. Other requirements, restrictions same as for Drawing.

PAINTING CONTEST: Acrylic, Oil, Watercolor Representational. No wet or sticky paintings. Other requirements, restrictions same as for Drawing.

SCULPTURE CONTEST: Representational. Other requirements, restrictions same as for Drawing.

AWARDS: HVAA Gold Medal of Honor (at discretion of Board of Directors). Honorary Mentions. Graphics: $100, $50 Awards. Oil: $500 Dumond Memorial Award to best light and atmospheric effect. 2 $100 Awards to portrait. $250, 2 $100, $75, 4 $50 Awards. Pastel: $100, $50 Awards. $50 Pastel Society of America Award. $150 Award to portrait. Sculpture: $250, $100 Awards. $50 Sculpture Associates Certificate Award. Watercolor: $250, $150, $75, 2 $50 Awards.

JUDGING: Entry review by HVAA Board of Directors. Awards by 9 jurors (3 each oils-pastels, watercolors-graphics, sculptures). May withhold awards. Not responsible for loss or damage.

SALES TERMS: Entries may be for

sale. 10% commission charge (donated to HVAA Scholarship Fund).

ENTRY FEE: $12 plus return postage and $35 for delivery and storage.

DEADLINES: Entry, April. Event, May.

107

New England Exhibition of Painting, Drawing and Sculpture
Silvermine Guild Center for the Arts
Virginia Mann, Gallery Director
1037 Silvermine Road
New Canaan, Connecticut 06840
U.S.A. Tel: (203) 966-5617

Entry May

Regional; **entry open to New England, New York, New Jersey, Pennsylvania;** annual in May-June; established 1948. Purpose: to provide meaningful showcase for emerging artists. Sponsored by Silvermine Guild. Average statistics: 2000 entries, 1500 entrants, 10 awards, 5000 attendance, $15,000 total sales. Held at Silvermine Guild Center in New Canaan for 3 weeks. Also sponsor National Biennial Print Exhibition, music concerts, educational programs, summer exhibitions of fine crafts.

DRAWING CONTEST: Pastel General, maximum 60x72 inches, wired with screw eyes, ready to install; unlimited entry. Completed in previous 5 years. No prints, multiples.

PAINTING CONTEST: Casein, Oil, Polymer, Watercolor General. Requirements, restrictions same as for Drawing.

SCULPTURE CONTEST: Any medium General, maximum 8 feet (height or width), 16 square feet, 300 pounds; wall reliefs maximum 60x72 inches (width x height), 100 pounds. Indoor sculpture to be fully assembled; entries exceeding maximum dimensions may be exhibited outdoors. No multiples.

MIXED MEDIA CONTEST: General. Requirements same as for Drawing. No prints, multiples, photographs, crafts.

AWARDS: $1000 Silvermine Guild Award; $500 New England Exhibition Award; $250 New York (Greenwich) Graphic Society Award; 1 $250, 10 $150 Awards to painting. $1000 Silvermine Guild Award; $500 Readers Digest Award; 2 $250, 1 $200, 3 $150 Awards to drawings and mixed media. $1000 Albert Jacobson Memorial Award; $500 Molly Jacobson Memorial Award; 1 $300, 2 $250, 2 $200, 1 $175, 4 $150 Awards to sculpture (including outdoor, cast bronze, traditional). 2 $150 Special Awards.

JUDGING: Entry review and awards by 1 juror. Not responsible for loss or damage on works not accepted for exhibition; sponsor insures accepted works.

SALES TERMS: 35% commission charge.

ENTRY FEE: $15 each entry.

DEADLINES: Entry, May. Event, May-June.

108

Palm Beach International Art Competition
Palm Beach Art Galleries
Holly Daly Herman, Director
240 Worth Avenue
Palm Beach, Florida 33480 U.S.A.
Tel: (305) 655-9364

Entry August

International; entry open to all; annual in November; established 1979. Purpose: to seek out talented artists. Sponsored by Palm Beach Art Galleries. Average statistics (all sections): 400 entries, 200 entrants, 6 countries, 14 awards, 1000 attendance. Held in Palm Beach for 4 days. Have lectures, seminars.

DRAWING CONTEST: **Pastel, Pen and Ink General,** 3x3 feet maximum; limit 2 (all sections) per entrant. Submit resume or brochure. Competition includes photography.

PAINTING CONTEST: **Acrylic, Oil, Watercolor General.** Requirements same as for Drawing.

SCULPTURE CONTEST: **General.** Requirements same as for Drawing.

AWARDS: $500 and 1-person show, First. Second, Third, Fourth Place, group show. Honorable Mentions.

JUDGING: By 1 artist. Based on creativity, imagination, subject matter.

SALES TERMS: 40% commission charge.

ENTRY FEE: $25 plus return postage.

DEADLINES: Entry, August. Event, November.

DRAWING, PRINTS

Drawing and Prints, including ENGRAVING. (Also see other DRAWING, PRINT CATEGORIES.)

109

Arkansas Arts Center Prints, Drawings and Crafts Exhibition
Townsend Wolfe, Director
MacArthur Park, P. O. Box 2137
Little Rock, Arkansas 72203 U.S.A.

Entry April

Regional; **entry open to South-Central U.S.;** annual in May-June; established 1968. Sponsored by Arkansas Arts Center, founded in 1941 to establish and maintain growth, understanding of arts. Supported by City of Little Rock. Recognized by Arkansas State Board of Education, American Association of Museums. Held at Arkansas Arts Center in Little Rock for 4 weeks. Have book and film library, traveling seminars, concerts, workshops, sales, visiting artists programs. Also sponsor Delta Art Exhibit, Toys Designed by Artists Exhibition; instruction, exhibitions and scholarships in photography, filmmaking, drama, dance, arts and crafts.

DRAWING CONTEST: **Any Medium General** (except watercolor); limit 2 per entrant (all sections). Also have crafts, photography sections.

PRINT CONTEST: **Any Type General,** limit 2 per entrant.

ELIGIBILITY: U.S. residents residing in Arkansas, Louisiana, Mississippi, Missouri, Oklahoma, Tennessee, Texas.

AWARDS: $200 each section. $2000 in Purchase Awards (all sections).

JUDGING: By 1 judge. Sponsor retains winning entries for permanent collection.

ENTRY FEE: $7.50 per work.

DEADLINES: Entry, April. Event, May-June.

110

Dulin National Print and Drawing Competition
Dulin Gallery of Art
Roxanne May, Director of Development

3100 Kingston Pike
Knoxville, Tennessee 37919 U.S.A.
Tel: (615) 525-6101

Entry February

National; **entry open to U.S.;** annual in Spring; established 1965. Sponsored by and held at Dulin Gallery of Art for 5 weeks. Also sponsor regional High School Print and Drawing Competition and Exhibition.

DRAWING CONTEST: Any Medium General, original, maximum 30x40 inches, unmounted, unbacked; limit 2 per entrant. Completed in previous 2 years. Competition includes prints.

PRINT CONTEST: Any Type General. Requirements, restrictions same as for Drawing.

AWARDS: $2000 in Purchase Awards.

JUDGING: By 1 nationally prominent judge. Sponsor may reproduce accepted works for catalog, press purposes; insures works while on exhibit, not responsible for loss or damage during transportation or judging.

ENTRY FEE: $15 plus return postage (carrier-delivered), $10 (hand-delivered). 25% sales commission charge.

DEADLINES: Entry, judging, February. Notification, March. Event, April-May.

111

North Dakota Annual Print and Drawing Show
University of North Dakota (UND)
Visual Arts Department
Ronald Schaefer, Chair
Box 8134-UND Station
Grand Forks, North Dakota 58202
U.S.A. Tel: (701) 777-2257

Entry February

National; **entry open to U.S.;** annual in Spring; established 1956. Began as mixed media exhibit to 1968. Purpose: to bring national exhibition of contemporary works to rural community, university setting. Sponsored by UND Visual Arts Department. Supported by UND. Average statistics (all sections): 1300 entries, 650 entrants, 100 finalists, 1500-2000 attendance. Held at UND Art Galleries for 4 weeks. Also sponsor workshops, exhibitions, classes conducted by visiting artists.

DRAWING CONTEST: Any Medium General, on paper, on white mats covered with acetate, unframed, without glass; limit 2 per entrant. Submit 35mm color slides for entry review. Competition includes prints.

PRINT CONTEST: Any Type General, including monoprints. Nonpaper prints acceptable. Requirements, restrictions same as for Drawing.

AWARDS: Minimum $2500 in Purchase Awards.

JUDGING: Entry review and awards judging by 1 judge. Sponsor insures during exhibition only.

SALES TERMS: 20% commission charge.

ENTRY FEE: $8 plus return postage.

DEADLINES: Entry, February. Notification, March. Accepted works, April. Event, April-May.

112

SECCA Southeastern Competition
Southeastern Center for
Contemporary Art (SECCA)
750 Marguerite Drive
Winston-Salem, North Carolina
27106 U.S.A. Tel: (919) 725-1904

Entry June

Regional; **entry open to Southeastern U.S. residents over age 18;** annual in August-September; established 1933. Average statistics (all sections): 1000 entries, 400 entrants, 11 states. Sponsored by and held at SECCA in Winston-Salem for 8 weeks.

DRAWING CONTEST: General, matted or mounted, covered with acetate or glazed and framed; limit 3 per entrant (all sections). Produced in previous 2 years. No plastic or metal clip frames, works requiring special installation. Competition includes photography.

PRINT CONTEST: General. Requirements same as for Drawing.

ELIGIBILITY: Residents (over age 18) of North Carolina, South Carolina, Georgia, Virginia, West Virginia, Tennessee, Kentucky, Louisiana, Mississippi, Alabama, Florida.

AWARDS: Up to $3000 in Purchase Awards.

JUDGING: By 1 judge. Sponsor reserves right to photograph entries for publicity, educational purposes; insures work during exhibition; not responsible for in-transit loss or damage.

SALES TERMS: 33-1/3% commission charge.

ENTRY FEE: $6 plus return postage.

DEADLINES: Entry, June. Judging, awards, July. Event, August-September. Materials returned, October.

113

Second Street Gallery National Juried Exhibition
116 N. E. Second Street
Charlottesville, Virginia 22901 U.S.A.

Entry March

International; **entry open to U.S. residents or U.S. agents of foreign residents;** annual in April-May; established 1974. Purpose: to present, promote work of new innovative artists. Sponsored by and held at Second Street Gallery for 5 weeks.

DRAWING CONTEST: Any Medium General, unframed, covered with acetate; limit 2 per entrant (all sections). Produced in previous 2 years. Submit 1 slide per work for entry review. Also have photography section.

PRINT CONTEST: Any Type General. Requirements, restrictions same as for Drawing.

AWARDS: $2500 in Cash and Purchase Awards, includes $400 Purchase Award to best of show (all sections). 2 $250 Honorable Mention Purchase Awards.

JUDGING: By 1 judge. Sponsor may reproduce entries for publicity; insures during exhibition.

SALES TERMS: 30 commission charge.

ENTRY FEE: $10 plus $5 shipping charge.

DEADLINES: Entry, acceptance, March. Event, April-May.

114

Waukesha National Print and Drawing Show
University of Wisconsin-Waukesha (UWW)
Stephanie Selle, Gallery Director
Art Department
1500 University Drive
Waukesha, Wisconsin 53186 U.S.A.
Tel: (414) 548-5886

Entry November

National; **entry open to U.S. residents age 18 and over;** biennial (odd years) in Winter; established 1978. Began as annual show, became biennial 1981. Sponsored and supported by UWW. Average statistics (all sections): 150 entries, 10 awards. Held at Waukesha Commons Gallery, UWW, for 1-2 months.

DRAWING CONTEST: General, matted or mounted with firm backing, protected with acetate. No photographs, glazed or framed works.

PRINT CONTEST: General. Requirements, restrictions same as for Drawing.

AWARDS: Over $750 in Purchase Awards. 2 1-person shows in UWW Commons Gallery.

JUDGING: By 1 out-of-state judge. Sponsor may reproduce accepted works; insures entries at exhibition.

ENTRY FEE: $10 plus return postage. No sales commission charge.

DEADLINES: Entry, November. Event, December-February.

115

Arteder International Graphic Arts Exhibition

Feria Internacional de Muestras de Bilbao
Roberto Velasco Barroetabena, Director
Plaza P. M. Basterrechea, 2
Apartado 468
Bilbao 13, SPAIN Tel: 441-54-00

Entry January

International; entry open to all; annual in March-April. Purpose: to contribute to greater appreciation of artistic work and research; increase cultural understanding among people. Sponsored by Foral Diputation of Vizcaya. Supported by Department of Culture of Basque Government. Held at Bilbao International Exhibition Center fairgrounds for 2-1/2 weeks.

DRAWING CONTEST: General, mounted on 50x70cm white bristol board, dated and signed; limit 2 per entrant per section. Produced in previous 2 years. Submit 18x24cm photo of work, documentation (optional). Also have photography section.

PRINT CONTEST: Engraving General. Requirements, restrictions same as for Drawing. No monotype or 3D exhibits.

AWARDS: Purchase Awards: 1,000,000 Pts. First, 300,000 Pts. Second, 200,000 Pts. Third, each section.

JUDGING: By international jury of specialists. Sponsor may reproduce accepted entries for promotion, publicity; insures during exhibition.

SALES TERMS: All work must be valued in pesetas. 25% commission charge.

ENTRY FEE: Not specified. Sponsor pays return postage.

DEADLINES: Entry, January. Event, March-April.

DRAWING, SCULPTURE

Drawing and Sculpture in any medium. (Also see other DRAWING, SCULPTURE CATEGORIES.)

116

Ball State University (BSU) Drawing and Small Sculpture Show

BSU Art Gallery

Betty Magill, Secretary
Muncie, Indiana 47306 U.S.A.
Tel: (317) 285-5242

Entry January

National; **entry open to U.S.;** annual in May-June; established 1955. Recognized by American Association of Museums. Average statistics: 600 entries, 400 entrants, 200 finalists, $1500 in awards, $1500 total sales. Held at Ball State University Art Gallery in Muncie for 8 weeks.

DRAWING CONTEST: General, maximum 84 inches packaged size (length plus girth), mounted or matted with heavy back-boarding, covered with acetate, unframed; limit 2 per entrant (drawing or sculpture). Fixative recommended on charcoal, pastels, other soft pencil drawings. No glass-covered entries, prints.

SCULPTURE CONTEST: General, maximum 84 inches (length plus girth, dismantled) packaged size, 40 pounds; limit 2 per entrant. Submit 2 color slides of each work for entry review.

AWARDS: $3000 in Purchase and Cash Awards.

JUDGING: Entry Review (sculpture) and awards judging by 1 art expert. Works insured while in gallery's possession and during return shipping. Sponsor may photograph entries for catalog, publicity.

ENTRY FEE: $10. Sponsor pays return postage. No sales commission charge.

DEADLINES: Entry, January (sculpture), March (drawings). Event, May-June.

117

Del Mar College National Drawing and Small Sculpture Show

William E. Lambert, Chair
Department of Art
Corpus Christi, Texas 78404 U.S.A.
Tel: (512) 881-6216

Entry January

National; **entry open to U.S.;** annual in April; established 1966. Held at Del Mar College in Corpus Christi for 1 month.

DRAWING CONTEST: General, on paper, maximum 84 inches crated size (length plus girth), matted or mounted on corrugated heavy cardboard, unframed, acetate covering, sprayed with fixative; limit 2 per entrant (both sections).

SCULPTURE CONTEST: General, maximum 84 inches crated size (length plus girth); limit 2 per entrant (both sections). Submit 2 slides each (different views) for entry review.

AWARDS: Over $3000 in Awards, Purchases, Prizes. $700 Joseph Cain Memorial Purchase Award to sculpture. $400 Del Mar College Purchase Award to drawing. Invitation for One Man Show (includes both sections).

JUDGING: Entry review and awards judging by 1 juror. Sponsor retains slides of accepted sculptures. Not responsible for loss or damage.

SALES TERMS: All work must be for sale. No commission charge.

ENTRY FEE: $15.

DEADLINES: Entry, January. Judging, February. Event, April.

118

Westwood Center of the Arts (WCA) National Small Sculpture and Drawing Exhibition
Selma B. Lokitz, President
1355 Westwood Boulevard
Los Angeles, California 90024 U.S.A.
Tel: (213) 477-2668

Entry March

International; **entry open to U.S., Canada;** annual in April-June; established 1961. Purpose: to further professional opportunities for artists; offer community service. Sponsored by WCA (founded 1947), formerly Westwood Art Association. Supported by membership dues, entry fees, donations. Average statistics: 100 entries, 50 entrants, 8 finalists, 5 awards, 50 attendance, 20 sales. Held in West Los Angeles for 2 months. Publish *WCA Newsletter.* Also sponsor Open Watermedia Exhibition, Open Painting on Canvas Exhibition, Open Print Show, other monthly exhibitions, scholarships-financial aid.

DRAWING CONTEST: Any Medium General, 16x16 to 60x60 inches; limit 3 per entrant (both sections). Submit slides for entry review.

SCULPTURE CONTEST: Any Medium General, maximum 6 feet high, 30 inches wide, 100 pounds. Hanging pieces acceptable. No installation pieces. Submit slides for entry review.

AWARDS: (Both sections): Two-Week Solo Exhibition to best in show. $200 First, $100 Second, $75 Third Awards. $15 Zora's Art Supplies Award. 3 Honorable Mention Ribbons.

JUDGING: By 1 artist. Not responsible for loss or damage.

SALES TERMS: 25% commission charge.

ENTRY FEE: $15.

DEADLINES: Entry, March. Judging, awards, April. Event, April-June.

GRANTS, LOANS (General)

Grants, Fellowships, Equipment-Facilities Loans primarily for RESEARCH, PRODUCTION, DEVELOPMENT and AID in Printmaking, Sculpture, and Visual Arts. Includes EMERGENCY ASSISTANCE, FOLK ARTS, and for CUBANS, WOMEN. (Also see RESIDENCE GRANTS, SCHOLARSHIPS, FELLOWSHIPS.)

119

Adolph and Esther Gottlieb Foundation Grants for Visual Artists
380 West Broadway
New York, New York 10012 U.S.A.

Entry December

International; **entry open to 20-year professionals;** annual; established 1977. Foundation (nonprofit) founded 1976 by provision of Adolph Gottlieb's will. Purpose: to provide financial assistance to continue careers of established artists. Average statistics: 300 entrants, 20 countries, 20 finalists, 5-8 awards.

VISUAL ARTS GRANTS: Professional Work. Several grants available to artists professionally involved for minimum of 20 years, who are currently in need of funds to continue work.

JUDGING: By Foundation's Board of Directors. Based on examination, evaluation of submitted materials.

DEADLINES: Application, December.

120

Betty Brazil Memorial Fund Woman Sculptor Grant
P. O. Box 221
Tarrytown, New York 10591 U.S.A.

Entry March

International; **entry open to women sculptors;** annual in May; established 1979. Named after Betty Brazil, sculptor, painter, feminist. Grant endowed by her friends, admirers. Purpose: to aid career development of women sculptors. Sponsored and supported by Betty Brazil Memorial Fund. Average statistics: 200 entrants, 31 finalists, 1 award. Held in Tarrytown, New York.

SCULPTURE GRANT: Woman Sculptor Career Development. 1 $2500 grant to woman sculptor for career development (unrestricted use of materials, style). Submit 2-page application, background essay, maximum 10 slides or photographs. No entrants affiliated with commercial galleries, full-time undergraduate students.

JUDGING: By 4 artists. Based on excellence in sculpture, career potential.

DEADLINES: Application, March. Notification, May.

121

Change Inc. Emergency Assistance Grants
Susan Lewis, Secretary
Box 705, Cooper Station
New York, New York 10276 U.S.A.
Tel: (212) 473-3742

Continuous

National; **entry open to U.S. professionals;** continuous; established 1970. Purpose: to award emergency grants to professional artists in all fields. Sponsored by Change Inc. Second contact: P. O. Box 480027, Los Angeles, California 90048.

ART GRANTS: Emergency Assistance. $100-$500 to professional artists in need of emergency assistance resulting from utility turn-off, eviction, unpaid medical bills, fire, illness. Submit detailed letter describing situation, proof of professional status, 2 recommendation letters from people in applicant's field, outstanding bills substantiating amount needed. Competition includes fine and commercial art, film, video, photography.

JUDGING: By Board of Directors.

DEADLINES: Continuous.

122

Cintas Fellowship Program
Institute of International Education
Robert F. Morris, Arts Program Administrator
809 United Nations Plaza
New York, New York 10017 U.S.A.
Tel: (212) 883-8454

Entry January-February

International; **entry open to Cuban (by citizenship or lineage) professional artists residing outside Cuba;** annual for 1 year. Named for late Oscar B. Cintas, industrialist and former Cuban Ambassador to U.S. Purpose: to foster, encourage professional development-recognition of literature, other creative arts. Sponsored by Institute of International Education (private, nonprofit organization administering, distributing information on international educational-cultural exchanges between U.S. and 100 other countries). Supported by Cintas Foundation. Average 13 fellowships to creative artists.

VISUAL ARTS GRANTS: Graphics, Painting, Sculpture Professional Work. Minimum 8 grants of $5000 each (in quarterly payments for 12 consecutive months) to Cuban citizen-lineage professional artists (primarily to young artists with completed academic, technical training) for arts activities in U.S. or other approved countries. Submit maximum 8 slides (35mm, 2x2 inches, cardboard-mounted), maximum 8 photos (up to 8x10 inches), or 1 portfolio of work (up to 15x20x4 inches) for entry review; reference letters; press criticisms; other evidence of artistic contributions-expertise (sponsor not responsible for loss or damage of review materials). Require report, work contributions at conclusion of fellowship. No professional-academic study or research, scholarly, academic writing; no performing artists. Competition includes architecture, creative writing, music composition.

ENTRY FEE: None.

DEADLINES: Entry, January-February. Acceptance, August. Grants begin, September.

123

Eben Demarest Trust Fund Grants

Anne Shiras, Secretary
4609 Batard Street, Apt. 81
Pittsburg, Pennsylvania 15213 U.S.A.

Entry May

International; **entry open to all (nominated by organizations);** annual in January for 1 year. Created by Elizabeth Demarest, history of civilization teacher at Carnegie Institute. Purpose: to free artist from livelihood dependence on sale, approval of work. Sponsored and supported by Eban Demarest Trust.

VISUAL ARTS GRANTS: General. 1 or more grants up to $7000 total to gifted artists (preferably but not exclusively U.S. citizens) who have produced works of recognized worth; have no other income to equal grant; are nominated by organizations, institutions, or Demarest Advisory Council member. No applications from individuals. Competition includes archaeology, music, performing arts, photography, writing.

JUDGING: By 5-member council. Based on ability, financial need.

DEADLINES: Application, May. Notification, Summer. Grant, January.

124

Guggenheim Memorial Fellowships

John Simon Guggenheim Memorial Foundation
90 Park Avenue
New York, New York 10016 U.S.A.
Tel: (212) 687-4470

Entry September

International; **entry open to U.S., Canada, Caribbean, Philippines, Latin America;** annual in October; established 1922. Purpose: to provide freest possible conditions in furthering development of scholars', artists' research in fine arts. Average statistics: 3017 applicants, 285 fellowships (U.S., Canada) totaling $5,040,000.

ART GRANTS: Research, Creative Work. 330 $15,000 (average) grants of 6-12 months (not immediately renewable) to scholars and artists for research and creation in any fine art. No other concurrent fellowships allowed. Competition includes science, social science, humanities.

ELIGIBILITY: Citizens and residents of U.S., Canada; all other American states of the Caribbean, Philippines; French, Dutch, British possessions in Western Hemisphere; of high intellectual and personal qualifications, having demonstrated ability for productive scholarship or unusual creative ability in the arts. Teachers on paid sabbatical leave are eligible.

JUDGING: By responsible scholars, artists.

DEADLINES: Application, September (U.S., Canada), November (Latin America, Caribbean, Philippines). Judging, March. Grants, October, December.

125

Ludwig Vogelstein Foundation Grants

Douglas Turnbaugh, Treasurer
Box 537
New York, New York 10013 U.S.A.

Entry various

International; entry open to all; semiannual; established 1940. Purpose: to support original projects by individuals in arts and humanities. Average statistics (all sections): 35 awards per year, $3000 each.

VISUAL ARTS GRANTS: Original Project. Up to $5000 to individuals to support original project. Submit evidence of achievement in field, importance of project to field, financial need. Also have crafts, music, performing arts, photography, writing grants.

DEADLINES: Various.

126

Massachusetts Bay Transportation Authority (MBTA) Arts on the Line Program

Cambridge Arts Council
Pallas Lombardi, Administrator
City Hall Annex
57 Inman Street
Cambridge, Massachusetts 02139
U.S.A. Tel: (617) 846-5150

Continuous

International; entry open to all; continuous; established 1978. Purpose: to support artists, enhance public environments (subway stations), encourage collaboration between artists and architects by making artwork an integral part of station structure. Sponsored and supported by Urban Mass Transportation Administration, Cambridge Arts Council, MBTA, NEA. Recognized by U.S. Department of Transportation. Held in Cambridge, Somerville, and Boston, Massachusetts. Have temporary art projects, exhibitions. Second contact: MBTA, Charlie Steward, 50 High Street, Boston, Massachusetts 02110.

ART GRANTS: Commissioned for Mass Transit System. $10,000-$100,000 grants to artists for incorporating art into subway system in Massachusetts. Submit 20 slides maximum in 8-1/2x11-inch clear acetate sheet, resume of involvement with this project, 2-page future objectives. Require contract between artist and MBTA. Categories: Open Competition (from unsolicited, unpaid proposals, 1 proposal is commissioned), Limited Competition (from paid proposals, 1 proposal is commissioned), Invitation (solicited and paid proposals, 1 paid commission), Direct Purchase (installation of already completed works). Competition includes photography.

JUDGING: By 3 art professionals advised by 5 representatives (architectural, demographic, historical, sociological). Based on information obtained from artist and slides. Sponsor retains entries. Not responsible for loss or damage.

DEADLINES: Continuous.

127

National Endowment for the Arts (NEA) Visual Arts Fellowships and Grants to Individuals and Organizations

2401 E Street N.W.
Washington, DC 20506 U.S.A.
Tel: (202) 634-6044

Entry Various

National; **entry open to U.S. citizens, residents, and nonprofit tax-exempt organizations;** annual; established 1965. Sponsored by NEA (independent agency of U.S. government) to encourage and assist U.S. cultural resources, make arts widely available, strengthen cultural organizations, preserve cultural heritage, develop creative talent. Supported by annual appropriations from U.S. Congress, private donations. Address inquiries to program *italicized.*

VISUAL ARTS FELLOWSHIP: Career Development *(Visual Arts Program).* $12,500 fellowships (some limited $4000 fellowships) to visual artists (including painters, printmakers, sculptors) of demonstrated talent for materials, time to pursue work. Require 10 slides of recent work, 2 catalogs of recent exhibitions, 3 reviews. Application once in only 1 medium. No students; not for projects. Application, February. Original works, May. Notification, January.

Contemporary Visual Arts Criticism *(Visual Arts Program).* $10,000 fellowships to critics for projects investigating, evaluating, analyzing contemporary visual arts; travel expanding critic's knowledge of art (limited $3000 travel fellowships also available). Require copies of 3 recent articles or essays, maximum 5000 words each. Not for primarily art-historical research. Application, December. Notification, July.

VISUAL ARTS GRANTS: Art in Public Places *(Visual Arts Program).* Up to $5000 on nonmatching basis to individuals; and up to $50,000 (for commercial works), $25,000 (purchases), $10,000 (public site planning, design) on matching basis to state or local governments, nonprofit organizations for making contemporary art accessible in public places. Require 10 slides of recent work (individuals); 8x10-inch monochrome prints, 35mm slides, and-or drawings of proposed site, resumes, plans to obtain community support (organizations). Have planning-design grants for artists' fees. No exhibitions, museum acquisitions, historical or commemorative projects. Application, May (individuals), December (organizations). Notification, January (individuals), July (organizations).

Services to the Visual Arts Field *(Visual Arts Program).* Up to $15,000 on nonmatching basis to individuals, and on matching basis to nonprofit organizations, for projects with direct, immediate effect on professional lives of visual artists, for financial-legal-technical assistance, information-resource-advisory services, publications. No students, amateurs, newsletters; not for major equipment, conferences, symposia, restricted programs. Application, June (Artists' organizations, spaces), October (other). Notification, July.

APPRENTICESHIP GRANT: Folk Arts Education *(Folk Arts Program).* Up to 25 $1000 once-only Heritage

Awards to nominated individuals of demonstrated talent who wish to learn traditional arts from master folk artists. Generally not for school study or ongoing training programs. Application, April. Notification, December.

ARTIST EXCHANGE FELLOWSHIP: Between U.S. and England-Japan *(International Activities Program).* 6-9-month stipend and round-trip transportation to American mid-career artists for exchange with British or Japanese artists. Priority to those with specific purpose who have not recently resided in chosen country.

ELIGIBILITY: Require (from individuals) project description, career summary, 35mm slide work samples; (organizations) project description, dissemination plans, detailed budget, secured sources of matching grants, IRS certification of tax-exempt status. Supplementary documentation depending on program. Application usually limited to 1 per year. Final reports required after project-program completion.

JUDGING: Application review by Program Panel. Recommendation by National Council on the Arts. Final by NEA Chair. Review criteria vary by program but generally include demonstrated quality of previous work, merit of and ability to realize proposed project, potential contribution to national and NEA program goals, budget feasibility.

DEADLINES: Vary by program. Application, 6-12 months before notification.

128

National Endowment for the Arts (NEA) Visual Arts Grants to Organizations

2401 E Street N.W.
Washington, DC 20506 U.S.A.
Tel: (202) 634-6044

Entry various

National; **entry open to U.S. citizens, residents, and nonprofit, tax-exempt organizations;** annual; established 1965. Sponsored by NEA (independent agency of U.S. government) to encourage and assist U.S. cultural resources, make arts widely available, strengthen cultural organizations, preserve cultural heritage, develop creative talent. Supported by annual appropriations from U.S. Congress, private donations. Address inquiries to program *italicized.*

VISUAL ARTS GRANTS: Artists' Spaces *(Visual Arts Program).* Up to $20,000 on matching basis to organizations providing structure, atmosphere conducive to artistic dialog, experimentation, for exhibitions, access to working facilities-equipment, visiting artists' series (up to $10,000 on nonmatching basis for artists' honoraria). No amateurs, students; not for real estate, construction, maintenance, major equipment, creation of new organizations. Application, June. Notification, April.

Visual Arts Education *(Visual Arts Program).* Up to $5000 on matching basis to nonprofit organizations for visiting artists' lectures, seminars, short-term workshops, artist-in-residence programs. Require 5 slides of artists' work, biographies, other documentation. Not for faculty positions, equipment purchase, regular educational curricula, administrative salaries, exhibition, receptions. Application, February. Notification, September.

ARTS GRANTS: Arts Education *(Expansion Arts Program).$* $5000-$30,000 on matching basis to nonprofit community-based arts organizations, consortia for regional arts education programs, festivals. Includes instruction-training, community cultural centers, arts exposure programs, summer projects, regional touring events, services to neighborhood arts organizations. Application, October-November. Notification, June-September.

Arts Development *(Challenge Arts Grants).* $30,000 to $1.5 million on matching basis to arts centers, cultural groups consortia for fund raising, other activities contributing to organization's long-term financial stability. Application, June. Notification, February.

Folk Arts Preservation, Presentation *(Folk Arts Program).* Up to $50,000 on matching basis to nonprofit organizations for media exhibits, distribution projects to document folk-art work methods, repertoires, performance styles. Require resumes, up to 10 photos demonstrating technical competency, sensitivity to needs of folklore documentation. Application, January, April, October. Notification, 6 months later.

Museum Development *(Museum Program).* $4000-$100,000 on matching basis to museums for special exhibitions, permanent collections catalogs, contemporary arts purchases, visiting specialists, collection development-maintenance, internships. Deadlines vary by subprogram.

Special Arts Projects *(Inter-Arts Program).* Up to $50,000 to artists' colonies, interdisciplinary arts projects, and presenting organizations, and up to $40,000 to art services organizations for programs involving 2 or more arts that are ineligible for funding under other NEA programs. Deadlines vary by subprogram.

ELIGIBILITY: Require (from individuals) project description, career summary, 35mm slide work samples; (organizations) project description, dissemination plans, detailed budget, secured sources of matching grants, IRS certification of tax-exempt status. Supplementary documentation depending on program. Application usually limited to 1 per year. Final reports required after project-program completion.

JUDGING: Application review by Program Panel. Recommendation by National Council on the Arts. Final by NEA Chair. Review criteria vary by program but generally include demonstrated quality of previous work, merit of and ability to realize proposed project, potential contribution to national and NEA program goals, budget feasibility.

DEADLINES: Vary by program. Application, 6-12 months before notification.

129

National Endowment for the Humanities (NEH) Grants

806 15th Street N.W.
Washington, DC 20506 U.S.A.

Entry various

National; **entry open to U.S. individuals, nonprofit organizations;** semiannual; established 1965. Sponsored by NEH (independent federal grant-making agency) to support research, education, public activity in the humanities (modern, classical languages; linguistics; literature; history; jurisprudence; philosophy; archaeology; comparative religion; ethics; art history, criticism, theory; historical, philosophical, social sciences with humanistic content, methods; human environment, condition; national life). Supported by annual appropriations from U.S. Congress, private donations. NEH "does not offer support for creative, original works in the arts or for performance or training in the arts. Historical, theoretical, and critical studies in the arts are, however, eligible for Endowment support. Projects dealing with appreciation of the arts may also be suitable for support if they clearly relate art appreciation to other fields of the humanities rather than to fields of the creative and performing arts." Among NEH programs that might offer support to humanities projects using or related to fine arts are those of the *Division of Fellowships and seminars* (supporting individuals in their work as scholars, teachers); the *Division of Research Programs* (supporting long-range, multiyear projects to prepare archival-research materials, preserve collections, publish scholarly humanities works); the *Division of Special Programs* (supporting youth humanities projects, humanities dissemination-development, experimental activities, promotion of science-technology understanding of U.S. citizens); and the *Challenge Grants Program* (on matching basis to institutions for long-term development, financial stability). Address inquiries to division *italicized.*

ART GRANT: Humanities Interpretive Projects *(Division of Public Programs)* grants on matching (minimum 20%) basis to museums, historical organizations, other cultural institutions for activities, exhibitions conveying ideas, stimulating learning through use of artifacts, art objects. Categories: Temporary, Permanent.

ELIGIBILITY: Fresh approach to humanities subject, evidence of potential for new uses of humanities resources. Require proposal, work plan, resumes, recommendations, third-party support for gifts-and-matching funding. Funds for approved budget only; NEH approves distribution and publicity. Grantee owns grant products (possibility of sharing income over $50,000 with Federal Treasury). No projects advocating single viewpoint or social programs; only describing current events or experimenting with technology; presenting uninterpreted information; addressing regions or youth exclusively; requiring extensive preproject research, permanent facilities, equipment, training.

JUDGING: By 4-stage review: NEH Panel (subject-area experts), Individual Review (external experts), National Council on the Humanities (26 presidential appointees), NCH Chair (makes final funding decisions). Based on proposal clarity, logic; use of humanities resources; interpretive nature; appeal to large audience (including English and Spanish speakers, blind, hearing-impaired); outreach to underserved social groups; feasibility, planning efficiency, budget.

DEADLINES: Application, January, July. Notification, 6 months later.

130

Sculpture Space Facilities Loans for Professional Sculptors

Sylvia de Swaan, Executive Director
800 Whitesboro Street
Utica, New York 13502 U.S.A.
Tel: (315) 724-8381

Entry Continuous

International; **entry open to professional sculptors;** continuous; established 1975. Purpose: to provide sculptors with resources for development and experimentation; expose completed work to public. Supported by NEA, New York State Council on the Arts, private sources. Average statistics: 50 entrants, 6 countries. Held at Sculpture Space, Utica.

SCULPTURE FACILITIES LOANS: Professional Work. 4 4-month maximum loans of studio, access to steel and steel plate fabricating plant ($16 per hour), technical assistance, free-inexpensive housing to professional sculptors for work in environment free of everyday distractions. Submit 35mm slides, resume, project description.

JUDGING: By 6 judges.

DEADLINES: Application, continuous. Notification, within 3 months of application.

131

Veterans Administration (VA) Art-in-Architecture Program (083)
Leonore H. Jacobs, Coordinator
810 Vermont Avenue N.W.
Washington, DC 20420 U.S.A.
Tel: (202) 389-3420, 389-3398

Continuous

National; **entry open to U.S.;** continuous. Purpose: to provide VA Medical Centers, clinics, other facilities with art works as integral part of architectural design concept. Sponsored by VA. Recognized by NEA.

VISUAL ARTS GRANTS: Commissioned for Veterans Administration Facilities. 1/2% of estimated construction cost of each VA facility (maximum $50,000) to U.S. artists for works of art as integral part of project's architectural design. Submit maximum 20 35mm slides, resume for entry review. Categories: Painting (Abstract, Figurative), Sculpture (Abstract, Figurative, Light, Water), Mosaics, Other. Competition includes photo murals, craft work.

JUDGING: Entry review by VA, project architects, art professionals appointed by NEA. Awards judging by Veteran Affairs Administrator.

DEADLINES: Application, open.

132

Washington State Arts Commission Art in Public Places Program
Sandra A. Percival, Visual Arts Coordinator
9th & Columbia Building
Mail Stop GH-11
Olympia, Washington 98504 U.S.A.
Tel: (206) 753-3860

Entry August

National; **entry open to U.S.;** continuous; established 1974. Formerly called ART IN NEW STATE BUILDING PROGRAM to 1980. Sponsored by Washington State Arts Commission.

ART GRANTS: Commissioned for Public Places (including mural and other 2D wall treatments, low reliefs, interior-exterior sculpture, and environmental treatments). Submit 10 slides maximum (additional accepted for 3D) in 8-1/2x11-inch clear plastic sheet; proposal (each project), resume, drawing or sketches (optional). No 3D submissions (models). Applicant encouraged to visit project sites and-or architect for detailed information.

JUDGING: By Art Selection Panel. Not responsible for loss or damage.

DEADLINES: Entry, August. Judging, November.

133

Women's Studio Workshop (WSW) Facilities Loans
Tatana Kellner, Coordinator
P. O. Box V
Rosendale, New York 12472 U.S.A.
Tel: (914) 658-9133

Continuous

International; **entry open to women;** continuous; established 1974.

Purpose: to provide supportive atmosphere for art work creation and exhibition. Sponsored and supported by NYSCA, NEA. Have WSW Print Center, classes, workshops in printmaking, painting, photography, papermaking, drawing, collage-mixed media, graphic design. Also sponsor W.I.N.G.S. Exhibition Outreach Program, film and video program, visiting artists.

PRINTMAKING EQUIPMENT-FACILITES LOANS: Intaglio, Silkscreen. 6 month-1 year equipment and facilities loans to women artists with expertise for full-time work at WSW printmaking studios. Submit 5 slides, resume, project proposal for entry review. Also have graphic design, offset printing, papermaking, photography equipment.

JUDGING: Not specified.

DEADLINES: Application, open.

134

Lowick House Printmaking Workshops Equipment and Facilities Loans
John Sutcliffe, Director
Lowick Green, Nr. Ulverston
Cumbria LA12 8DX, ENGLAND
Tel: (0229) 85 698

Entry not specified

International; entry open to all; annual in October-June; established 1975. Purpose: to stimulate, preserve, promote printmaking; provide comprehensive printmaking facilities. Sponsored and supported by Lowick House Printmaking, Northern Arts, Arts Council of Great Britain. Have various accommodation facilities. Also sponsor summer workshops, traveling collection, loan service, resident grants.

PRINTMAKING EQUIPMENT-FACILITIES LOANS: Intaglio, Lithography, Relief, Screen, Photo-Related Techniques. Up to 3 2-8-week loans (per month, October-June) to artists and printmakers for use of printmaking facilities (sundry materials included) at Lowick House to expand image-making, experimental printmaking, edition work. Submit 12 slides, drawings, or prints (20x30 inches maximum), resume, return postage with application. Require applicant to bear cost of major materials, food and accommodation.

JUDGING: By Lowick House Director. Sponsor withholds 3 prints from each edition for Northern Arts, traveling collection, loan service.

DEADLINES: Application, not specified.

GRANTS (regional-State)

Limited to specific Region, State. Primarily for RESEARCH, PRODUCTION, and DEVELOPMENT in Graphics, Painting, Printmaking, Sculpture, and Visual Arts. Includes CALIFORNIA, MINNESOTA REGION, NEW YORK, OHIO SOUTHEAST, SOUTHWEST, CANADA. (Also see RESIDENCE GRANTS, SCHOLARSHIPS, FELLOWSHIPS.)

135

Bush Foundation Fellowships for Artists
E-900 First National Bank Building
St. Paul, Minnesota 55101 U.S.A.
Tel: (612) 227-0891

Entry October

State; **entry open to Minnesota;** annual in March; established 1975. Purpose: to help artists work full-time. Sponsored by Bush Foundation. Also sponsor Leadership Fellows Program (to prepare mid-career persons for high responsibility through academic-internship training).

VISUAL ARTS GRANTS: Graphics, Painting, Sculpture Professional Work. 10 $15,000 maximum fellowships for 12-18 months or $1250 per month for 6-12 months to help artists pursue full-time work ($3000 maximum for programs, travel expenses). Submit 35mm slides of work, reference letters, evidence of professional status (publications, exhibition catalogs, recent work samples). Not for academic training. Competition includes fiction, film, photography, poetry, video.

ELIGIBILITY: Professional artist age 25 and over residing in Minnesota for 1 continuous year minimum. No students.

JUDGING: Entry review by panel. Awards judging by interdisciplinary panel. Based on demonstrated artistic ability. Applicant should show strong leadership capabilities.

DEADLINES: Application, October. Entry review, January. Notification, March.

136

Creative Artists Public Service (CAPS) Program Fellowship Grants

Creative Artists Program Service
250 West 57th Street, Room 1424
New York, New York 10019 U.S.A.
Tel: (212) 247-6303

Entry May

State; **entry open to New York;** annual for 1 year; established 1970. Purpose: to aid individual creative artists in creating new work, completing work in progress. Sponsored by CAPS, nonprofit arts service organization. Supported by NEA, NYSCA. Average 200 awards (all sections). Have community service program, visual arts and playwriting referral services. Also sponsor other media fellowship grants.

VISUAL ARTS GRANTS: Graphics (includes drawing, prints, watercolor, collage). $3500-$5000 for 12 months to create new work or complete work in progress. Submit maximum 4 color slides of recent work for entry review; 3 unframed original works, 7x7 feet maximum for semifinal judging. Competition includes crafts, dance, film, fiction writing, photography, video.

Painting. $3500-$5500. Submit maximum 4 color slides of recent work (if textured, at least 1 close-up) for entry review; 2 original works, 7x7 feet maximum for semifinal judging.

Sculpture. $3500-$6500. Submit maximum 8 color slides of 4 recent works (2 different views of each).

Multimedia. $3500-$6500. Submit work (or arrange audit or studio visit).

ELIGIBILITY: New York residents willing to perform community-related service. May apply in 2 sections maximum. No matriculated graduate, undergraduate students. No proposals for travel, study, teaching, equipment, publication-production of completed work.

JUDGING: By professionals (vary yearly). Sponsor keeps copy of work. Not responsible for loss or damage.

DEADLINES: Application, May. Materials (on request), November. Notification, March.

137

Dallas Museum of Fine Arts (DMFA) Awards to Artists
Sue Graze, Curator of Contemporary Art
P. O. Box 26250
Dallas, Texas 75226 U.S.A.
Tel: (214) 421-4187

January

Regional; **entry open to Southwest U.S.;** annual in March; established 1980. Purpose: to encourage talent and promise in young visual artists. Sponsored by DMFA. Supported by Clare Hart DeGloyer, Anne Giles Kimbrough Memorial Funds. Average statistics (all sections): 500 entries, 100 entrants, 2 awards. Publish *DMFA Bulletin* (quarterly).

VISUAL ARTS GRANTS: **Travel, Independent Study, Special Project.** 2 awards ($1000 maximum *Clare Hart DeGloyer Award;* $3000 maximum *Anne Giles Kimbrough Award)* to young artists with ability, to be used in same calendar year (not for tuition). Submit 5-10 35mm slides or videotape of work; current curriculum vitae, residency information, 2 recommendation letters; project, budget statement. Competition includes photography.

ELIGIBILITY: Clare Hart DeGloyer Award: age 15-25, residing in Texas, Oklahoma, New Mexico, Arizona, Colorado. Anne Giles Kimbrough Award: age 35 and under, resident of Texas for past 3 years.

JUDGING: By committee. Based on abilities, intelligence, talents, convictions, continuing endeavors. Applicant's need is considered but is not determining factor. May withhold awards.

DEADLINES: Application, January. Notification, March.

138

Forecast Outdoor Art Projects Competition
Forecast Public Artspace Productions
Jack Becker, Project Director
2301 East Hennepin Avenue
P. O. Box 3194
Minneapolis, Minnesota 55403 U.S.A. Tel: (612) 331-4674

Entry January

Regional; **entry open to 5-state Minnesota region:** biennial (even years) in June-August; established 1980. Formerly called ENVIRONMENTAL ART & SCULPTURE COMPETITION to 1981. Purpose: to provide opportunity for emerging artists to demonstrate that new art forms can co-exist in environment. Sponsored by Forecast Public Artspace Productions. Supported by NEA, Jerome Foundation. Average statistics (all sections): 140 entries, 80 entrants, 13 finalists, 11 awards, 10,000 attendance. Held in Minneapolis-Saint Paul area for 3 months.

ART GRANTS: **Outdoor Works Production.** 7 $2000 maximum grants to produce proposed works. Submit written, drawn proposal for review (2 maximum). Applicant required to select suitable available site.

JUDGING: By 3-5 visual arts professionals (museum curators, art historians, critics). Based on quality of proposed project, suitability to site.

DEADLINES: Application, judging, January. Exhibition, June-August.

139

Inter-Arts of Marin Public Art Competition
Kerry Vander Meer, Director
1000 Sir Francis Drake Blvd.

San Anselmo, California 94960
U.S.A. Tel: (415) 457-9744

Entry November

State; **entry open to Marin County, California;** annual; established 1979. Purpose: to increase interaction between artists and community, create public art works. Sponsored and supported by San Francisco Foundation, Inter-Arts of Marin. Average statistics: 800 entries, 43 entrants, 4 finalists.

SCULPTURE GRANT: Commissioned for Public Places. 1 grant (including all expenses) to Marin County artist to design and execute art project for public place. 2 $250 Cash Awards to 2 finalists. Submit 20 slides maximum of work completed within previous 3 years, resume for entry review. 3 semifinalists submit detailed models of proposal.

JUDGING: By 5 members elected by sponsoring agency and 2 advisors from Inter-Arts Board of Directors. Based on originality, permanence of materials, aesthetics, resisitance to vandalism, low maintenance cost, site appropriateness, project budget.

DEADLINES: Application, November. Notification, January.

140

Ohio Arts Council Aid to Individual Artists

Denny Griffith, Coordinator
727 East Main Street
Columbus, Ohio 43206 U.S.A.
Tel: (614) 466-2613

Entry January

State; **entry open to Ohio;** annual in June; established 1978. Purpose: to provide direct, nonmatching grants to artists for creation of new work. Sponsored by Ohio Arts Council. Average statistics (all sections): 590 entries, 110 grants. Second contact: 50 West Broad Street, Columbus, Ohio 43215.

VISUAL ARTS GRANTS: Graphics, Painting, Sculpture, Multimedia New Work (including conceptual art). $500-$6000 to Ohio residents for planning, supplies, facilities-services, rental, research, presentation, reproduction, documentation, publication expenses for creating new work. Submit maximum 10 slides of work or portfolio of 10 photographs (16x20 inches maximum including mat). Artists encouraged to indicate direction, focus, concepts they will employ and showcase through exhibitions, publications. No students. Competition includes architecture-design, crafts, creative writing, music, performing arts, photography.

JUDGING: Based on creative, technical excellence. Preference given to work advancing art.

DEADLINES: Application, January. Notification, June.

141

Southeastern Center for Contemporary Art (SECCA) Grants

Vicki Kopf, Curator
750 Marguerite Drive
Winston-Salem, North Carolina
27106 U.S.A. Tel: (919) 725-1904

Entry October

Regional; **entry open to U.S. professionals residing in Southeastern states;** annual for 1 year; established 1976. Purpose: to enable Southeastern artists to advance their careers. Sponsored and supported by SECCA, NEA. Average statistics (all sections): 6000 entries, 1000 entrants. Have rental gallery. Also sponsor exhibitions, traveling shows, children's summer programs, art sales.

VISUAL ARTS GRANTS: Painting, Printmaking, Sculpture Career Advancement. 7 $2000 grants to Southeastern artists to set aside time and-or purchase materials and advance their careers. Submit maximum 6 35mm slides for entry review. Competition includes photography.

ELIGIBILITY: U.S. citizens and professional artists over age 18 residing in Alabama, Florida, Georgia, Kentucky, Louisiana, Mississippi, North Carolina, South Carolina, Tennessee, Virginia, West Virginia, Washington, D.C.

JUDGING: By 4 distinguished national judges. Not responsible for loss or damage.

DEADLINES: Application, October. Notification, January. Materials returned, March.

142

Canada Council Grants
Robert Kennedy, Head, Arts Awards Service
P. O. Box 1047
255 Albert Street
Ottawa, Ontario K1P 5V8 CANADA
Tel: (613) 237-3400

Entry April, October

National; **entry open to Canada;** semiannual for 3-12 months; established 1957. Sponsored by Canada Council, founded 1957 by Act of Parliament to foster and promote study, enjoyment, production of art in Canada. Have architecture, art criticism, dance, film, music, photography, video, theater, writing, multidisciplinary and performance art sections. Also sponsor Aid to Arts Organizations, scholarships, fellowships, academic exchanges, research grants.

ART GRANTS: General *(under Aid to Artists Branch)* to Canadian citizens, landed immigrants with 5 years' residence. Submit 30 work samples. Categories: **Arts Grants A:** up to $19,000 for living expenses, project, travel costs for 4-12 months to senior artists with record of significant contributions. **Arts Grants B:** up to $11,000 for living expenses, project costs (possible added travel allowance) for 4-12 months to professional artists. **Short-Term Grants:** $800 per month and travel allowance (up to $800 possible project allowance) for 3 months to artists for specific project. **Project Cost Grants:** up to $2700 for goods, services, travel (no living expenses) for completion of project. **Travel Grants:** for travel (up to $100 possible living expenses). Competition includes film, music, performing arts, photography, video, writing.

JUDGING: Entry review by outside juries. Based on artistic merit, potential, significance, project value, artistic quality, relevance. First awards judging by 28-member Advisory Arts Panel. Final awards judging by 31-member Canada Council.

DEADLINES: Application, April, October. Notification, September, March.

GRAPHICS, PAINTING

Graphics, Painting, including Acrylic, Oil, Watercolor. (Also see other GRAPHICS, PAINTING CATEGORIES.)

143

Hill Country Arts Foundation Photography-Graphics Exhibition
Jeanne Bowman, Art Director

P. O. Box 176
Ingram, Texas 78025 U.S.A.
Tel: (512) 367-5121

Entry May

National; **entry open to U.S.;** biennial (even years) in May; established 1958. Alternates with Biennial Craft Exhibition. Purpose: educational. Sponsored and supported by and held at Hill Country Arts Foundation for 3 weeks. Average statistics (all sections): 150 entries, 100 entrants, 5 awards. Also sponsor Juried Arts Exhibition, summer photography and arts seminars, drama productions.

GRAPHICS CONTEST: General, original, framed, ready for hanging; limit 3 per entrant. Categories: Portrait-Pictorial, Scenic-Wildlife, Unclassified. Competition includes photography.

AWARDS: 5 Awards totaling $1000.

JUDGING: By 1 judge. Not responsible for loss or damage.

SALES TERMS: 20% commission charge.

ENTRY FEE: $5 plus return postage.

DEADLINES: Entry, event, May.

144

Ozark Writers and Artists Guild Art Show
Maggie Smith, Director
P. O. Box 411
Siloam Springs, Arkansas 72761
U.S.A. Tel: (501) 524-3591

Entry June

International; entry open to all; annual in July; established 1935. Purpose: to provide workshop of idea-exchange in friendly atmosphere. Sponsored by Ozark Writers and Artists Guild. Supported by Siloam Springs banks, savings and loans, individual donations. Held at John Brown University, Mabee Center for 1 day. Tickets: $6 (luncheon).

GRAPHICS CONTEST: General, dimensions not specified, framed; unlimited entry. Require hand-delivery.

PAINTING CONTEST: Acrylic, Oil, Watercolor, Mixed Media General. Requirements, restrictions same as for Graphics.

AWARDS: $100 First to each of 5 media. Ribbons. Up to $1000 in Cash Awards.

JUDGING: By 3 professionals. Not responsible for loss or damage.

SALES TERMS: Work need not be for sale. No commission charge.

ENTRY FEE: $4 up to 4 works, $1 each additional work.

DEADLINES: Entry, June. Event, July.

145

Spectrum Magazine Art Contest
Associated Students: UC Santa Barbara (UCSB)
Joan L. Chappell, Managing Editor
Box 14800, UCSB
Santa Barbara, California 93107
U.S.A.

Entry January

International; **entry open to students, nonprofessionals;** annual in May; established 1957. Purpose: to publish student, nonprofessional work. Sponsored by UCSB English Department, Associated Students, Alumni Association. Supported by UCSB sales of *Spectrum Magazine.* Average statistics (all sections): 700 entries, 250 entrants, 50 awards. Also sponsor poetry-fiction readings. Second contact: Ellen Girardeau, 6504 Seville, Apartment 7, Goleta, California 93017.

GRAPHICS CONTEST: **Black-and-White General,** reducible; unlimited entry; published or unpublished. No simultaneous submissions. Competition includes photography, fiction and nonfiction writing.

AWARDS: 50 winning works published in *Spectrum Magazine.*

JUDGING: By 8-10 student-staff judges. Entrant retains copyright after publication. Not responsible for loss or damage.

ENTRY FEE: None. Entrant pays return postage.

DEADLINES: Entry, January. Judging, February-March. Notification, April. Awards, May.

146

Washington Metropolitan Area Exhibition of Paintings and Graphics
Fairfax County Council of the Arts (FCCA)
4601 Green Spring Road
Alexandria, Virginia 22312 U.S.A.
Tel: (703) 941-6066

Entry January

State; **entry open to Washington metropolitan area;** annual in February-March. Sponsored and supported by FCCA, Northern Virginia Community College. Held at Godwin Library, Virginia Community College, Annandale campus for 3 weeks.

GRAPHICS CONTEST: **General,** 72 inches maximum width including frame, ready for hanging; limit 2 per entrant. Produced in previous 2 years. No wires. Require hand-delivery. Competition includes all 2D works except photography.

PAINTING CONTEST: **General,** no wet entries. Requirements, restrictions same as for Graphics.

AWARDS: $125 First, $75 Second, $50 Third Place Merit Awards. 4 $25 Honorable Mentions. Purchase Awards.

JUDGING: By 1 curator. Not responsible for loss or damage.

SALES TERMS: Works need not be for sale. 25% commission charge.

ENTRY FEE: $3 first, $2 second work.

DEADLINES: Entry, January. Judging, event, February-March.

GRAPHICS, PAINTING SCULPTURE, MIXED MEDIA

Graphics, Painting, Sculpture, and Mixed Media. (Also see other GRAPHICS, SCULPTURE CATEGORIES.)

147

Beverly Art Center Art Fair and Festival
Beverly Art Center and Vanderpoel Art Association
Pat McGrail, Manager
2153 West 111th Street
Chicago, Illinois 60643 U.S.A.
Tel: (312) 445-3838

Entry April

International; entry open to all; annual in June; established 1975. Purpose: to bring art to people and people to art. Sponsored and supported by

Beverly Art Center and Vanderpoel Art Association. Average 130 entries (all sections). Held at Beverly Art Center for 2 days. Have 2-story gallery, 460-seat theater, classrooms, workshops. Also sponsor drama, film, literature, music contests.

GRAPHICS CONTEST: **General,** original; unlimited entry (all sections). Submit 5 2x2-inch 35mm slides (4 full view, 1 detail) for entry review. No copies, kits, stencils. Competition includes photography.

PAINTING CONTEST: **General.** Requirements, restrictions same as for Graphics.

SCULPTURE CONTEST: **General,** original; unlimited entry (all sections). Submit 5 2x2-inch 35mm slides (4 full view, 1 detail) for entry review. No copies, commercial molds. Competition includes photography.

AWARDS (all sections): $400 Best of Show. 8 $200 Excellence Awards.

JUDGING: Entry review by 5 art professionals; awards judging by 3 judges. Sponsor may withhold awards. Not responsible for loss or damage.

ENTRY FEE: $15 (refundable if not accepted) plus return postage. $7.50 jury fee. No sales commission charge.

DEADLINES: Entry, April. Acceptance, May. Judging, event, June.

148

La Mirada Festival of Arts Art Competition and Exhibition

Sheila Krotinger, Publicity Director
P. O. Box 233
La Mirada, California 90637 U.S.A.
Tel: (213) 941-3066, 943-0627

Entry May

National; **entry open to U.S.;** annual in June; established 1960. Formerly called LA MIRADA FIESTA DE ARTES to 1980. Purpose: to provide opportunity for artists to compete. Sponsored by City of La Mirada. Average statistics (all sections): 1000 entries, 500 entrants, 21 awards. Held at La Mirada Civic Theatre and grounds for 10 days. Have theatre, food facilities, entertainment. Tickets: $1. Also sponsor annual Artists Village.

GRAPHICS CONTEST: **Any Type General,** original, 72 inches maximum any dimension, framed, ready for hanging, portable by one person (can be exceeded by special arrangement). No unprotected smearable surfaces, fragile entries. Divisions: Juried (unlimited entry), Open (limit 3 per section-category), Young Artists (limit 3 per entrant, all sections). Competition includes photography, crafts in Juried, Young Artists shows. Also have photography, crafts in Open show.

PAINTING CONTEST: **Any Medium General,** dry. Restrictions, divisions same as for Graphics. Open Division Categories: Realistic, Impressionistic, Nonobjective.

SCULPTURE CONTEST: **Any Medium General,** 72 inches maximum any dimension, portable by one person (may be exceeded by special arrangement). Divisions same as for Graphics.

AWARDS: Juried Show (all sections): $2000 Purchase Award. 2 $500 Jurors' Awards, 6 Honorable Mentions. Open Show: 2 $100 Awards, 3 Honorable Mentions in each section-category. Young Artists (all sections): $100 Best of Show. Seniors (14-18): $75 Award, 2 $40 Awards, 6 Honorable Mentions; Juniors (9-13): $35 Award, 2 $20 Awards, 6 Honorable Mentions. La Mirada Mall Purchase Award (includes Open and Juried Shows).

JUDGING: Entry review (Juried Show) and awards judging (Juried, Open Shows) by 3 judges from different art disciplines. Awards judging (Young Artists) by art educator. Not responsible for loss or damage.

SALES TERMS: Work need not be for sale. 30% commission charge.

ENTRY FEE: $5 per work plus $2 handling charge for Juried, Open Shows. $1 per work plus $2 handling charge for Young Artists.

DEADLINES: Entry, May. Event, June.

149

Lodi Art Center (LAC) Annual Show
Bill Chapman and Donna Korphage, Directors
14-1/2 West Pine Street
P. O. Box 45
Lodi, California 95241 U.S.A.
Tel: (209) 368-4925

Entry April

International; entry open to all; annual in May; established 1960. Purpose: to bring art to public; enable artists to exhibit, sell works, compete for awards. Sponsored by LAC. Supported by local individuals, organizations. Average statistics (all sections): 600 entries, 50 total sales. Held at Barengo Vineyards Acampo, California for 4 days. Have free wine tasting. Also sponsor monthly artist demonstrations.

GRAPHICS CONTEST: General, original 6x6 feet maximum, glassed, framed, wired, ready for hanging; unlimited entry. Require hand-delivery. Also have pottery section.

PAINTING CONTEST: Acrylic, Oil, Watercolor General. Watercolors must be glassed and framed. Other requirements, restrictions same as for Graphics.

SCULPTURE CONTEST: General, original, minimum 15 inches any direction (including attached base); maximum 75 pounds per section, 300 pounds total weight, 75 pounds optional display stand; unlimited entry. Require hand-delivery. No soft sculpture, unassembled items.

MIXED MEDIA CONTEST: General. Requirements, restrictions same as for Graphics, Sculpture.

AWARDS: $100 Award of Excellence (includes all sections). $75 First, $50 Second, $25 Third, 2 Honorable Mentions each to best graphics, acrylics-oils, watercolors, sculptures, mixed media. 38 Special Purchase Awards ($100-$450 each) totaling $4100.

JUDGING: By 3 judges. Sponsor reserves right to refuse works based on handling facilities. Not responsible for loss or damage.

SALES TERMS: 25% commission charge (includes special purchase awards).

ENTRY FEE: $3.50 per item.

DEADLINES: Entry, April. Judging, event, May.

150

Mamaroneck Artists Guild Open Juried Exhibition
Cynthia Doyle, Chair
150 Larchmont Avenue
New York, New York 10538 U.S.A.
Tel: (914) 834-1117, 948-8385, 961-9050

Entry various

International; **entry open to U.S.;** annual in Spring; established 1953. Purpose: to show best available work covering broad spectrum of styles. Sponsored by Mamaroneck (cooperative, nonprofit organization), Community Unitarian Church. Average statistics (all sections): 850 entries, 500 entrants, 220 finalists, 23 awards, 550 attendance. Held at Community Lutheran Church, White Plains, for 2 weeks. Also sponsor solo show, lectures, demonstrations.

GRAPHICS CONTEST: **General,** original, maximum 50 inches in longest dimension (second entry may be greater), 75 pounds, ready for hanging; limit 2 per entrant (all sections). Recent works. Require hand-delivery. Competition includes photography.

PAINTING CONTEST: **Acrylic, Oil, Watercolor General.** Requirements, restrictions same as for Drawing.

SCULPTURE CONTEST: **General,** original, attached to base; limit 2 per entrant (all sections). Submit 3 8x10-inch photographs (different views) of sculptures over 150 pounds. Recently produced. Require hand-delivery. Competition includes photography.

MIXED MEDIA: **General.** Requirements, restrictions same as for Drawing, Sculpture.

AWARDS: $1500 minimum in Cash Awards.

JUDGING: By 3 judges. Entry review by point count. Not responsible for loss or damage.

SALES TERMS: Work need not be for sale. 30% commission charge.

ENTRY FEE: $12, 1 entry; $15, 2 entries.

DEADLINES: Entry, event, various.

151

Orange County Art Association (OCAA) All Media Juried Exhibition

Harmon Avery, Coordinator
P. O. Box 3279
Fullerton, California 92631 U.S.A.

Entry October

National; **entry open to U.S.;** annual in November-December; established 1966. Purpose: to provide juried exposure to artists in all media. Sponsored by OCAA, City of Brea. Supported by OCAA. Average statistics (all sections): 625 entries, 335 entrants. Held at Brea Civic Cultural Center Art Gallery for 5 weeks. Have 5800 square feet of gallery space.

GRAPHICS CONTEST: **Any Type General,** maximum 60x60 inches (including frame), 100 pounds, framed or edged, wired, ready for hanging; unlimited entry. No wet works. Competition includes crafts.

PAINTING CONTEST: **Any Medium General.** Requirements, restrictions same as for Graphics.

SCULPTURE CONTEST: **Any Medium General,** maximum 60 inches any side, framed or edged, wired, ready for hanging (hanging works); maximum 6x8 feet (installation works); unlimited entry. Submit slides, description and(or) diagram with explanation of unusual media or installation. No wet works.

AWARDS: $300 Juror's Award. $200 OCCA Award. $50 Popular Choice Award.

JUDGING: By 1 nationally prominent juror. Sponsor may photograph works for publicity. Not responsible for loss or damage; insures during exhibition only.

SALES TERMS: 30% commission charge.

ENTRY FEE: $10 each plus shipping.

DEADLINES: Entry, October. Event, November-December.

152

River City Arts Festival Visual Arts Competition
Arts Assembly of Jacksonville
632 May Street
Jacksonville, Florida 32204 U.S.A.
Tel: (904) 633-3748

Entry January

Regional; **entry open to Southeastern U.S. residents age 18 and over;** annual in April; established 1972. Formerly called JACKSONVILLE ARTS FESTIVAL. Purpose: to provide opportunity for artists to compete for prize money. Sponsored by Arts Assembly of Jacksonville, Fine Arts Council of Florida. Supported by NEA. Held in Jacksonville for 5 days. Also sponsor concurrent Street Artist Market, Film-Video Contest, Poetry Contest.

GRAPHICS CONTEST: **General,** framed, ready for hanging; limit 2 per entrant (maximum 5 all sections, 100 entrants). Submit 5 35mm slides for entry review. Competition includes crafts, photography.

PAINTING CONTEST: **General.** Requirements, restrictions same as for Graphics.

SCULPTURE CONTEST: **General,** 100 pounds maximum. Other requirements, restrictions same as for Graphics.

ELIGIBILITY: Residents of Florida, Georgia, North Carolina, South Carolina, Alabama, Louisiana, Mississippi, age 18 and over.

AWARDS: $6000 in Cash Awards.

JUDGING: Entry review and awards judging by 1 juror. May withhold awards. Not responsible for loss or damage. Work need not be for sale.

ENTRY FEE: $20 plus return postage. $10 additional per category (refundable).

DEADLINES: Entry, January. Judging, event, April.

153

Wind River Valley National Art Exhibit
Wind River Valley Artists' Guild (WRVAG)
Eugenia Christensen, Secretary
P. O. Box 26
Dubois, Wyoming 82513 U.S.A.
Tel: (307) 455-2693

Entry July

International; entry open to all; annual in July-August; established 1947. Purpose: to encourage art, art education. Sponsored by WRVAG. Supported by Wyoming Council of the Arts, membership fees. Average statistics: 300 entries, 150 entrants, 12 awards, 2000 attendance, $10,000 total sales, $100 average sale per entrant. Held at Dubois High School for 1 week. Tickets: $1.50. Also sponsor workshops.

GRAPHICS CONTEST: **General,** in any fine arts medium, original, ready for hanging; limit 3 per entrant (all sections). No photographs. Divisions: Professional, Advanced Amateur, Amateur, Teen, Child (to age 12).

PAINTING CONTEST: **Oil, Watercolor General.** Requirements, restrictions, divisions same as for Graphics.

SCULPTURE CONTEST: **Any Medium General,** original, with

pedestal. Restrictions, divisions same as for Graphics.

AWARDS: Up to $3000 in Cash Awards. Sweepstakes, First, Second, Third and Honorable Mention Award to each division. Purchase awards: Fremont County Library Award to best picture representative of Wyoming (must be framed); Dale Warren Wildlife Award; WRVAG Award; $100 Door Prize. Popular Award Ribbons to most popular work in each division.

JUDGING: By 3 nationally prominent judges. Sculpture judged separately. Not responsible for loss or damage.

SALES TERMS: Sales handled through Snowshoe Gallery at 30% commission (donated to Guild).

ENTRY FEE: Membership fee for first entry: $5 adult, $2.50 teen, $1 child. Each additional entry: $5 Professional and Advanced Amateur, $2.50 Amateur, $1.25 Teens, 50¢ Child. Entrant pays return shipping plus $3 handling charge.

DEADLINES: Entry, judging, July. Event, July-August.

HISTORICAL, SCENIC

Drawing, Painting, Prints, Sculpture, and Visual Arts, including CLEVELAND PARKS, COLONIAL AMERICA, FOLKLORE, HISTORICAL PRESERVATION, LINCOLN THEME, LONDON, MARINE, OLD COLORADO. (Also see OTHER CATEGORIES.)

154

Civil War Round Table of New York Awards

George M. Craig, Chair
83-12 St. James Street
Elmhurst, New York 11373 U.S.A.
Tel: (212) NE9-1172

Entry December

International; entry open to all; annual in February; established 1960. Purpose: to facilitate greater appreciation of life and works of Lincoln. Sponsored and supported by Civil War Round Table of New York, Barondess family. Held at Round Table dinner meeting in New York City. Also sponsor Fletcher Pratt Award (to best book on civil war topic). Second contact: Arnold Gates, 168 Weyford Terrace, Garden City, New York 11530.

VISUAL ARTS: Lincoln Theme. Competition includes writing, music, TV, radio.

AWARDS (all sections): $100, copy of Volk bust of Lincoln, plaque to winner.

JUDGING: By 3 judges.

ENTRY FEE: None.

DEADLINES: Entry, December. Awards, February.

155

Emerald Necklace Juried Art Competition

Baycrafters, Inc.
Sally Price
28795 Lake Road
Huntington Metropark
Bay Village, Ohio 44140 U.S.A.
Tel: (216) 871-6545

Entry March

Regional; **entry open to Ohio resi-**

dents age 18 and over; annual in March. Named after Cleveland Metropark System. Sponsored by Baycrafters (founded 1948), arts and crafts organization. Supported by Great Northern Management Company. Held at Great Northern Mall in North Olmstead for 2 weeks. Have shops, art classes, touring exhibition, scholarships, Picture Rental Gallery. Also sponsor Renaissance Fair, Octoberfair, Higbee Show, Baycrafters Annual Juried Art Competition.

VISUAL ARTS CONTEST: Inspired by Cleveland Park System (paintings, prints, drawings, watercolors), original, paintings 5x5 feet maximum, framed, backed, ready for hanging; limit 4 per entrant. Completed in previous 2 years. Class work must be indicated. Competition includes photography. Also have sculpture, crafts sections.

AWARDS: $500 in Cash Prizes, Purchase Awards.

JUDGING: By jury. Sponsor may photograph accepted entries for publicity. Not responsible for loss or damage.

SALES TERMS: Work need not be for sale. 25% commission charge.

ENTRY FEE: $5 per work.

DEADLINES: Entry, March. Event, March-April.

156

Lincoln Days Celebration Annual Tri-State Art Show

Iris LaRue, Executive Secretary
58 Lincoln Square
P. O. Box 176
Hodgenville, Kentucky 42748 U.S.A.
Tel: (502) 358-3411

Entry September

International; entry open to all; annual in October; established 1972 in Hodgenville, birthplace of Abraham Lincoln. Purpose: to celebrate birth of Lincoln. Sponsored by Lincoln Days Celebration, Inc. Recognized by Kentucky Festival Association. Held at Hodgenville Christian Church for 2 days. Have entertainment, food booths, Pioneer Games.

DRAWING CONTEST: Charcoal, Ink, Pencil, Scratchboard, Silverpoint Lincoln Theme, original, suitably framed, ready for hanging; limit 2 per entrant. Completed in previous 2 years. Categories: Lincoln's Birth-Childhood; Lincoln as Youth, Young Politician, President, Family Man; Civil War; Slavery; Lincoln Trail.

PAINTING CONTEST: Acrylic, Oil Lincoln Theme. Requirements, restrictions same as for Drawing.

Casein, Tempera, Watercolor Lincoln Theme. Requirements, restrictions same as for Drawing.

PRINT CONTEST: Lincoln Theme. Requirements, restrictions same as for Drawing.

AWARDS: $300 Purchase Award to best of show. $50 First, Ribbon Second to acrylic or oil; watercolor, tempera or casein; charcoal, ink, pencil, scratchboard, silverpoint or printmaking.

JUDGING: By experienced judge. Based on historical authenticity.

SALES TERMS: Work need not be for sale. No commission charge.

ENTRY FEE: $10 first, $5 each additional work.

DEADLINES: Entry, September. Judging, event, October.

157

Maritime International Art Awards Show

Mystic Seaport Museum Store
Mary Lou Smith, Gallery Director
39 Greenmanville Avenue
Mystic, Connecticut 06355 U.S.A.
Tel: (203) 536-9688

Entry April

International; entry open to all; annual in May-June; established 1980. Purpose: to exhibit contemporary marine artists' works. Sponsored by Mystic Seaport Museum Store. Recognized by American Society of Marine Artists, Royal Society of Marine Artists. Average statistics (all sections): 250 entries, 150 entrants, 6 countries, 13 awards. Held at Marine Art Gallery, Mystic, Connecticut for 6 weeks.

DRAWING CONTEST: **Marine,** relating to water, ships, and-or boats; 78 inches combined length and width (including frame) maximum, ready for hanging; limit 2 per entrant (all sections). Submit biography. Also have scrimshaw section.

PAINTING CONTEST: **Acrylic, Oil, Watercolor Marine.** Requirements same as for Drawing.

PRINT CONTEST: **Marine** (including etchings, lithographs, serigraphs), original. Requirements same as for Drawing. No photographic reproductions.

SCULPTURE CONTEST: **Marine,** maximum 78 inches combined length and width, 250 pounds; mounted; limit 2 per entrant (includes other sections). Submit biography.

AWARDS: (each section): $500 First, $300 Second, $150 Third Prize. Honorable Mentions. $1000 Schaefer International Maritime Art Award.

JUDGING: Entry review, awards judging by panel of 6 maritime art specialists. Sponsor insures works on premises.

SALES TERMS: All entries must be for sale. 40% commission charge.

ENTRY FEE: $15 first, $11 second entry, plus return postage.

DEADLINES: Entry, April. Event, May-June.

158

Old Colorado City Historic Juried Art Show

Arati Artists Gallery
Lucille Damico, Show Chair
2425 West Colorado Avenue
Colorado Springs, Colorado 80904
U.S.A. Tel: (303) 636-1901

Entry February

State; **entry open to Colorado;** annual in February-March; established 1978. Purpose: to show history, present rejuvenation of oldest town in region through artistic translation. Sponsored and supported by Arati Artists Gallery, West Colorado Springs Commercial Club. Average statistics (all sections): 70 entries, 55 entrants, 6 awards. Held at Arati Artists Gallery in Colorado Springs for 2 weeks.

VISUAL ARTS CONTEST: **Old Colorado City,** original, ready for hanging; limit 2 per entrant. Require hand-delivery. Categories: Old Colorado City (the Way It Was, the Way It Is). Competition includes photography.

AWARDS: Cash awards to both categories.

JUDGING: By 1 local historian and 1 professional artist. Based on artistic merit and historical validity. Not responsible for loss or damage.

SALES TERMS: Work need not be for sale. 20% commission charge.

ENTRY FEE: $3 first, $2 second entry.

DEADLINES: Entry, February. Event, February-March.

159

Society of Colonial Wars Awards
Joan Sumner, Executive Secretary
122 East 58th Street
New York, New York 10022 U.S.A.

Entry not specified

International; entry open to all; annual; established 1951. Purpose: to promote wider knowledge, encourage material on life and times of early America (1607-1775). Sponsored by Society of Colonial Wars.

VISUAL ARTS CONTEST: **Colonial Americana** (including drawing, painting, sculpture), original or reproduction with description of production, first use, present location. 75% of content in America's colonial period; completed in previous year. Competition includes literature, drama, music, photography.

AWARDS: Honor Citation on parchment and Bronze Medallion. Honorable Mention Citations.

JUDGING: By special Awards committee. May withhold awards.

ENTRY FEE: None.

DEADLINES: Not specified.

160

Suggin Folklife Society Art Show
Mildred M. Gregory, President
324 Walnut Street
Newport, Arkansas 72112 U.S.A.
Tel: (501) 523-6250

Entry April

State; **entry open to Arkansas-born artists;** annual in April; established 1971. Purpose: to preserve the old through painting. Sponsored by Suggin Folklife Society. Supported by State Matching Fund. Average statistics (all sections): 400 entries, 116 entrants. Held at First State Bank in Newport, Arkansas for 2 weeks.

DRAWING CONTEST: **Pastel, Pen and Ink Folklore, Historical Preservation.** 24x20 inches maximum, framed, ready to hang; limit 3 per entrant. New or recent vintage (preferably previous year). Categories: Landscape, Still-Life, Historical Landmarks, Biblical, Portraits, Wildlife and Animals, Theme. Competition for Purchase Prize includes painting. Also have photography section.

PAINTING CONTEST: **Acrylic, Oil, Watercolor Folklore, Historical Preservation.** Requirements, restrictions, categories same as for Drawing.

AWARDS: 12 Best of Show Monetary Prizes to oil, watercolor, acrylic, pen and ink, pastel. Purchase Prize to theme (includes both sections). Ribbons all categories.

JUDGING: By out-of-town judges.

SALES TERMS: Work need not be for sale. No commission charge.

ENTRY FEE: $1 per work. Free for elementary students.

DEADLINES: Entry, event, April.

161

Spirit of London Painting Competition
Greater London Council (GLC)
Norman Sutherland
Department for Recreation and Arts
RA-E1, Room 673, The County Hall
London SE1 7PB, ENGLAND
Tel: (01) 633-1686, 633-1705

Entry October

City; **open to Greater London residents over age 16;** annual in November-December; established 1978. Purpose: to encourage amateur and professional artists living in area; provide them with exhibition and sales opportunities. Theme: Spirit of London. Sponsored and supported by GLC, industrial, private donors. Average statistics: 1100 entries, 230 accepted entries, 558 entrants, 21 awards, 12,000 attendance. Held at Royal Festival Hall for 17 days and Stock Exchange for 20 days.

DRAWING CONTEST: Pastel London Spirit, 11x7-1/2 to 48x48 inches, matted, framed, suitable for hanging; limit 3 per entrant. Require hand-delivery. By those who live, work, study in GLC area.

PAINTING CONTEST: Oil, Tempera, Watercolor, Mixed Media, London Spirit. Watercolors must be glazed; tempera may be glazed. Other requirements same as for Drawing.

PRINT CONTEST: London Spirit. Requirements same as for Drawing.

AWARDS: (all sections): GLC Awards, £1500 First, 4 £750, and £350 Prizes. London Silver Vaults and Sterling Guards Limited Silver Prize valued at £250 to GLC first place winner. £250 Sports Council Prize, best on sporting topic. Galleon World Travel British Painting Holiday Prize of 1 week. £250 Felix Rosentiel Prize plus reproduction of work as commercial print with 10% commission on sales to artist. £250 Arthur Guinness Prize to painting by artist under 30. £250 Mrs. Jerry Archer Prize, best painting by artist under 30. £500 Rawney Oil Painting Prize, best oil. £250 Inveresk Prize, best watercolor.

JUDGING: By 3 professional artists. Sponsor may reproduce entries for publicity.

SALES TERMS: Work need not be for sale. 15% commission charge.

ENTRY FEE: £4 per entrant.

DEADLINES: Entry, October. Event, November-December.

MINIATURE

Drawing, Painting, Prints, Sculpture, Visual Arts and Mixed Media. Miniature Art usually defined as being 10x10 inches maximum framed (10x10x10 inches for sculpture), or with maximum framed perimeter of 44 inches, and 1/6 or less life size. However, these definitions may vary. (Also see SMALL WORKS.)

162

Cameo Art Gallery National Miniature Show
Patricia Lee Steele, Manager
7339 Parklane Road
Columbia, South Carolina 29204
U.S.A. Tel: (803) 788-1302

Entry December

National; **entry open to U.S.;** annual in January-February; established 1981. Purpose: to establish tradition of annual miniature contests in South Carolina. Sponsored and supported by Cameo Art Gallery. Average statistics (all sections): 400 entries, 3 awards. Held at Cameo Gallery in Columbia for 1 month.

DRAWING CONTEST: Miniature, original, 10x10 inches maximum including frame, ready for hanging; subject 1/6 or less of life size; limit 3 per entrant (all sections). Completed in previous 2 years. Competition includes photography.

PAINTING CONTEST: Acrylic, Oil, Watercolor, Mixed Media Miniature. Requirements, restrictions same as for Drawing.

PRINT CONTEST: Miniature. Requirements, restrictions same as for Drawing.

AWARDS: (all sections): $500 First, $300 Second, $200 Third Place Merit Awards. Purchase Awards. Plaques. Ribbons.

JUDGING: By 2 artists. Sponsor may photograph winning entries. Not responsible for loss or damage.

SALES TERMS: 25% commission charge.

ENTRY FEE: $5 1 item; $8.50 2; $10 3, plus $5 shipping and handling.

DEADLINES: Entry, December. Event, January-February.

163

Country Art Festival

Mrs. Peter Milano, General Chair
2626 Yellow Creek Road
Akron, Ohio 44313 U.S.A. Tel: (216) 867-3830

Entry September

International; **entry open to nonstudents;** annual in September; established 1958. Formerly called Bath Country Art Festival. Began as local miniature painting show; became international 1981. Purpose: to provide place to learn about, enjoy fine arts. Sponsored by Eastview School. Supported by private donations. Recognized by Akron Society of Artists. Average statistics (all sections): 5000 entries, 300 entrants, 2 countries, 21 awards, 3000 attendance, $32000 total sales. Held at Eastview School in Bath for 4 days. Have galleries. Tickets: $1-$1.50. Also sponsor local scholarships. Second contact: Diane Housley, Advisory Board, Country Art Festival, Eastview School, Corner of N. Revere and Spring Valley Road, Bath, Ohio 44210.

DRAWING CONTEST: Miniature, including pastel, original; 10x10 inches maximum including frame; limit 10 miniatures per entrant plus 1 large piece (no size restrictions). No student work; or large pieces without miniature entries. Competition includes enamels, scrimshaw, illuminated calligraphy. Also have crafts, ceramics, photography sections.

PAINTING CONTEST: Acrylic, Oil, Watercolor Miniature. Requirements, restrictions same as for Drawing.

PRINT CONTEST: Miniature. Requirements, restrictions same as for Drawing.

MIXED MEDIA CONTEST: Miniature. Requirements, restrictions same as for Drawing.

AWARDS: $1000 in Cash Prizes. Merit Ribbons. Purchase Awards. Only miniatures are eligible for prizes.

JUDGING: Entry review by 4 judges. Awards judging by juror. Based on quality of execution, good taste. May withhold awards. Sponsor insures return.

SALES TERMS: All work must be for sale. 25% commission charge.

ENTRY FEE: $7 (juried miniature show), $2 (nonjuried entries).

DEADLINES: Entry, event, September.

164

Dakota Center for the Arts Midwest Miniature Show
Lisa Furaro, Director
Sky Gallery
222 North Concord Exchange
South St. Paul, Minnesota 55075
U.S.A. Tel: (612) 457-1220

Entry January

Regional; **entry open to Midwest U.S.;** biennial (odd years) in February; established 1981. Purpose: to provide fine art competition for Midwest artists. Sponsored and supported by Dakota Center for the Arts. Average statistics: 100 entries, 40 entrants, 12 awards. Held at Sky Gallery, St. Paul for 3 weeks.

VISUAL ARTS CONTEST: Two-dimensional Miniature, any medium, original, maximum framed perimeter 44 inches, 2-1/2 inches deep, ready for hanging, works on paper under plexiglass; limit 3 per entrant. Completed in previous year. No copies, photography.

AWARDS: 6 Excellence Awards. 6 Merit Awards. Cash Awards. Ribbons.

JUDGING: By 1 judge. Not responsible for loss or damage.

SALES TERMS: Work need not be for sale. 30% commission charge.

ENTRY FEE: $3 per work plus return postage.

DEADLINES: Entry, January. Event, February.

165

Laramie Art Guild American National Miniature Show
Olive Cupal, Chair
Overland Trail Gallery
603-1/2 Ivinson Avenue
Laramie, Wyoming 82070 U.S.A.
Tel: (307) 742-5388

Entry September

International; entry open to all; annual in October; established 1975. Purpose: to recognize miniature art, artists, and public interest in small-sized art. Sponsored and supported by Laramie Arts Guild, Wyoming Council for the Arts. Held in Laramie for 1 month. Average statistics: 300 entries, 125 entrants, 25 awards, 1000 attendance, $60 sales per entrant. Have workshops, fieldtrips, demonstrations.

VISUAL ARTS CONTEST: All Media Miniature, original, maximum framed perimeter 44 inches, 2-1/2 inches deep, ready for hanging; limit 5 per entrant. No images created by photographic processes, copies.

SCULPTURE CONTEST: Miniature, 10x10x10 inches maximum on pedestal. Other requirements, restrictions, same as for Visual Arts.

AWARDS: $150 to best of show. $100 First, $50 Second Place Awards. Special Awards. Honorable Mentions. Ribbons.

JUDGING: By 3 recognized artists. Sponsor reserves right to photograph entries for news media, catalog. Not responsible for loss or damage.

SALES TERMS: All work must be for sale. 35% commission charge.

ENTRY FEE: $4 per work plus return postage.

DEADLINES: Entry, September. Event, October. Materials returned, November.

166

Montana Miniature Art Society International Show
Elsie Jackson, Secretary-Treasurer
223 Fair Park Drive
Billings, Montana 59102 U.S.A.
Tel: (406) 656-8073

Entry March

International; **entry open to artists of legal age;** annual in May; established 1979. Purpose: to promote growth of miniature painting movement. Supported by Montana Miniature Society members. Recognized by Miniature Art Societies of Florida, New Jersey, Washington, D.C., Wyoming, New Mexico. Average statistics: 1000 entries, 4 countries. Held at Castle Gallery in Billings for 1 month. Second contact: Joan Christensen, 3123 Marguerite. Billings, Montana 59102; tel: (406) 656-8396.

VISUAL ARTS CONTEST: **Miniature,** original, 10x10 inches maximum including frame, quality framing and matting; sculpture 10x10x10 inches including pedestal; limit 3 per entrant. Subject 1/6 or less of life size. No crafts, darkroom techniques, plastic shrinkwrap. Competition includes enamels, tapestry, scrimshaw sections.

AWARDS: (all sections): Best of Show Award. Collector's Choice Purchase Awards. Honorable Mention Ribbons. Cash Awards to First, Second Place in all major sections. Ribbons to all winners. Special Awards.

JUDGING: Entry review by 4 judges. Awards judging by 1 judge. Sponsor insures up to $200 at exhibition; not responsible for loss or damage.

SALES TERMS: All work must by for sale. 30% commission charge.

ENTRY FEE: $15 ($20 foreign). Sponsor pays return postage.

DEADLINES: Entry, March. Event, May. Materials returned, June.

PAINTING (All Media)

Painting in any medium. Includes LANDSCAPE, SEASCAPE, REPRESENTATIONAL. (Also see other PAINTING CATEGORIES.)

167

El Paso National Sun Carnival Art Exhibition
El Paso Museum of Art
Bill Rakocy, Curator of Collections
1211 Montana Avenue
El Paso, Texas 79902 U.S.A.
Tel: (915) 541-4040

Entry August

National; **entry open to U.S.;** biennial (even years) in December-January; established 1949. Became biennial 1974. Purpose: to offer exposure to struggling and unknown artists. Sponsored and supported by El Paso Museum of Art, El Paso Museum Association. Average statistics: 350 entries, 150 entrants, 5 awards, 4000 attendance. Held in El Paso Museum of Art for 2 months. Have Sun Bowl games, various festivities. Publish *Art Line* (quarterly).

PAINTING CONTEST: **Any Medium General,** original, maximum 60x60 inches, 200 pounds (including frame, crate, packaging), framed or suitable for presentation; limit 3 per entrant. Completed in previous 2 years. Submit slides for entry review, 1-page biography. No fragile entries or works produced under supervision.

AWARDS: $1500 in Purchase Prizes. $1500 in Cash Awards.

JUDGING: By noted art personage. Sponsor may reproduce entries for records, publicity; owns slides of accepted works. Not responsible for loss or damage.

SALES TERMS: All work must be for sale. 25% commission charge.

ENTRY FEE: $5 per work plus return postage.

DEADLINES: Entry, August. Acceptance, October. Awards, December. Event, December-January. Materials returned, February.

168

Judith Selkowitz Fine Arts Annual Competition for Representational Painters

65 East 55th Street
P. O. Box 5268
New York, New York 10150 U.S.A.
Tel: (212) 838-3706

Entry April

National; **entry open to U.S.;** annual in April; established 1981. Named after and sponsored by Judith Selkowitz Fine Arts, Inc.

PAINTING CONTEST: Representational. Submit maximum 10 slides for entry review. No works previously exhibited in New York, or by artists affiliated with commercial New York gallery.

AWARDS: $2500 in Prizes.

JUDGING: By 2 art professionals.

ENTRY FEE: None.

DEADLINE: Entry, event, April.

169

Ogunquit Art Center National Exhibition of Paintings

Florence White Nims, Director
Hoyt's Lane
Ogunquit, Maine 03907 U.S.A.
Tel: (207) 646-2453

Entry May

National; **entry open to U.S.;** annual in Summer; established 1921. Purpose: to encourage the arts. Sponsored by Florence and Fredrick Nims. Average statistics: 300 entries, 200 entrants. Held in Ogunquit for 12 weeks. Second contact: 31 Golden Ball Road, Weston, Massachusetts 02193.

PAINTING CONTEST: Acrylic, Oil, Watercolor, Mixed Media General, 9x12 to 40x40 inches including frame (no raw wood, chalky white, colored frames), original; limit 2 per entrant. Request photo of exhibit for possible reproduction in newspapers, catalogs.

AWARDS: *Judges' Cash Awards:* $50 each to landscape (any season), marine subject, impressionistic work. $25 each to landscape (acrylic or watercolor), small marine (20x24 inches maximum), still life. *Visitors' Vote Cash Awards:* $100 to outstanding oil. $50 each to outstanding watercolor, still life (any medium). $25 to outstanding landscape.

JUDGING: Entry review by 6 judges. Awards judging by 3-5 judges. Not responsible for loss or damage.

SALES TERMS: 25% commission charge.

ENTRY FEE: $12. $3.50 per package handling charge on material in excess of 1 package

DEADLINES: Entry, May. Event, Summer.

170

Ozarks Annual Painting Exhibit

School of the Ozarks Art Department
Dr. Kenneth E. Burchett, Chair
Point Lookout, Missouri 65726
U.S.A. Tel: (417) 334-6411

Entry June

Regional; **entry open to artists living within 150 miles of Point Lookout;** annual in July-August; established 1963. Formerly called ART SHOW OF THE OZARKS to 1980. Sponsored by School of Ozarks Art Department. Supported by Missouri Arts Council. Average statistics: 200 entries, 115 entrants, 50 finalists, 10 awards, 4000 attendance, $2500 total sales. Held at School of the Ozarks in Point Lookout for 5 weeks.

PAINTING CONTEST: General (including acrylic, oil, watercolor), original; limit 2 per entrant. Completed in previous 2 years.

AWARDS: 6 $100 Cash Awards. $2000 in Purchase Awards.

JUDGING: By 1 prominent art professional. Based on quality. Sponsor may photograph entries.

ENTRY FEE: None. No sales commission charge.

DEADLINES: Entry, June. Event, July-August.

171

Tolley Galleries Annual Landscape Competition

Elinor Tolley
821 15th Street N.W.
Washington, DC 20005 U.S.A.
Tel: (202) 347-0003

Entry March

International; **entry open to North America;** annual in June; established 1981. Tolley Galleries specializes in 19th century American landscape, seascape paintings and commensurate quality of 20th century art. Purpose: to stimulate painting of realistic landscapes. Sponsored and supported by Tolley Galleries. Average statistics: 40 entries, 20 semifinalists, 3 awards. Held at Tolley Galleries for 20 days.

PAINTING CONTEST: Oil Landscape, 11x14 to 24x30 inches, framed, ready for hanging (prefer lightweight frame); limit 3 per entrant. Submit 3 slides for entry review.

AWARDS: $300 First, $200 Second, $100 Third Prize.

JUDGING: By local judges, gallery owner. Sponsor insures entries while on premises.

SALES TERMS: 33-1/3% commission charge on sales.

ENTRY FEE: $15 plus return postage.

DEADLINES: Entry, March. Acceptance, April. Event, June.

172

Washington and Jefferson National Painting Show

Washington and Jefferson (W & J) College
Paul B. Edwards, Chair
South Lincoln Street
Washington, Pennsylvania 15301
U.S.A. Tel: (412) 222-4400

Entry January

National; **entry open to U.S. residents age 18 and over;** annual in April; established 1967. Purpose: to increase permanent collection. Sponsored by W & J College, Committee on Intellectual Life and Resources. Supported by W & J College. Average statistics: 800 entries, 450 entrants, 4 finalists, 3500 attendance, $500 sales each entrant. Held in W & J College new art gallery for 20 days.

PAINTING CONTEST: Any Medium General (permanent media); watercolors matted and framed (no glass); limit 2 per entrant. Submit 2 2x2-inch color slides for entry review. No copies, class work.

AWARDS: Over $2000 in Prizes.

JUDGING: Entry review by 2 jurors. Awards judging by 1 juror. Not responsible for loss or damage.

SALES TERMS: 10% commission charge.

ENTRY FEE: $5. Sponsor pays return postage.

DEADLINES: Entry, January. Event, April.

173

Westwood Center of the Arts (WCA) Open Paintings on Canvas Exhibition

Selma B. Lokitz, President
1355 Westwood Boulevard
Los Angeles, California 90024 U.S.A.
Tel: (213) 477-2668

Entry February

International; **entry open to U.S., Canada;** annual in March-May; established 1961. Purpose: to further professional opportunities for artists; offer community service. Sponsored by WCA (founded 1947) formerly Westwood Art Association. Supported by membership dues, entry fees, donations. Average statistics: 100 entries, 50 entrants, 2 countries, 8 finalists, 5 awards, 50 attendance, 20 sales. Held in Los Angeles for 2 months. Publish *WCA Newsletter.* Have Traveling Show. Also sponsor Open Watermedia Exhibition, Open Print Show, National Small Sculpture and Drawing Exhibition, other monthly shows, scholarships-financial aid.

PAINTING CONTEST: Any Medium General, on canvas (fabric or board), 16x16 to 60x60 inches framed size, strip frames only, ready for hanging, limit 3 per entrant. Require hand-delivery. No paper, works under glass-plexiglass, installation pieces.

AWARDS: Two-Week Solo Exhibition to best in show. Two-Artist Gallery Exhibition First, $125 Second, $75 Third Place Award. $15 Value Zora's Art Supplies Award. 2 Honorable Mention Ribbons.

JUDGING: By 1 artist. Not responsible for loss or damage.

SALES TERMS: $20 commission charge.

ENTRY FEE: $15.

DEADLINES: Entry, February. Judging, awards, March. Event, March-May.

174

The Artist Magazine Reader's Pictures Exhibited Contest

The Artist Publishing Company, Ltd.
Jill Whittle, Editorial Manager
102 High Street
Tenterden, Kent TN30 6HT,
ENGLAND Tel: (05806) 3673

Entry Continuous

International; entry open to all; continuous in alternate months. Sponsored by *The Artist* Magazine.

PAINTING CONTEST: Any Medium General, dimensions not specified. Produced in previous 18 months, exhibited at professional art societies; minimum 3 works per entrant. Submit photographs (black and white, color transparencies), details of paintings, exhibitions, artist for review, publication.

AWARDS: Up to £150 Purchase Prize to best works featured in yearly series.

JUDGING: By Editor of *The Artist* Magazine.

ENTRY FEE: Not specified. All work must be for sale. No commission charge.

DEADLINES: Entry, event, various.

175

John Moores Liverpool Art Exhibition
Walker Art Gallery
Timothy Stevens, Secretary
William Brown Street
Liverpool L3 8EL, ENGLAND
Tel: (051) 227-5234

Entry September

National; **entry open to U.K.;** biennial (even years) in November-February; established 1957. Included sculpture to 1963; now concentrate on developments in painting. Alternates with Peter Moores Liverpool Project (noncompetitive exhibition). Purpose: to expose people to painting exhibition of best, most vital work being done today; encourage contemporary artists. Sponsored and supported by Walker Art Gallery, Sir John Moores. Average statistics (all sections): 2000 entries, 13 awards, 25,000 attendance. Held at Walker Art Gallery for 3 months. Exhibition tickets: 10p-20p. Also sponsor Exhibition of Contemporary and Older Art.

PAINTING CONTEST: General (oil, emulsion, other modern techniques), 10x12 inches maximum, 6-inch maximum projection; framed, ready for hanging; limit 1 per entrant. No watercolor, rings, projections on backs of works.

AWARDS: £6000 Purchase Award to First, £3000 Second, £2000 Third Place. 10 £250 Prizes.

JUDGING: By 3-5 judges (includes artist, art administrator, dealer, sponsor-founder). Sponsor claims First Prize entry, may photograph winners for catalog. Not responsible for loss or damage.

ENTRY FEE: £3 plus return shipping. No sales commission charge.

DEADLINES: Entry, September. Judging, event, November-February.

176

Laing Painting Competition
John Laing Limited
Norma Keatley, Public Relations Officer
14 Regent Street
London SW1Y 8PJ, ENGLAND
Tel: (01) 930 7271, ext. 42

Entry January

National; **entry open to U.K.;** annual in March; established in 1973. Purpose: to select pictures for company's calendar. Sponsored and supported by John Laing Limited. Average statistics: 1000 entries, 800 entrants. Held at Mall Galleries in London for 1 week.

PAINTING CONTEST: Acrylic, Gouache, Oil, Watercolor Landscape-Seascape, width 18-36 inches, depth approximately 2/3 of width, framed; limit 2 per entrant (only 1 hung). British or continental landscapes, seascapes; horizontal formal. Require hand-delivery. No square paintings or metal frames.

AWARDS: £1500 in Cash Awards.

JUDGING: By 4 members of Royal Academy. Sponsor may purchase entries or copyrights of entries for calendar. Not responsible for loss or damage.

SALES TERMS: Work need not be for sale. 25% commission charge.

ENTRY FEE: None.

DEADLINES: Entry, January. Judging, February. Event, awards, March.

PAINTING (Watercolor, Water Media)

Painting in Watercolor and Water Media, including TRANSPARENT WATERCOLOR. (Also see other PAINTING CATEGORIES.)

177

Eastbay Watercolor Society (EWS) Annual Exhibition

Jean Warren, President
28 Lost Valley Drive
Orinda, California 94563 U.S.A.

Entry September

State; **entry open to California;** annual in Fall; established 1968. Purpose: to foster excellence in watercolor through demonstrations, workshops, scholarships and shows. Sponsored and supported by EWS, Pleasant Hill Recreation Department, City of Walnut Creek, Bay Area businesses. Average statistics: 200 entries, 100 entrants. Held at Crown Zellerbach in San Francisco for 2 weeks. Have EWS Portfolio (members' works for sale or rental). Also sponsor monthly watercolor demonstrations, lectures, workshops, $500 scholarship to high school senior, member shows and exhibits. Second contact: Jim Glanton, Show Chair, Eastbay Watercolor Society, P.O. Box 4631, Walnut Creek, California 94596.

PAINTING CONTEST: Watercolor General, original, 30x40 inches maximum, framed (all edges) under glass, ready for hanging; limit 2 per entrant. Require hand-delivery. No pastels, graphics, copies, class work.

AWARDS: $300 City of Walnut Creek Purchase Award. $175 First, $125 Second, $75 Third Prize. $150 Flax Artists' Mart Purchase Award. $200 Harold Gretzner Award to member. Honorable Mentions. Merchandise, Merit Awards.

JUDGING: By 3 watercolor artists. Sponsor may reproduce entries for publicity. Not responsible for loss or damage.

SALES TERMS: Work need not be for sale. 15% commission charge (20% from portfolio).

ENTRY FEE: $5.

DEADLINES: Entry, September. Judging, event, October.

178

Houston Watercolor Art Society Spring Open Exhibition

Jackie Menefee, Chair
1738 Sunset Blvd.
Houston, Texas 77005 U.S.A.
Tel: (713) 524-6736

Entry April

International; entry open to all; annual in April-May; established 1969. Sponsored by Watercolor Art Society-Houston, nonprofit organization founded to further interest in watercolor through teaching, programs, demonstrations, exhibitions. Supported by local businesses, Cultural Arts Council of Houston. Average statistics: 300 entries, 100 entrants, 90 finalists. Held at International Bank

Plaza, Houston for 3 weeks. Also sponsor membership only fall show in October.

PAINTING CONTEST: Watercolor General, (any water-soluble medium) on paper, original concept, maximum 45 inches any dimension, framed, under plexiglass, wired, ready for hanging, unvarnished; limit 3 per entrant. No pastels, direct copies of work (including photographs), student work, work previously exhibited in Houston.

AWARDS: $1000 in Cash Awards.

JUDGING: By nationally known professional artist. Not responsible for loss or damage.

ENTRY FEE: $8 per work.

DEADLINES: Entry, April. Event, April-May.

179

Midwest Watercolor Society Open Juried Show

Lu Penner
Box 192
Hudson, Wisconsin 54016 U.S.A.
Tel: (715) 386-2560

Entry April

International; **entry open to U.S., Canada;** annual in August; established 1977. Purpose: to advance stature of transparent watercolor as major painting medium. Sponsored by Midwest Watercolor Society (founded 1975) and sponsoring museum. Supported by members and businesses. Average statistics: 900 entries, 450 entrants, 48 states and provinces, 100 acceptances. Held at different locations throughout Midwest. Also sponsor annual watercolor workshop. Second contact: Vivian Chevillon, President, 111 West Washington Blvd., Lombard, Illinois 60148; tel: (312) 629-0443.

PAINTING CONTEST: Transparent Watercolor General, 36x42 inches maximum outside dimensions including frame, under glass or plexiglass (if shipped), backed, glazed, ready for hanging; limit 1 per entrant. Submit 2 35mm full-framed slides for entry review. No opaque, mixed media, collage, copies.

AWARDS: $250, $225, 6 $200 Excellence Awards. 2 $150, $111, 11 $100 Special Merit Awards. $75, 5 $50 Merit Awards. 3 $50 Merchandise Awards.

ENTRY FEE: $10.

DEADLINES: Entry, April. Acceptance, May. Judging, July. Event, August.

180

National Arts Club (NAC) Open Watercolor Exhibition

Moses Worthman, Chair
3027 Brighton 5th Street
Brooklyn, New York 11235 U.S.A.
Tel: (212) 646-2385

Entry December

International; **entry open to Canada, Mexico, U.S.;** annual in May; established 1900. Purpose: to stimulate, foster, promote public interest in the arts; educate Americans in fine arts. Sponsored and supported by NAC (founded 1898 by Charles de Kay, *New York Times* art critic). Average statistics: 75 entries, 3 countries, 10 awards. Held at NAC Galleries, New York, for 3-4 weeks (awards event for 1 evening). Have demonstrations. Also sponsor NAC Gold Medal of Honor Awards in Literature, Music, Visual Arts, Drama (to distinguished arts figures); scholarships and prizes. Second contact: Fay Moore, Exhibition Committee Chair, 15 Gramercy

Park South, New York, New York 10003.

PAINTING CONTEST: Water Media General (watercolor, gouache, tempera, acrylic, or casein), in color, maximum 44 inches per side framed size, framed under glass or plexiglass, wired for hanging; limit 1 per entrant. Submit 1 cardboard-mounted 35mm slide (not glass) for entry review.

AWARDS: $500 First, $200 Second, $100 Third NAC Awards. $100 Popular Prize Award. $50 Frame Allowance Award. President's Award and Exhibition Committee Award (1-week 1-person show in Gregg Galleries, each). Winsor & Newton Materials Award. Percy R. Baker Award. 4 Grumbacher Award Plaques.

JUDGING: Entry review and awards judging by 3 art professionals. Popular Prize Award by ballot at close of exhibition. Not responsible for loss or damage.

ENTRY FEE: $10 handling charge. Sponsor expects 20% donation from all sales.

DEADLINES: Entry, December. Entry review, January. Awards, event, May.

181

New Jersey Water Color Society Open Exhibition
Dorothy Dallas
378 Eastwood Court
Englewood, New Jersey 07631
U.S.A. Tel: (201) 567-5725

Entry September

Regional; **entry open to present and former New Jersey residents;** annual in September-November; established 1942. Purpose: to encourage watercolor painting art in New Jersey. Sponsored by New Jersey Water Color Society. Supported by local businesses. Recognized by Federated Art Associations of New Jersey. Average statistics: 450 entries, 250 entrants, 20 awards. Held in Morristown and Lincroft alternately for 1 month each. Have watercolor demonstration. Tickets: $1. Second contact: June Benson, 71 Old Orchard Court, Cedar Grove, New Jersey 07009; tel: (201) 239-3174.

PAINTING CONTEST: Watercolor General, on paper, original, maximum width 42 inches including frame, under glass or plexiglass, unvarnished, ready for hanging; limit 2 per entrant. Mixed media with watercolor dominant acceptable. Require hand-delivery. No class work.

AWARDS: Over $1200 in Cash Awards. New Jersey Water Color Society Silver Medal to member.

JUDGING: Entry review by 6 American Watercolor Society (AWS) members. Awards judging by 2 AWS members. Not responsible for loss or damage.

SALES TERMS: 20% commission charge. Work may be for sale.

ENTRY FEE: $8 one entry, $12 two entries.

DEADLINES: Entry, judging, September. Event, September-November.

182

Northwest Watercolors Annual Exhibition
Northwest Watercolor Society
Francine Porad, Show Chair
6944 South East 33rd
Mercer Island, Washington 98040
U.S.A. Tel: (206) 232-3239

Entry March

Regional; **entry open to Washington, Oregon, Idaho, Montana, Alaska, British Columbia (Canada);**

annual in Spring; established 1939. Purpose: to promote interest in watercolor, encourage new approaches. Sponsored by Northwest Watercolor Society, Bellevue Art Museum. Supported by various memorial funds, art galleries, art associations. Average 385 entrants. Held in Bellevue, Washington for 5 weeks. Have traveling exhibition for 50 selected entries.

PAINTING CONTEST: **Watercolor General,** on paper (or illustration board), original, 12-45 inches wide, framed (plexiglass recommended with metal frames), ready for hanging; limit 1 per entrant. Produced in previous 2 years. Entrants outside 200-mile radius of Seattle submit slides for entry review. No class work or work previously shown in Seattle or King County area juried exhibition.

AWARDS: $500 Northwest Watercolor Society Award to best transparent watercolor. $400 Puget Sound Group of Painters Award. $300 Fisher Award. 5 $200 Awards. 5 Cash Awards. $800 Safeco, 2 $500 Craftsman Press, 1 $300 Purchase Awards. 10 Merchandise Awards. 50 paintings selected for 2-week exhibition at Federation of Canadian Artists Gallery in Vancouver, British Columbia.

JUDGING: By 3 artists. Not responsible for loss or damage.

SA[illegible] TERMS: All work must be [illegible] [illegible]0% commission charge.

[illegible] $5 plus $15 handling charge ([illegible]nts $20).

DEADL[illegible]arch. Judging, event, [illegible]

183

Rocky Mountain National Watermedia Exhibition
Foothills Art Center
Marian J. Metsopoulos, Executive Director
809 15th Street
Golden, Colorado 80401 U.S.A.
Tel: (303) 279-3922

Entry May

National; **entry open to U.S.;** annual in August-September; established 1974. Purpose: to expose some of nation's best artists. Sponsored by Foothills Art Center. Supported by private donations. Average statistics: 1500 entries, 125 finalists, 20 awards, 7000 attendance, $60,000 total sales. Held at Foothills Art Center for 5 weeks. Also sponsor Energy Art Exhibition, Foothills Art Center North American Sculpture Exhibition; workshops.

PAINTING CONTEST: **Water Media General** (acrylic, ink, watercolor) on paper, original, signed, unvarnished, under glass or plexiglass, framed ready for hanging; limit 3 per entrant. Submit 35mm slides for entry review. Request resumes of accepted artists. No pastels; collage material other than original watermedia on paper.

AWARDS: $9000 in 20 Cash Awards.

JUDGING: Entry review and awards judging by 2 nationally known jurors. Sponsor may photograph accepted paintings for catalog, publicity; keeps slides of accepted works for permanent collection; insures during exhibition.

SALES TERMS: All work must be for sale. 30% commission charge.

ENTRY FEE: $7.50 each plus shipping and handling.

DEADLINES: Entry, judging, May. Notification, June. Awards, August. Event, August-September.

184

Texas Watercolor Society Annual Exhibition
Norma Cox Miller, Chair
2927 Quail Oak
San Antonio, Texas 78232 U.S.A.
Tel: (512) 494-8173

Entry January

State; **entry open to adult Texas residents;** annual in February; established 1950. Purpose: to encourage Texas watercolor artists; interest public in medium. Sponsored by Texas Watercolor Society. Supported by businesses. Average 600 entries. Held at University of Texas Health Science Center in San Antonio for 3 weeks. Have traveling exhibition. Second contact: Betty Coakley, Exhibition Co-Chair, 6205 Rue Sophie, San Antonio, Texas 78238; tel: (512) 684-0517.

PAINTING CONTEST: Watercolor General, original, transparent or opaque, on paper, framed, under 1/16-inch minimum plexiglass, ready for hanging; limit 3 per entrant. Completed after January previous year. Collages with paper and water-soluble media accepted. No printed matter, commercially colored papers, varnish, pastel, crayola, foreign substances adhering, plexiglass box-type frames, or work under supervision.

ELIGIBILITY: Resident or former resident of Texas (for 6 consecutive months at any one time), age 18 or older.

AWARDS: $2000 to best of show. $1000 George Pinca Memorial Award. $500 to transparent watercolor. 12 $300 Purchase Awards. $1900 other cash awards. Society membership offered after acceptance of 1 work in annual show. Traveling exhibition of some winning entries.

JUDGING: By distinguished critic-artist-teacher. Purchase Awards selected by juror. Not responsible for loss or damage.

SALES TERMS: Work need not be for sale. 15% commission charge.

ENTRY FEE: $7.50 per work.

DEADLINES: Entry, judging, January. Event, February.

185

Watercolor Oklahoma Open Exhibition
Oklahoma Watercolor Association
Anna Belle Birckett
417 North West 41
Oklahoma City, Oklahoma 73118
U.S.A. Tel: (405) 524-2105

Entry July

International; **entry open to artists age 18 or over;** annual in September-October; established 1975. Purpose: to promote sales of watercolor media. Sponsored by Oklahoma Watercolor Association. Supported by local businesses. Average statistics: 400 entries, 185 entrants, 3 countries, $12,875 total sales. Held at The House Gallery, Oklahoma City for 4 weeks. Second contact: The House Gallery, 5536 North Western, Oklahoma City, Oklahoma 73118.

PAINTING CONTEST: Wa[illegible] color General, original, trans[illegible]ed opaque, on paper, framed [illegible]ass, (with protective covering [illegible]) ready to hang; unlimit[illegible] [illegible]om-pleted after January [illegible]ears. No [illegible] Submit 2x2-inch [illegible] varnish, pastels, crayola, foreign substances adhering or non-water-soluble media.

AWARDS: $5000 in Purchase, Merchandise Awards. $100 First, $75 Second, $50 Third, $25 Fourth Prize.

JUDGING: By 1 artist. Sponsor may photograph entries for publicity. Not responsible for loss or damage.

SALES TERMS: All work must be for sale. 33-1/3% commission charge.

ENTRY FEE: $6 per work.

DEADLINES: Entry, July. Event, September-October.

186

Watercolor West Annual Transparent Watercolor Exhibition

Beryl Larkin, Secretary
P. O. Box 213
Redlands, California 92373 U.S.A.

Entry January

International; entry open to all; annual in April. Purpose: to promote interest in, present best of recent purely transparent watercolor painting. Sponsored by Watercolor West (founded 1967). Average 500 entries. Held at Riverside Art Center and Museum, Riverside for 1 month. Also sponsor exhibits of members' work, scholarships.

PAINTING CONTEST: Transparent Watercolor General, on untreated paper, original, 45 inches maximum (including frame), under glass or plexiglass; limit 3 per entrant. Submit 3 slides maximum for entry review. No work previously exhibited in any juried show; no gesso, other opaque ground or buildup, embossing, collage, pastel, acrylic, ink, mixed media, varnished work, white or opaque color.

AWARDS: $400 First, $300 Second, $200 Third Place Prize. $200 National Watercolor Society Award. $150 Crafton Hills College Watercolor Seminar Award. $150 Strathmore Paper Award. $125 San Diego Watercolor Society Award. $125 and Grambacher Silver Medallion. $111 Arches Paper Award, $100 Winsor & Newton Award. $100 Challis Gallery Award. $100 Mersereau and O'Neill Award. $250 Santa Fe Federal Purchase Award. 2 $300 Purchase Selections.

JUDGING: By well-known watercolor artist. Sponsor may photograph entries for publicity; rent slides of accepted entries to teachers, organizations. Not responsible for loss or damage.

SALES TERMS: 33-1/3% commission charge

ENTRY FEE: $4 per work.

DEADLINES: Entry, judging, January. Event, April.

187

Westwood Center of the Arts (WCA) Open Watermedia Exhibition

Selma B. Lokitz, President
1355 Westwood Boulevard
Los Angeles, California 90024 U.S.A.
Tel: (213) 477-2668

Entry September

International; **entry open to U.S., Canada;** annual in November-December; established 1961. Purpose: to further professional opportunities for artists; offer community service. Sponsored by WCA (founded 1947), formerly Westwood Art Association. Supported by membership dues, entry fees, donations. Average statistics: 100 entries, 50 entrants, 2 countries, 8 finalists, 5 awards. Held in Los Angeles for 1 month. Publish *WCA Newslet-*

ter. Also sponsor Open Paintings on Canvas Exhibition, Open Print Show, National Small Sculpture and Drawing Exhibition, other monthly shows, scholarships-financial aid.

PAINTING CONTEST: Water Media General, on paper, water-soluble, 16x16 to 48x48 inches unframed size, framed, under glass or plexiglass; limit 3 per entrant. Submit slides for entry review. Require shipping, handling by specified agent.

AWARDS: Two-Week Solo Gallery Exhibition to best in show. $100 Luv-It Jeans Company Award. $100 WCA Award. $50 President's Award. $15 value Zora's Art Supplies Award. 3 Honorable Mention Ribbons.

JUDGING: By prominent art professional. Not responsible for loss or damage.

SALES TERMS: 25% commission charge.

ENTRY FEE: $15 first entry, $5 each additional.

DEADLINES: Entry, September. Notification, October. Judging, November. Event, November-December.

188

Zaner Gallery National Watermedia Biennial Exhibition

John Haldoupis, Director
100 Alexander Street
Rochester, New York 14620 U.S.A.
Tel: (716) 232-7578

Entry February

National; **entry open to U.S. residents over age 18;** biennial (even years) in May-June; established 1982. Purpose: to encourage appreciation of American watercolor. Sponsored by and held at Zaner Gallery in Rochester for 1 month. Also sponsor Small Works National, ongoing exhibitions.

PAINTING CONTEST: Water Media General, on paper, original, maximum 60 inches any dimension including frame, ready for hanging; limit 3 per entrant. Executed in previous 2 years. Submit 2x2-inch cardboard or plastic-mounted slide of each entry for entry review.

AWARDS: $1500 in Cash Awards.

JUDGING: By 1 artist. Sponsor retains slides for documentation, may reproduce entries in catalog and press. Not responsible for loss or damage.

SALES TERMS: Work may be for sale. 30% commission charge.

ENTRY FEE: $10 each work plus return postage.

DEADLINES: Entry, February. Event, judging, May-June.

PAINTING, SCULPTURE

Painting and Sculpture in any medium. (Also see other PAINTING, SCULPTURE CATEGORIES.)

189

Arkansas Arts Center Delta Art Exhibition

Townsend Wolfe, Director
MacArthur Park
P. O. Box 2137
Little Rock, Arkansas 72203 U.S.A.

Entry August

Regional; **entry open to South and Southwestern U.S.;** annual in October-November; established 1958. Sponsored by and held at Arkansas Arts Center for 1 month. Also sponsor Prints, Drawing, and Crafts Exhibition; Toys Designed by Artists Exhibition; Young Arkansas Artists Competitive Exhibition.

PAINTING CONTEST: Any Medium General; limit 2 per entrant. Submit 35mm slides for entry review.

SCULPTURE CONTEST: General, 500 pounds maximum weight; limit 2 per entrant. Submit 35mm slides for entry review.

ELIGIBILITY: Artists born or residing in Arkansas, Louisiana, Mississippi, Missouri, Oklahoma, Tennessee, Texas.

AWARDS: $1000 First Pyramid Life Insurance Co. of America Purchase Award. $3000 in other Purchase Awards.

JUDGING: By nationally recognized artist.

ENTRY FEE: $7.50 per work.

DEADLINES: Entry, August. Judging, September. Event, October-November.

190

Art on the Green Juried Show
Citizens Council for the Arts
Sue S. Flammia
P. O. Box 901
Coeur d'Alene, Idaho 83814 U.S.A.
Tel: (208) 667-3561

Entry April

International; entry open to all; annual in August; established 1968. Purpose: to celebrate arts through displays, demonstrations, performances. Sponsored and supported by Citizens Council for the Arts (nonprofit). Held at North Idaho College, Coeur d'Alene for 3 days. Have arts and crafts booths, Clothesline Sales, minibooths for high school students or younger, Children's Art Corner, entertainment, food booths.

PAINTING CONTEST: All Media General, original, 48 inches maximum outside dimensions, framed; limit 2 per entrant (all sections). Produced in previous 2 years. No copies, commercial kits. Competition includes photography. Also have crafts sections.

SCULPTURE CONTEST: General, original, 150 pounds maximum; limit 2 per entrant (all sections). No copies, molds, fragile entries. Competition includes crafts. Also have photography.

AWARDS: 11 $100 Awards to painting. (Includes crafts): $250 North Idaho College Presidents Purchase Award; $250 Community Purchase Award; $175 Ralph E. Holmberg Memorial Award. Also have $200 Best Decorated Booth Award.

JUDGING: By 3-person jury. Not responsible for loss or damage.

SALES TERMS: Work must be for sale. Overpriced items rejected. 20% commission charge.

ENTRY FEE: $3 each work.

DEADLINES: Entry, April. Judging, event, August.

191

Harrisburg Art Association Juried Exhibition
Charles A. Schulz, Executive Director
21 North Front Street
Harrisburg, Pennsylvania 17101
U.S.A. Tel: (717) 236-1432

Entry February

National; **entry open to Eastern U.S.;** annual in March; established 1927. Purpose: to bring quality art to Harrisburg area. Sponsored by and held at Art Association of Harrisburg for 3 weeks. Supported by local business and members. Average statistics (all sections): 175 entries, 115 entrants, 85 finalists. Also sponsor 12-week school program through Fall and Spring; workshops in Summer; lectures.

PAINTING CONTEST: **General,** 72x72 inches maximum, framed, matted, under glass or plexiglass, ready for hanging; limit 2 per section. Completed in previous 2 years. Submit slides for entry review. No wet paintings. Competition for some awards includes photography.

SCULPTURE CONTEST: **General,** mounted on base, may be under glass. Other requirements same as for Painting.

AWARDS: $200 Best of Show. $200 First, $100 Second, $50 Third Prize each section. 2 Grumbacher Medallions for oil and watercolor. Purchase Awards, Honorable Mentions (all sections).

JUDGING: By 1-3 judges. Sponsor may photograph entries for publicity; insures work during exhibition only.

SALES TERMS: 25% commission charge.

ENTRY FEE: $10 plus postage.

DEADLINES: Entry, February. Event, March.

192

Marietta National Painting and Sculpture Exhibition

Marietta College Art Department
Arthur Howard Winner, Director
Marietta, Ohio 45750 U.S.A.
Tel: (614) 373-4643, ext. 275

Entry February

National; **entry open to U.S. amateurs, students;** annual in April; established 1967. Formerly called MAINSTREAMS (1967-1977). Purpose: to display and reward creative efforts of artists throughout U.S. Sponsored and supported by Marietta College. Average statistics (all sections): 1872 entries, 713 entrants, $3500 in awards. Held at Marietta College for 1 month. Also sponsor Marietta College Crafts National Exhibition.

PAINTING CONTEST: **Any Medium General,** original; limit 3 per entrant, 1 set constitutes 1 entry (all sections). May submit 1 slide for entry review. No class work. Competition includes photography, crafts.

SCULPTURE CONTEST: **Any Medium General,** original; limit 3 per entrant, 1 set constitutes 1 entry (all sections). Submit 4 35mm slides for entry review and awards judging. No molds, classwork. Competition includes photography, crafts.

AWARDS: $1000 Painting Award. $1000 Sulpture Award. $1500 in Purchase Awards. Plaques of Distinction.

JUDGING: By 3 nationally known judges. Based on merit. Purchase Prizes selected by Marietta College Art Department. Sponsor insures during exhibition only; not responsible for loss or damage.

SALES TERMS: Work need not be for sale. 25% commission charge (including purchase prize).

ENTRY FEE: $15 plus return postage.

DEADLINES: Entry, February. Event, April. Materials returned, July.

193

Mint Museum Biennial Exhibition of Piedmont Painting and Sculpture

Jane Kessler, Assistant Curator
501 Hempstead Place
P. O. Box 6011

Charlotte, North Carolina 28207
U.S.A. Tel: (704) 334-9723

Entry October

Regional; **entry open to Southeast U.S. adults;** biennial (odd years) in January-March; established 1963. Alternates with Mint Museum Biennial Exhibition of Piedmont Crafts (even years). Purpose: to identify best work produced in Southeast U.S. Sponsored by the Mint Museum. Recognized by American Association of Museums. Supported by Mint Museum Woman's Auxiliary. Average statistics: 1000 entries, 250 entrants, 30 finalists, 10 awards. Held in Charlotte for 7 weeks

PAINTING CONTEST: **Any Medium General,** original; limit 3 per entrant (all sections) of which maximum 2 may be accepted for exhibit. Produced in previous 2 years. Submit 1-3 35mm slides, cardboard or plastic mounted, of each work for entry review. No extraordinary installation requirements, electrical devices.

SCULPTURE CONTEST: **Any Medium General.** Requirements, restrictions same as for Painting.

ELIGIBILITY: Artists age 18 years or older, living in Alabama, Florida, Georgia, Kentucky, Louisiana, Mississippi, North Carolina, South Carolina, Tennessee, Virginia, West Virginia.

AWARDS: $6000 in Purchase Awards.

JUDGING: Entry review and awards judging by 1 nationally recognized art professional. Sponsor may photograph, reproduce entries for catalog, educational, publicity purposes. Not responsible for loss or damage.

SALES TERMS: 30% commission charge (except on Purchase Awards).

ENTRY FEE: $10 per entrant plus return shipping costs.

DEADLINES: Entry, October. Notification, December. Event, January-March.

194

Union Street Gallery Annual Competition
Jill Manton, Director
1909 Union Street
San Francisco, California 94123
U.S.A. Tel: (415) 921-7160

Entry April

International; entry open to all; annual in July-August; established 1981. Purpose: to provide opportunity for new artists to exhibit their work. Sponsored and supported by Union Street Gallery. Held in San Francisco for 2 months.

PAINTING CONTEST: **General,** on paper 6x6 feet maximum, framed, ready to hang; limit 10 per entrant. Submit 10 slides for entry review. Require hand-delivery. Request entrant attendance.

SCULPTURE CONTEST: **General,** 6 feet maximum any dimension; limit 10 per entrant. Other requirements same as for Painting.

ELIGIBILITY: No artists affiliated with art galleries in San Francisco.

AWARDS: $100 Cash Award. 1 or 2 Person Show.

JUDGING: By 3-member Gallery Board of Directors.

SALES TERMS: All work must be for sale. 50% commission charge.

ENTRY FEE: $10.

DEADLINES: Entry, April. Judging, event, July-August.

PRINTS

Prints of any type. (Also see other PRINT CATEGORIES.)

195

Boston Printmakers National Exhibition

Sylvia Rantz, Treasurer
P.O. Box 161
Lexington, Massachusetts 02173
U.S.A. Tel: (617) 444-2696,
862-2658

Entry January

International; **entry open to U.S. and Canada;** annual in Spring; established 1948. Purpose: to promote development, high standards of original printmaking; provide showcase for artists, public. Sponsored and supported by Boston Printmakers, museums, Massachusetts Council on the Arts and Humanities. Average statistics: 1500 entries, 500 entrants, 150 finalists, 10 awards, $5000 total sales, $150 average sale per entrant. Held at various locations in Eastern Massachusetts for 4-6 weeks. Have traveling exhibition. Second contact: H. C. Boodman, 4 Linmoor Terrace, Lexington, Massachusetts 02173.

PRINT CONTEST: Any Type General, original, maximum 4x4 inches matted size, in hinged mats; limit 2 per entrant. Completed in previous 2 years. No colored mats.

AWARDS: $5000 minimum in Prizes, Purchases.

JUDGING: By 2 art professionals of national reputation. All entries viewed twice. Sponsor insures during event only; not responsible for in-transit loss or damage.

SALES TERMS: 33-1/3% commission charge (including patrons' selections).

ENTRY FEE: None. Entrant pays return postage.

DEADLINES: Entry, January. Event, awards, Spring. Materials returned, May.

196

Hunterdon Art Center Annual Print Exhibition

A. S. Marsh
7 Center Street
Clinton, New Jersey 08809 U.S.A.
Tel: (201) 735-8415

Entry February

National; **entry open to U.S.;** annual in Spring. Sponsored by and held at Hunterdon Art Center (nonprofit organization to provide education and participation in the arts) for 2 weeks. Have traveling show to September.

PRINT CONTEST: Any Type General except monotypes; limit 2 per entrant.

AWARDS: Purchase Awards.

JUDGING: By jury.

SALES TERMS: 25% commission charge.

ENTRY FEE: $15.

DEADLINES: Entry, February. Event, March-May.

197

Miami International Print Biennial

Miami Art Center Helpers (Mach I)
Marilyn Liedman, Co-Chair
Metropolitan Museum and Art Center
1212 Anastasia Avenue
Coral Gables, Florida 33134 U.S.A.
Tel: (305) 442-1448, 233-0997

Entry November

International; entry open to all; biennial (even years) in March-May; established 1973. Formerly called MIAMI GRAPHICS BIENNIAL. Purpose: to recognize developing as well as established artists; benefit Miami's cultural growth. Sponsored by MACH I. Supported by NEA, Fine Arts Council of Florida, local businesses. Recognized by Metro-Dade Department of Tourism. Average statistics: 2000 entries, 1000 entrants, 30 countries, 180 finalists, 20 awards. Held at Metropolitan Museum and Art Center in Coral Gables for 6-8 weeks, Have lectures, seminars, displays of printmaking techniques, traveling exhibition.

PRINT CONTEST: Any Type General except monoprints, original, maximum 72x100 inches (282x254cm); limit 2 per entrant. Produced in previous 2 years. Submit 1-2-inch (5.08x5.08cm) 35mm, cardboard-mounted color slides for entry review. No frames; no paintings, drawings, photos.

AWARDS: 2 $1000, 2 $800, 2 $600, and 2 $400 Purchase Prizes. 10-12 $250 Merit Awards.

JUDGING: Entry review by 3 art professionals. Awards judging by 1 professional. Sponsor owns slides for educational or future exhibition use; may reproduce entries for publicity. Not responsible for loss or damage.

SALES TERMS: 25% commission charge.

ENTRY FEE: $10.

DEADLINES: Entry, November. Awards, judging, February. Event, March-May.

198

Oregon Printmakers Annual Juried Show

Mt. Hood Community College Art Mall Gallery
Deb Martz, Coordinator
26000 S. E. Stark Street
Gresham, Oregon 97030 U.S.A.
Tel: (503) 667-7303

Entry February

State; **entry open to Oregon:** annual in February-March; established 1976. Purpose: to bring together printmakers of all media; represent Oregon artists. Sponsored by and held at Mt. Hood Community College Art Mall Gallery for 4 weeks. Average statistics: 200 entries, 175 entrants, 5 awards, 500 attendance, $1200 sales.

PRINT CONTEST: Any Type General, Dimensions not specified, framed, ready for hanging; limit 2 per entrant. Produced in previous year. No class work.

AWARDS: $500 Purchase Awards.

JUDGING: By 1-2 judges. Sponsor insures during exhibition only.

SALES TERMS: 25% commission charge. Work need not be for sale.

ENTRY FEE: None. Entrant pays return postage on mailed entries.

DEADLINES: Entry, February. Judging, event, February-March.

199

Potsdam National Print Exhibition

State University of New York (SUNY)-Potsdam
Georgia Coopersmith, Gallery Director
Brainerd Art Gallery
College of Arts and Sciences
Potsdam, New York 13676 U.S.A.
Tel: (315) 268-2710

Entry February

National; **entry open to U.S.;** biennial (even years) in Winter, established 1976. Alternates with Potsdam National Drawing Exhibition (odd years). Sponsored by State University of Arts and Sciences. Held at Brainerd Art Gallery for 1 month (may travel). Second contact: Arthur Sennet, Chair, Art Department, SUNY Potsdam, New York 13676.

PRINT CONTEST: Any Type General (except monoprints), no size restrictions, matted or mounted on stiff board or otherwise presentable (no glass); limit 2 per entrant. No frames except to protect 3D prints.

AWARDS: Up to $2500 in Purchase Awards.

JUDGING: By 1 juror. Sponsor insures during exhibition.

SALES TERMS: 10% commission charge.

ENTRY FEE: $5 per work plus postage.

DEADLINES: Entry, February. Event, February-March.

200

Print Club International Competition

Ofelia Garcia, Director
1614 Latimer Street
Philadelphia, Pennsylvania 19103
U.S.A. Tel: (215) 735-6090

Entry October

International; **entry open to members (may join with entry);** annual in November; established 1925. Purpose: to educate, encourage, inform print collectors and public; support contemporary printmakers. Sponsored by Print Club, nonprofit, educational organization supporting printmaking (founded 1915). Average statistics (all sections): 1400 entries, 800 entrants, 20 countries, 119 finalists, 28 awards, 2000 attendance. Held at Print Club for 1 month. Have exhibitions, information-reference-referral services. Publish *NewsPRINT* (monthly), *CounterPROOF* (biannual). Also sponsor lectures, workshops, Print Appraisal Days.

PRINT CONTEST: Any Type General (including monotype, color Xerox, editions variable, hand-colored), backed, matted, acetated; limit 2 per entrant. Completed in previous 3 years. No frames. Also have photography section.

AWARDS: $8000 in Purchase, Cash and Professional Prizes. Patron and Special Awards.

JUDGING: By 3 artists and curators. Sponsor may photograph entries for publicity; insures entries on premises.

SALES TERMS: Work need not be for sale. 40%-50% commission charge (except Purchase Prizes).

ENTRY FEE: None. Membership $25, $15 (student, foreign, nonlocal artists), $20 (local artists).

DEADLINES: Entry, judging, October. Event, November.

201

Rocky Mountain Regional Print Show

Colorado Graphic Arts Center
Patricia A. Cronin, Director
2541 15th Street
Denver, Colorado 80211 U.S.A.
Tel: (303) 477-6570

Entry May

Regional; **entry open to working artists of Rocky Mountain states;** annual in May-June; established 1981.

Purpose: to promote interest and further understanding of limited edition, hand-pulled prints. Sponsored by Colorado Graphic Arts Center. Average statistics: 400 entries, 250 entrants, 3 awards, 1500 attendance. Held in Denver for 5 weeks.

PRINT CONTEST: General, limited editions or monoprints, 30x40, 20x30, 15x20, 8x10 inches, on white mount, covered with acetate; limit 2 per entrant. Produced in previous year. Require cost of glass if entry exceeds specified dimensions. No prints valued above $500.

ELIGIBILITY: Working artists in Colorado, Wyoming, Idaho, Utah, Arizona, New Mexico.

AWARDS: $1500 minimum in Prizes, Purchase Awards.

JUDGING: By historian and printmaker-college instructor. Based on technical, artistic excellence. Not responsible for loss or damage during shipping; insures work during show.

SALES TERMS: All work must be for sale. 30% commission charge.

ENTRY FEE: $8 plus return postage.

DEADLINES: Entry, judging, May. Event, May-June.

202

Tempo Gallery Annual Competitive Graphics Exhibit
Sarah E. King, Director
115 East College Avenue
Appleton, Wisconsin 54911 U.S.A.
Tel: (414) 733-7420

Entry March

International; **entry open to U.S. and Canada;** annual in April-May; established 1982. Sponsored by and held at Tempo Gallery for 4 weeks. Recognized by Professional Picture Framers Association.

PRINT CONTEST: Any Type General, except monoprints, maximum length and width within UPS or U.S. parcel post dimensions, framed under plexiglass, on white mount, ready for hanging; limit 3 per entrant. Produced since January 3 years prior. Submit 35mm color slides for entry review. No photocopies, photographs, drawings.

AWARDS: $2000 minimum in Awards.

JUDGING: By 1 university professor of graphic arts. Sponsor may photograph entries, retain slides of accepted entries. Not responsible for in-transit loss or damage; insured during exhibition only.

SALES TERMS: 25% commission charge. All work must be for sale.

ENTRY FEE: $15 plus return postage.

DEADLINES: Entry, March. Judging, March. Event, April-May.

203

Westwood Center of the Arts (WCA) Open Print Show
Selma B. Lokitz, President
1355 Westwood Boulevard
Los Angeles, California 90024 U.S.A.
Tel: (213) 477-2668

Entry August

National; **entry open to continental U.S.;** annual in September-November; established 1961. Purpose: to further professional opportunities for artists; offer community service. Sponsored by WCA (founded 1947), formerly Westwood Art Association. Supported by membership dues, entry fees, donations. Average statistics: 100 entries, 50 entrants, 8 finalists, 5 awards, 20 sales. Held in Los Angeles for 2 months. Publish *WCA Newsletter.* Also sponsor Open Watermedia Exhibition, Open Paintings on Canvas Exhibition, National Small Sculpture and Drawing Exhibition, other monthly shows, scholarships-financial aid.

PRINT CONTEST: Any Type General; limit 3 per entrant. No photocopy or photography prints.

AWARDS: Two-Week Solo Exhibition to best in show. $125 First, $75 Second, $25 Third Place Award. $15 value Zora's Art Supply Award. Honorable Mention Ribbons.

JUDGING: By 1 artist. Based on clarity of presentation, originality, skill; whether work is compelling, imaginative. Not responsible for loss or damage.

SALES TERMS: 20% commission charge.

ENTRY FEE: $7 per work.

DEADLINES: Entry, August. Judging, September. Event, September-November.

204

Cracow International Print Biennale

Sekretariat Miedzynarodowego Biennale Grafiki
Prof. Andrzej Pietsch, President
P1. Szczepanski 3a
31-011 Cracow, POLAND
Tel: 22-19-03

Entry November

International; entry open to all; biennial (even years) in September-November; established 1966. Purpose: to gather artists from different cultures, societies to exchange ideas, display art. Sponsored and supported by Polish Artists' Union, Ministry of Culture and Art, Cracow City Council. Average statistics: 4000 entries, 110 entrants, 50 countries, 400 finalists with 100 final works, 10 awards, 4 exhibitions, 100,000 attendance. Held in Exhibition Hall, Cracow for 1 month. Have accompanying exhibitions.

PRINT CONTEST: Any Type General, original, unframed; limit 4 per entrant. Produced in previous 2 years. Submit 13x18cm photos or 3-5 slides of representative work (preferably entries) for entry review. Require entry form in Polish, English, French, or Russian. No copies.

AWARDS: 10 Cash Awards of 30,000 Zlotys (nontransferable to other countries). Expense-paid 1-person Exhibition at next international exhibition (Grand Prix) to cash winner most appreciated by jury. Honorable Mention Medals. Purchase Awards.

JUDGING: By international jury of artists, print experts from Poland and abroad. May reject entries offending morals, religion, nation. Sponsor may reproduce, publish entries for promotion. Not responsible for loss or damage.

SALES TERMS: 15% commission charge. Works sold to galleries, museums, private collections.

ENTRY FEE: None. Sponsor pays return postage.

DEADLINES: Entry, November. Materials, February. Entry review, April. Awards judging, September. Event, September-November. Materials returned, April.

RESIDENCE GRANTS, SCHOLARSHIPS, FELLOWSHIPS

Residence Grants, Scholarships, Fellowships, and Assistantships primarily for RESIDENCE STUDY, RESEARCH, and PRODUCTION in Collage, Painting, Printmaking, Sculpture, and Visual Arts. (Also see GRANTS, SCHOLARSHIPS, FELLOWSHIPS.)

205

Apeiron Workshops Artist-in-Residence Program
Peter Schlessinger, Director
Silver Mountain Road
Box 551
Millerton, New York 12546 U.S.A.
Tel: (518) 789-4495

Entry Continuous

International; entry open to all; continuous; established 1971. Purpose: to enable artists to work in supportive context without required teaching involvement or other demands. Sponsored by and held at Apeiron Workshops, Millerton. Supported by Apeiron Workshops, NEA, NYSCA. Have darkrooms, class-exhibition space, library-archives, dormitory. Also sponsor Traveling Exhibitions Program, field trips, publication projects. Publish photography books.

VISUAL ARTS RESIDENCE GRANTS: **Creative Project.** 5 1-6-month grants (include room, board, darkroom facility, studio space, small monthly material stipend) to painters, sculptors, critics, others, for pursuing independent project of any style or format. Artist expected to work relentlessly toward goals; participate in discussions; share maintenance-operational tasks; leave portfolio or project results for archives. Submit letter of intention and financial need, skills. Competition includes art theory, architecture, photography.

JUDGING: By staff and board of directors. Based on financial need, useful professional skills (including carpentry).

DEADLINES: Open.

206

Arrowmont School of Arts and Crafts Spring and Summer Assistantships
Sandra J. Blain, Director
P.O. Box 567
Gatlinburg, Tennessee 37738 U.S.A.
Tel: (615) 436-5860

Entry January, March

International; entry open to all; annual in Spring and Summer; established 1945. Purpose: to provide opportunity for artists to study, exchange ideas, perfect skills. Sponsored by and held at Arrowmont School of Arts and Crafts, located adjacent to Great Smoky Mountains National Park outside Gatlinburg for 2-5 weeks. Supported by Pi Beta Phi Fraternity, Tennessee Arts Commission, private and corporate donations. Recognized by University of Tennessee-Knoxville. Average 125 entrants (all sections). Have equipped studios, book-supply store, visiting artists, lectures, permanent collection.

VISUAL ARTS RESIDENCE ASSISTANTSHIPS: **Workshop Sessions** (including drawing, painting, printmaking, clay and metal work). 10-15 Spring, 12 Summer tuition grants plus room and board to artists with 4 years completed course work or equivalent in experience for 2 weeks in Spring (1 week class, 1 week for school), 5 weeks in Summer (3 weeks class, 2 weeks work for school). Submit 10-20 slides of recent work, 3 references. Graduate-undergraduate credit available through University of Tennessee-Knoxville. Assistants do work assignments related to general functions of school. Competition includes photography, crafts.

JUDGING: By director and program coordinator. Based on application form, references, slide portfolio.

ENTRY FEE: $10.

DEADLINES: Application, January (Spring), March (Summer). Acceptance, February, April. Assistantships, March-April, June-August.

207

Artists for Environment Foundation Artists-in-Residence Program

Kenneth N. Salins, Director
Box 44
Walpack Center, New Jersey 07881
U.S.A. Tel: (201) 948-3630

Entry November

National; **entry open to U.S. visual artists;** semiannual in Fall and Spring; established 1971. Purpose: to provide opportunity for professional artists to work unencumbered within national park setting; promote natural environment as source of inspiration. Sponsored by Department of Interior National Park Service, Union of Independent Colleges of Art. Supported by NEA, New Jersey State Council on the Arts. Average statistics (all sections): 80 entrants, 2 grants. Held at Delaware Water Gap National Recreation Area at Walpack Center, for 3 months. Have art gallery. Also sponsor 1-semester college landscape painting program for students from prominent U.S. art colleges, 8-week summer art program in cooperation with Maryland Institute College of Art.

VISUAL ARTS RESIDENCE GRANTS: **Professional Work.** 2 grants of unspecified value, including house with paid utilities and studio space, to visual artists for opportunity to work without financial concerns for 3 months. Submit resume, statement of purpose, samples of recent work (6 35mm slides in 8x11-inch clear plastic sheet) for review. Competition includes photography.

JUDGING: By review committee. Sponsor keeps slides of accepted applicants. Not responsible for loss or damage.

ENTRY FEE: None. Entrant pays return postage.

DEADLINES: Application, November. Notification, February. Residencies, Fall, Spring.

208

Cummington Community of the Arts Artist in Residence Scholarships

David Thomson, Director
Potash Hill Road
Cummington, Massachusetts 01026
U.S.A. Tel: (413) 634-2172

Entry Continuous

International; entry open to all; continuous; established 1923. Formerly called THE MUSIC BOX (1923-30), PLAYHOUSE IN THE HILLS (1930-53), CUMMINGTON SCHOOL OF THE ARTS (1953-68). Purpose: to stimulate artistic growth by providing living and studio space to artists, especially those recently committed to the arts or disadvantaged by race, sex, age, economic status. Sponsored and supported by Cummington Community of the Arts. Supported by NEA, Massachusetts Council on the Arts and Humanities. Average 75 artists. Held on 150-acre site in Cummington, Massachusetts (Berkshire Mountains). Have individual living accommodations, kitchen, dining hall, library, darkrooms, kiln, studios, concert shed, garden, workshops, readings, shows at local galleries, summer children's program (ages 5-14). Publish *Cummington Journal.*

VISUAL ARTS RESIDENCE SCHOLARSHIPS: **Artistic Development.** Several partial tuition abatements per month (1 month minimum, 7 months maximum) to painters, sculptors, other artists, based on financial need. Submit 10-12 slides of work, resume, work plan, complete financial statement (including past 2 years' income, tax forms, savings, holdings, projected income, expenses). Require interview. Competition includes film, video, writing, photography, performing arts.

JUDGING: By professional artists appointed by Board of Trustees. Based on work, interview. All entries viewed in entirety.

DEADLINES: Application, 2 months before desired residency (continuous).

209

Fine Arts Work Center in Provincetown Fellowships

Susan B. Slocum, Director
24 Pearl Street
P. O. Box 565
Provincetown, Massachusetts 02657
U.S.A. Tel: (617) 487-9960,
487-9351

Entry January

International; entry open to all; annual from October to April; established 1968. Purpose: to encourage, support artists through give and take of shared experiences. Sponsored by and held at Fine Arts Work Center in Provincetown (America's first art colony on Cape Cod). Supported by NEA, Massachusetts Council on the Arts and Humanities, CCLM. Average statistics (all sections): 800 entrants, 20 fellows. Have live-in studios, general equipment, exhibitions at Hudson D. Walker Gallery, readings, discussions, resident staff artists for consultations, visiting guest artists, darkroom. Publish *Shankpainter* (annual prose, poetry magazine). Also sponsor 10 writing fellowships.

VISUAL ARTS RESIDENCE GRANTS: **Painting, Sculpture, Multimedia Creative Growth.** 10 fellowships (including room and studio space) in unspecified monthly stipends to artists for 7-month residencies to pursue own work in congenial, stimulating environment free from distraction. Applicant must provide any special equipment needed. Submit 10 slides maximum in 11x9-inch plastic slide sheet for entry review, original works (6-12 drawings, 5 maximum paintings, 3 pieces sculpture) second stage entry review. Competition includes photography.

JUDGING: All entries viewed by jury. Based on work quality; preference to young artists who have completed formal taining and are working on their own. Not responsible for loss or damage.

ENTRY FEE: $15 plus return postage.

DEADLINES: Application, January (slides), March (works). Notification, May. Residency, October-April.

210

Fontainebleau Fine Arts and Music Schools Association Residence Scholarships

Mrs. John N. Crawford, Executive Secretary
47 Fifth Avenue
New York, New York 10003 U.S.A.
Tel: (212) 691-2869

Entry March

National; **entry open to U.S. residents age 30 and under;** annual in July-August; established 1980. Sponsored by Edward Maverick Fund, Fontainebleau School of Fine Arts. Held at Fontainebleau School of Fine Arts, Fontainebleau, France for 2 months. Have studios, seminars, excursions, music concerts. Also sponsor music scholarships. Second contact: Marion Tournon-Branly, 228 BD Raspail, 75014 Paris, France; tel: 320-75-55.

PAINTING RESIDENCE SCHOLARSHIP: **Summer Study in Paris** *(Edward Maverick Fund Scholarship).* 1 or 2 $2000 scholarships (including registration fees, tuition, room and board, day trips, 1 4-day trip, and New York to Paris round-trip airfare) to U.S. architectural student age 30 or under for study at Fontainebleau School for 2 months. Submit 5-10 monochrome photographs (may send color transparencies in addition) of works completed in previous 4 years, 2 personal photographs, transcripts from school or college last attended, 2 reference letters, resume for entry review. Require regular attendance. Competition includes architecture-design.

JUDGING: Not specified. Not responsible for loss or damage.

ENTRY FEE: $100 registration ($75 refundable).

DEADLINES: Application, March. Event, July-August.

211

Fulbright-Hays Grants
Institute of International Education (IIE)
Theresa Granza, Manager
809 United Nations Plaza
New York, New York 10017 U.S.A.
Tel: (212) 883-8265

Entry November

National; **entry open to U.S.;** annual in April-June; established 1946 by legislation authorizing use of foreign currencies accruing to U.S. abroad for educational exchanges. Named after Senator J. William Fulbright. Purpose: to increase mutual understanding between U.S. and other nationals through foreign study. Sponsored by IIE (founded to promote peace, understanding through educational, cultural exchanges in all academic fields), U.S. International Communication Agency (USICA). Supported by annual appropriations from U.S. Congress, other governments. Average 3000 entrants (all sections). Also sponsor grants to visiting scholars, American scholars-professionals, predoctoral fellowships, teacher exchanges, Hubert H. Humphrey North-South Fellowship Program (study-internships), Faculty Research Abroad Program, Doctoral Dissertation Research Abroad Program, Group projects Abroad, Fulbright Awards for University Teaching and Advanced Research Abroad. Second contact: USICA, 1776 Pennsylvania Avenue N.W., Washington, D.C. 20547.

CREATIVE ARTS RESIDENCE GRANTS: **Foreign Study.** Round-trip transportation, language and orientation course, tuition, books, health-accident insurance, single-person maintenance for 6-12 months' study in 1 foreign country (doctoral candidates may receive higher stipends). Competition includes all media.

ELIGIBILITY: U.S. citizens with majority of high school, college education in U.S., B.A. or equivalent (or 4 years professional experience-study in proposed creative art field). Require host-country language proficiency, certificate of good health, study plan, project proposal, reasons for choosing particular country, what contribution foreign experience will make to professional development, work samples, possible interview.

JUDGING: Professional juries and binational commissions in field of expertise prepare nominations to Fulbright agencies abroad, U.S. Board of Foreign Scholarship.

DEADLINES: Application, November. Judging, November-December. Preliminary notification, January. Awards, April-June.

212

Fulbright Awards for University Teaching and Advanced Research Abroad

Council for International Exchange of Scholars (CIES)
Suite 300
Eleven Dupont Circle
Washington, DC 20036 U.S.A.
Tel: (202) 833-4950

Entry June, July

National; **entry open to U.S.;** annual, for academic year; established 1946 by legislation authorizing use of foreign currencies accruing to U.S. abroad for educational exchanges. Named after Senator J. William Fulbright. Purpose: to increase mutual understanding between U.S. and other nationals through foreign study, teaching. Sponsored and administered by CIES and U.S. International Communication Agency (USICA). Supported by annual appropriations from U.S. Congress, other governments. Average statistics (all grants): 2500 entrants, 1000 semifinalists, 500 awards, 100 countries. Also sponsor Fulbright-Hays Grants, other grants for teacher-scholar exchanges, research abroad. Second contact: USICA, 1776 Pennsylvania Avenue N.W., Washington, D.C. 20547.

CREATIVE ARTS RESIDENCE GRANTS: University Teaching, Advanced Research. Stipend (in lieu of salary), round-trip transportation, other allowances for 1 academic year or less for university teaching and-or postdoctoral research abroad. Applicant must rank countries and openings of major interest from Fulbright list. Competition includes all media.

ELIGIBILITY: U.S. citizens, scholars, creative artists, professionals, institutions. Require demonstrated training-experience in appropriate subject, language (academic degrees, university teaching, publications, etc.); doctorate, if specified by host country (for teaching); doctorate or recognized professional standing evidenced by faculty rank, publications, exhibition record (for research); project presentation; other documentation.

JUDGING: 50 discipline-area committees and binational commissions assist CIES in preparing nominations to Fulbright agencies abroad and U.S. Board of Foreign Scholarship.

DEADLINES: Application, June (American Republics, Australia, New Zealand), July (Africa, Asia, Europe). Judging, September-December. Notification, January-April. Awards given 12-18 months following notification, usually for September-October to June-July academic terms of host institution.

213

Haystack Mountain Residence Grants

Haystack Mountain School of Crafts
Howard M. Evans, Director
Deer Isle, Maine 04627 U.S.A.

Entry March

International; **entry open to age 18 and over;** annual for Summer. Purpose: to provide artists sustained exhilaration, respect for individual uniqueness, regard for potential of personal capacity. Sponsored by and held at Haystack Mountain School of Crafts, on wooded slope overlooking Penobscot Bay, Deer Isle. Average statistics: maximum 65 residents, 10 day-students. Have courses, workshops in crafts, photography; undergraduate, graduate course credit available.

VISUAL ARTS RESIDENCE GRANTS: **Printmaking, Sculpture, Collage Studio-Coursework.** Free tuition ($100 per week for up to 6 weeks), room and board to candidates qualifying as technical assistants. Require 1 year graduate specialization or equivalent. Competition includes crafts, graphics, photography.

JUDGING: Partly based on need, consider geographical range, maintain men-women ratio and age differential.

ENTRY FEE: $15.

DEADLINES: Application, March. Residence, 6 weeks in Summer.

214

Helene Wurlitzer Foundation of New Mexico Residencies

Henry A. Sauerwein, Jr., Executive Director
P. O. Box 545
Taos, New Mexico 87571 U.S.A.
Tel: (505) 758-2413

Continuous

International; entry open to all; continuous for 3-12 months. Sponsored by Helene Wurlitzer Foundation. Have 12 studio-apartments.

VISUAL ARTS RESIDENCE GRANTS: **All Media** (including painting, sculpture, allied fields). Furnished studio-apartment (including linen and utilities) in Taos for 3-12 months. Residents responsible for cleaning apartment. No families, transportation, material, or living expenses provided. Competition includes choreography, photography, writing, and allied fields.

ENTRY FEE: $150 refundable damage deposit.

DEADLINES: Continuous.

215

Institute of American Indian Arts Residence Scholarships

Ramona M. Tse Pe, Admissions Director
Cerrillos Road
Santa Fe, New Mexico 87501 U.S.A.
Tel: (505) 988-6493

Entry March

National; **entry open to Native American students;** annual. Purpose: to assist Native Americans develop leadership, promote self-determination, increase employment opportunities in professional fields. Sponsored by Bureau of Indian Affairs. Held at Institute of American Indian Arts, Santa Fe. Have placement services. Second contact: Mary E. Ross, Education Specialist, U.S. Department of the Interior, Bureau of Indian Affairs, Washington, D.C. 20245.

VISUAL ARTS RESIDENCE SCHOLARSHIPS: **Native American**

Artistic Development, Cultural Heritage Study (including drawing, painting, print making, sculpture, museum training, art history study). Limited number of yearly scholarships (renewable, including on-campus room and board, tuition, limited classroom material, $60 miscellaneous expenses) to full-time, unmarried, Native American students for study at Institute of American Indian Arts, Santa Fe. Submit certificate of degree of Indian blood, letter of acceptance into accredited degree program, grades or transcripts from previous semester. Require student pay transportation costs, personal expenses, laboratory fees. Competition includes photography, film, crafts. Also have liberal arts program.

ELIGIBILITY: Full-time, unmarried students with at least 1/4 degree blood quantum American Indian, Eskimo, Aleut, of tribes federally recognized and served by Bureau of Indian Community, enrolled or accepted for enrollment in accredited college or university leading to bachelor degree, demonstrating financial need.

JUDGING: By Bureau of Indian Affairs Area Agency office.

DEADLINES: Application, March.

216

MacDowell Colony Residence Fellowships

Christopher Barnes, General Director
100 High Street
Peterborough, New Hampshire
03458 U.S.A. Tel: (603) 924-3886

Entry quarterly

International; **entry open to professionals;** quarterly; established 1907 by American composer Edward MacDowell. Purpose: to help artists pursue work under optimal conditions. Sponsored by and held at MacDowell Colony, Peterborough (nonprofit membership corporation). Supported by NEA, small endowment, private donors. Average statistics (all sections): 650 entrants, 5 countries, 175 residents. Have 30 isolated studios, 3 residence halls, pianos, graphics workshops, library, main hall, on 450 acres of fields, woods. Publish *MacDowell Colony Newsletter* (triannual). Also sponsor Edward MacDowell Medal (presented annually in August to major artist), MacDowell Corporate Award (annually to individual in corporate life who exemplifies patronage of the arts). Second contact: Charles Edwards, Director of Development, MacDowell Colony, 163 East 81st Street, New York 10028.

VISUAL ARTS RESIDENCE GRANTS: Painting, Printmaking, Sculpture, Professional Work. 5-8 week grants to professional artists for working, living accommodations and solitude (no instruction). Submit 5 color slides of work completed in previous 3 years (sculptors may include 1 8x10-inch monochrome photo of any work represented on slides), resume of art schools attended, 3 references. Competition includes film, writing, photography, composition.

JUDGING: By professional artists. Based on talent shown in submitted work samples (slides and references; number of accepted applicants; financial need for room, board, private studio (1 residence per year). Entrant pays return postage.

ENTRY FEE: $5 (filing fee). Accepted residents asked to make contributions if able.

DEADLINES: Entry, January (for June-August), April (September-November), July (December-February), October (March-May).

217

Montalvo Artist-in-Residence Program

Montalvo Center for the Arts
Harriet Leman, Publicity Director
P. O. Box 158
Saratoga, California 95070 U.S.A.
Tel: (408) 867-3586

Continuous

International; entry open to all; continuous for 1-3 months; established 1948. Named after Garcia Ordonez de Montalvo, sixteenth-century Spanish novelist. Sponsored by Montalvo Association (private, nonprofit corporation). Supported by Montalvo Center for the Arts Air Committee, trust endowment investment income. Held at *Montalvo,* 19-room Mediterranean-style villa on 175-acre estate of late James D. Phelan, U.S. senator and San Francisco mayor. 5 artists (all sections) accepted at any one time. Have exhibition gallery, lectures, classes, workshops, readings, seminars, competitions, field trips, art sales, visiting artists, arboretum, indoor-outdoor theaters for plays, pavilion for recitals, concerts, library. Also sponsor Montalvo Summer Music Festival.

VISUAL ARTS RESIDENCE GRANTS: **Creative Project.** Limited funds available (up to $75 per month for single; $90 for married couple) for 1-3-month residency at Montalvo Villa, plus extension of 3 months (if needed and agreeable), including apartment, linens, laundry room, utilities except telephone, to artists unable to pay residency cost to work on new projects or complete projects already started. Submit samples, resume, 1-page publicity summary, work proposal, 3 recommendations from professionals in field, personal photo. Provide own equipment, food, materials. No children, pets, overnight guests. Competition includes music, photography, writing.

JUDGING: By Board of Trustees at first monthly meeting following receipt of application.

ENTRY FEE: $30 (cleaning-breakage deposit).

DEADLINES: Application, 6 months prior to desired residency.

218

New York State Summer School of the Arts School of Visual Arts Scholarships

New York State Education Department
Charles J. Trupia, Executive Director
NYSSA, Room 679 EBA
Albany, New York 12234 U.S.A.
Tel: (518) 474-8773

Entry January

State; **entry open to New York high school students ages 14-17;** annual in July-August; established 1976. Purpose: to provide intensive training in professional atmosphere to talented high school students. Sponsored by Division of Humanities and Arts, New York State Education Department, Chautauqua Institution. Held at State University College at Fredonia for 4 weeks. Have room, board, facilities, art supplies, lectures, screenings. Also sponsor Schools of Film/Media, Visual Arts, Choral Studies, Dance, Theater, Orchestral Studies.

VISUAL ARTS RESIDENCE SCHOLARSHIPS: **Summer School Intensive Training.** $75-$650 to New York high school students for summer school giving exposure to variety of art disciplines and techniques and study under direction of nationally known artists. Submit portfolio containing 8-10 works.

JUDGING: Based on need, ability.

DEADLINES: Application, January. Judging, February-March. Residence, July-August.

219

Northwood Institute Creativity Fellowships
Alden B. Dow Creativity Center
Judith O'Dell, Director
3225 Cook Road
P. O. Box 1406
Midland, Michigan 48640 U.S.A.
Tel: (517) 631-1600, ext. 208

Entry December

National; **entry open to U.S. mainland, English-speaking persons;** annual in June-August; established 1979. Purpose: to encourage creative thought; provide time, work facilities for creative persons to concentrate on ideas without financial worries; establish internationally recognized center for creative technology. Sponsored by Northwood Institute, Alden B. Dow. Average 6 fellowships. Held at Northwood Institute, Midland, Michigan.

VISUAL ARTS RESIDENCE FELLOWSHIPS: Creative Project, all disciplines. 3-month study at Northwood Institute (including room, board, travel expenses, professional council) for study, creation, innovation, appreciation. Submit description of proposed project, resume, budget projection. Require personal interview. College credit arranged upon request. Special certificates, recognition, recommendations upon successful completion. Competition includes film, video, writing, photography, commercial and performing arts.

JUDGING: By Board of Directors, Advisory Panel, Northwood Institute, Alden B. Dow Creativity Center. Ideas remain property of applicant. Not responsible for loss or damage.

DEADLINES: Application, December. Judging, December-March. Notification, April. Fellowships, June-August.

220

Rome Prize Fellowships
American Academy in Rome
Executive Secretary
41 East 65th Street
New York, New York 10021 U.S.A.
Tel: (212) 535-4250

Entry November

National; **entry open to U.S. Ph.D.'s or art graduates;** annual for academic year. Purpose: to promote study and practice of fine art, archaeology, literature, history. Sponsored by and held at American Academy in Rome (founded 1894). Supported by the American Academy in Rome, NEA, National Institute for Architectural Education.

VISUAL ARTS RESIDENCE FELLOWSHIPS: Painting, Sculpture Advanced-Independent Work. Approximately 22 $7200 1-year residencies (including $450 monthly stipend, $1400 travel and $400-$900 supply allowance, housing allowance to married fellows with children) to graduates in scholarly field for study of fine art, archaeology, literature, history of classical and later periods. Competition includes architecture, photography, music, humanities, art history, literature, archaeology.

JUDGING: Based on outstanding promise or achievement.

ENTRY FEE: $15 each field of application.

DEADLINES: Application, November. Notification, April.

221

United States and Japan Exchange Fellowship Program
Japan-United States Friendship Commission
Francis B. Tenny, Executive Director
1875 Connecticut Avenue N.W., Suite 709
Washington, DC 20009 U.S.A.
Tel: (202) 673-5295

Entry March, September

National; **entry open to mid-career U.S. artists;** semiannual beginning in April, October; established 1977. Purpose: to aid education and culture at highest level; enhance reciprocal people-to-people understanding; support close friendship and mutuality of interests between U.S. and Japan. Sponsored by Japan-United States Friendship Commission; NEA (U.S.), Agency for Cultural Affairs (Japan). Also sponsor Book Translation Awards, American Performing Arts Tours in Japan, Japanese Cultural Performances in U.S. Second contact: Nippon Press Center Building, 201 Uchisaiwai-cho, 2 chome, Chiyoda-ku, Tokyo; tel: 508-2380.

VISUAL ARTS RESIDENCE GRANTS: **Work, Study in Japan.** 5 fellowships of $1600 monthly stipends plus round-trip transportation, overseas travel fare for spouse and children to age 18, baggage allowance and additional expenses for language training, interpreter, etc. to creative and practicing artists well established in field, to observe Japanese traditional and contemporary artistic developments. Require completed training, written report at conclusion of residency. No applicants working or residing in Japan at time of application; no historians, scholars, art critics, students, groups of 6 or fewer. Competition includes crafts, dance, design, journalism, literature, music composition, photography, theater, writing.

JUDGING: Entry review by private citizen advisory panels of experts in respective fields. American selection committee chooses semifinalists. Final awards judging by Japanese awards committee. Priority to projects that involve art forms or artists not well known in Japan, exchanges not viable on self-supporting basis, and arts characteristic of contemporary or historical national traditions.

DEADLINES: Application, March, September. Notification, April, October.

222

Virginia Center for the Creative Arts (VCCA) Residence Fellowships
Sweet Briar College
William Smart, Director
Mt. San Angelo
Box VCCA
Sweet Briar, Virginia 24595 U.S.A.
Tel: (804) 946-7236

Entry Continuous

International; **entry open to professionals;** continuous for 6 weeks; established 1971. Purpose: to provide dedicated, talented professionals with uninterrupted time, adequate space to concentrate on their art. Sponsored by VCCA. Supported by NEA, Virginia Commission for the Arts, foundations. Average statistics (all sections): 100 entrants, 5 countries, 18 residencies. Have studios, pool, 450 acres of pasture and woodlands, library, recreation facilities, cultural events. Held at Mt. San Angelo Estate, adjacent to Sweet Briar College, for about 6 weeks. Residency costs: $10 per day.

VISUAL ARTS RESIDENCE GRANTS: **Professional Work.** Up to $40 per day for 6 weeks' room, board, studio space. Submit slides of work, 2 professional recommendations, curriculum vitae, project description. Competition includes music, photography, writing.

JUDGING: By 5 professional artists, professors. Based on talent, dedication, promise of professional achievement, financial need. Entrant pays return postage.

DEADLINES: Entry, continuous. Notification within 6 weeks.

223

William Flanagan Center for Creative Persons Residencies
Edward F. Albee Foundation
14 Harrison Street
New York, New York 10013 U.S.A.

Entry April

International; entry open to all; annual in June-October; established 1978. Sponsored by Edward F. Albee Foundation. Held at William Flanagan Memorial Creative Persons Center on Long Island in New York.

VISUAL ARTS RESIDENCE GRANTS: **Painting, Sculpture.** 1-month (extendable) room and board, daily transport to Saratoga Springs to artists. Submit letter of intent, recommendation, work samples. Competition includes writing, music, photography.

JUDGING: Based on artistic merit rather than popular appeal.

DEADLINES: Application, April. Residency, June-October.

224

Lowick House Printmaking Workshops Residencies
John Sutcliffe, Director
Lowick Green, Nr. Ulverston
Cumbria LA12 8DX, ENGLAND
Tel: (0229) 85 698

Entry October

National; **open to regions of U.K.;** annual in Winter-Spring. Supported by Northern Arts, Greater London Arts Association (GLAA), Arts Council of Great Britain. Have printmaking equipment; living accommodations. Also sponsor Lowick House Printmaking Workshops Equipment and Facilities Loans, 15 traveling exhibitions, loan service, summer workshops.

PRINTMAKING RESIDENCE GRANTS: **Workshop Use** (intaglio, lithography, relief, screen printing, photo-related techniques). 2 £1000 short-term residencies (including £ 500 bursary, living accommodations, 24-hour use of workshop equipment and facilities, materials, technical expertise, travel expenses) to artists in Northern Arts and GLAA Areas for use in Lowick House Printmaking Workshops. Submit 12 transparencies of work and-or maximum 6 prints (20x30 inches maximum), summary of commitments. No outside commitments during residency.

JUDGING: By Lowick House Director. Based on application content and-or subsequent interview. Sponsor withholds 3 prints from each edition for Northern Arts Traveling Exhibition.

ENTRY FEE: None. Entrant pays return postage.

DEADLINES: Application, October. Event, Winter-Spring.

225

Harriet Hale Woolley Scholarships
Fondation des Etats-Unis
R. Frazer, Director
15, boulevard Jourdan
75690 Paris-Cedex 14, FRANCE
Tel: 589-35-79

Entry January

National; **entry open to U.S. citizens age 21-34;** annual for academic year; established 1929. Sponsored by Fondation des Etats-Unis. Average statistics (all sections): 40 entrants, 6 awards. Held in Paris.

VISUAL ARTS RESIDENCE FELLOWSHIPS: **Painting, Printmaking, Sculpture Graduate Study in Paris.** 5-6 scholarships of $3800 each (payable in francs in 5 installments during academic year) for room, board, transportation within Paris, some miscellaneous expenses; not for training fees (estimated $2000 extra) or transportation to and from Europe. Submit statement of foreign-study project (including Paris school or instructor preferred), income statement, French language proficiency by qualified teacher, minimum 3 recommendation letters from professors, college transcript, medical certificate, identification photographs, supplementary materials (reviews, up to 12 slides of art works). Competition includes music.

ELIGIBILITY: U.S. citizens age 21-34 who have graduated from accredited American college, university, or professional school with high standing, show evidence of artistic accomplishment, have capacity for graduate-level study, good moral character, adaptability, good physical health, emotional stability. No performing arts students; not for art history research. Applicants' projects must be approved by director of Fondation des Etats-Unis.

JUDGING: By 3 judges.

ENTRY FEE: None.

DEADLINES: Entry, January. Scholarships, October-June.

226

Tyrone Guthrie Centre Creative Artists Residence Grants
Bernard Loughlin, Resident Director
Annaghmakerrig
Newbliss
County Monaghan, IRELAND

Entry Continuous

National; **entry open to Ireland (facilities open to all);** continuous; established 1981. Purpose: to offer peaceful, secluded working environment to creative artists. Sponsored by Arts Council of Northern Ireland, An Chomhairle Ecilaion, Dublin. Held at Annaghmakerrig. Average 100 entrants. Have living, food preparation facilities, library, painters' studio, rehearsal room (with piano). Also sponsor workshops, conferences.

VISUAL ARTS RESIDENCE GRANTS: **Creative Project.** 200-300 residencies per year (3 weeks to 3 months), including meals, to artists showing evidence of sustained dedication, high level of achievement. May apply as group. Submit 5 color slides or photographs of previous work plus outline of proposed project; work samples. Require applicant to contribute to cost of stay. Competition includes writing, music, drama, dance.

JUDGING: By panel of writers, painters, composers. Based on merit and number of residencies available (11 maximum at any one time).

ENTRY FEE: None. Entrant pays return postage.

DEADLINES: Continuous. Judging, quarterly. Materials returned, 1 month after judging.

SCHOLARSHIPS, FELLOWSHIPS

Scholarships, Fellowships, Assistantships, Internships, Work-Study Programs primarily for STUDY and RESEARCH in Drawing, Graphics, Painting, Printmaking, Sculpture, Visual Arts, and Art History. Includes MOSAIC, MURAL PAINTING. (Also see RESIDENCE GRANTS and ART HISTORY FELLOWSHIPS.)

227

Brooklyn Museum Art School Painting and Sculpture Scholarships
M. Stephens, Registrar
188 Eastern Parkway
Brooklyn, New York 11238 U.S.A.
Tel: (212) 638-4486

Entry April

International; **entry open to college graduates;** annual for academic year. Purpose: to give advanced students opportunity to continue studies in New York. Sponsored by Brooklyn Museum Art School, founded in early 19th century as part of Brooklyn Institute of Arts and Sciences. Also sponsor BACA Honors Painting Scholarships, Alan B. Rothenberg Memorial Scholarship.

VISUAL ARTS SCHOLARSHIPS: Painting, Sculpture Advanced Study *(Max Beckmann Memorial Scholarships in Painting, Robert Smithson Memorial Scholarships in Sculpture).* Approximately 22 $650 scholarships to college or professional art school graduates for tuition and registration fees at Brooklyn Museum Art School.

JUDGING: Based on portfolios.

DEADLINE: Application, April. Scholarships for academic year.

228

Cooper Union for the Advancement of Science and Art Scholarships
Dean of Admissions and Records
41 Cooper Square
New York, New York 10003 U.S.A.
Tel: (212) 254-6300

Entry December

National; **entry open to U.S. high school graduates;** annual for academic year. Sponsored by Cooper Union (coeducational college established 1859 with enrollment of 900 students).

VISUAL ARTS SCHOLARSHIPS: College, Graduate Study. Approximately 1000 full tuition renewable scholarships ($2700 equivalent) to U.S. citizen high school graduates for art study. Competition includes architecture, engineering.

DEADLINES: Application, December. Scholarship for academic year.

229

Edwin Austin Abbey Memorial Scholarship for Mural Painting
National Academy of Design
John H. Dobkin, Director
1083 Fifth Avenue
New York, New York 10028 U.S.A.
Tel: (212) 369-4880

Entry December

National; **entry open to U.S. citizens under age 35;** biennial. Named after Edwin Austin Abbey, 19th-century mural and easel painter. Purpose: to advance study of mural painting. Sponsored by National Academy of Design. Also sponsor National Academy of Design Annual Exhibition.

PAINTING SCHOLARSHIP: Mural Painting Study. 1 $6000 1-year stipend to student who has completed formal art education, for continuation of mural painting study in U.S. or abroad.

JUDGING: By 5-member Board of Directors.

DEADLINE: Application, December.

230

John F. and Anna Lee Stacey Scholarship Fund

R. Brownell McGrew, Chair
P. O. Box 2
Quemado, New Mexico 87829
U.S.A.

Entry October

National; **entry open to U.S. citizens age 18-35;** annual for academic year; established 1946. Named after John F. and Anna Lee Stacey, artists and educators. Purpose: to foster high standard in study of form, color, drawing, painting, design, technique in classical, conservative tradition of Western culture. Sponsored by John F. and Anna Lee Stacey Fund.

DRAWING-PAINTING SCHOLARSHIPS: Conservative Tradition Art Study. 1-3 $4000 1-year appointments (made in quarterly installments) to U.S. citizens age 18 to 35 for furtherance of art education along conservative lines in U.S. or abroad. Submit 8x10 glossy black and white photographs of work (painting from life, nude, composition, or landscape), photograph of self, letter outlining ambitions, plans, preferred location of work or study, 4 reference letters.

JUDGING: By Selection Committee. Based on merit, research capacity, ability to take advantage of scholarship.

DEADLINES: Application, October. Scholarships for academic year.

231

Johnson Atelier Sculpture Apprenticeship Program Tuition Scholarships

Johnson Atelier Technical Institute of Sculpture
Brooke Barrie, Academic Director
743 Alexander Road
Princeton, New Jersey 08540 U.S.A.
Tel: (609) 452-2661

Entry continuous

International; **entry open to students;** continuous throughout year; established 1974. Institute founded by and named after J. Seward Johnson, Jr. to foster traditional sculpture casting technology; expanded to one of most sophisticated art foundries in world. Purpose: to restore link, interplay between sculptor and founder. Sponsored and supported by J. Seward Johnson, Jr. Recognized by New Jersey State Department of Education, Veterans Administration. Average 50 2-year apprentices. Have advanced equipment and technology for ceramic shell and bound sand metal casting.

SCULPTURE SCHOLARSHIPS: Technical Training. $4800 grants available to student-apprentices for tuition costs. Submit resume, slide portfolio of work. Require personal interview. Categories: Moldmaking, Waxworking, Resins, Ceramic Shell, Foundry, Sand, Chasing, Structures,

Modeling-Enlarging.

ELIGIBILITY: Advanced students preferably with BA, BFA, MFA in sculpture and interest in casting sculpture technology.

DEADLINES: Application, continuous.

232

Kate Neal Kinley Memorial Fellowship

University of Illinois at Urbana-Champaign College of Fine and Applied Arts
Jack H. McKenzie, Dean
110 Architecture Building
608 East Lorado Taft Drive
Champaign, Illinois 61820 U.S.A.
Tel: (217) 333-1661

Entry March

International; **entry open to college graduates;** annual for academic year; established 1931. Purpose: to help defray expenses of advanced fine arts study. Sponsored by University of Illinois College of Fine and Applied Arts. Supported by David Kinley bequest. Average statistics (all sections): 34 entrants, 1 award. Held at University of Illinois, Urbana-Champaign Campus. Have galleries, concert halls.

VISUAL ARTS FELLOWSHIP: **Art, Art History Study.** 1 $4000 fellowship for 1 academic year to art graduates (preferably under age 25) for defraying expenses of advanced fine arts study in U.S. or abroad. Submit 3 (minimum) recommendation letters from scholars; artwork or 2x2-inch slides in projection carousel (artists); examples of work, statement outlining proposal, preparations, accomplishments (art historians). Competition includes architecture design history, music.

JUDGING: By 3-member committee with specialist consultants. Based on suitability and merit of program, excellence of character, attainment in studies.

DEADLINES: Application, March. Judging, April. Materials returned, May. Award commencement, September.

233

Kearney State College Special Activities Grants Scholarships in Art

Kearney State College Art Department
Jerry Austin, Committee Chair
Kearney, Nebraska 68847 U.S.A.
Tel: (308) 236-4221

Entry March

State; **entry open to Nebraska high school graduates;** annual for academic year. Purpose: to recruit outstanding high school artists. Sponsored by Kearney State College. Average 40-60 entrants (all sections).

VISUAL ARTS SCHOLARSHIPS: **Freshman Year Study** (including drawing, painting and sculpture). 25 $200 tuition waivers to Nebraska students entering freshman year for art study at Kearney State College. Submit slides or photographs of representative selection of work in portfolio, 3 reference letters. Competition includes commercial art, ceramics, fiber arts.

JUDGING: By 5 faculty artists. Based on craftsmanship, technique, concept, originality, artistic merit.

DEADLINES: Application, March. Scholarships for academic year.

234

National League of American Pen Women Scholarships for Mature Women
1300 17th Street N.W.
Washington, DC 20036 U.S.A.
Tel: (717) 225-3023

Entry January

National; **entry open to U.S. women over age 35;** annual. Sponsored by National League of American Pen Women.

ART SCHOLARSHIP GRANTS: **General.** $1000 each to women over 35. Submit sample of artwork for entry review. Require age verification. Competition includes music, writing.

JUDGING: Not specified.

ENTRY FEE: $5.

DEADLINES: Application, January.

235

Pauly D'Orlando Memorial Art Scholarship
Religious Art Guild
Barbara M. Hutchins
Unitarian Universalist Association
25 Beacon
Boston, Massachusetts 02108 U.S.A.
Tel: (617) 742-2100

Entry October

International; **entry open to Unitarian Universalist Societies art students;** annual; established 1981. Named after Pauly D'Orlando, enamelist. Purpose: to aid art students' further study in their major. Sponsored and administered by Religious Art Guild. Supported by First Unitarian Church of New Orleans. Recognized by Unitarian Universalist Association. Also sponsor Religious Art Guild Drama, Poetry, Book Awards. Second contact: Rev. Edwin A. Lane, 3 Church Street, Cambridge, Massachusetts 02138.

VISUAL ARTS SCHOLARSHIP: **Drawing, Painting, Printmaking Study.** 1 $700 scholarship to art student for tuition fees, art supplies. Paid directly to student. Submit short essay outlining background, goals, needs; statement of tuition fees; photographs, slides of artwork (3 maximum); recommendation letter from Unitarian minister, officer; letter from minister who has viewed artwork. Competition includes enameling.

ELIGIBILITY: 1-year minimum members of Unitarian Universalist Society. Applicant may not be in receipt of other awards.

DEADLINES: Application, October. Notification, February. Materials returned, March.

236

Peters Valley Craftsmen Internship Program
Sherrie Posternak, Director
Star Route
Layton, New Jersey 07851 U.S.A.
Tel: (201) 948-5200

Continuous

International; **entry open to age 18 and over;** continuous; established 1970. Purpose: to serve as alternative or supplemental program to traditional education. Sponsored by Peters Valley Craftsmen. Supported by NEA, New Jersey State Council on the Arts, Dodge Foundation. Have workshops, living accommodations, studios, kitchen facilities, sales, auctions, demonstrations, performances. Also sponsor Summer studio assistantships, resident program.

SCULPTURE INTERNSHIPS: **Ceramic Studio-Outdoor Production.**

10-13-week internships to qualified individuals for opportunity to learn through observation and participation with resident teachers. Submit resume, slides of work, recommendation letters, letter of intent. College credit may be arranged. Competition includes photography, crafts.

ENTRY FEE: $15 for annual membership.

DEADLINES: Open.

237

Truro Center for the Arts at Castle Hill Work-Study Program

Joyce Johnson, Director
Box 756, Castle Road
Truro, Massachusetts 02666 U.S.A.
Tel: (617) 349-3714

Entry June

International; entry open to all; annual in Summer; established 1972. Purpose: to assist artists who are financially restricted to augment their experience, exposure. Sponsored by Truro Center for the Arts. Recognized by Massachusetts Council on the Arts and Humanities. Average 10 entrants (all sections). Held in Truro, Massachusetts for 10 weeks. Have studios, workshops, weekly concerts and lectures, films, classes, visiting artists.

VISUAL ARTS WORK-STUDY PROGRAM: **Drawing, Painting, Sculpture Summer Workshops.** 10 tuition waivers to students age 14 and over for 10 weeks of art instruction in exchange for minimum 5 weeks work at specific jobs in Center. Submit resume. Room and board not furnished. College credit may be arranged. Competition includes photography, crafts, writing.

JUDGING: By Director.

ENTRY FEE: $10.

DEADLINES: Application, June. Study program, Summer.

238

University of Wisconsin-Superior Visual Arts Graduate Assistantships

Mel Olsen, Coordinator
University of Wisconsin
Superior, Wisconsin 54880 U.S.A.
Tel: (715) 392-8101, ext. 391

Entry March

International; **entry open to bachelor's degree holders;** annual for academic year; established 1963. Purpose: to provide graduate assistantships; fill visual arts programming needs. Sponsored and supported by University of Wisconsin-Superior. Average statistics: 20 entrants, 4 awards. Held at Holden Fine Arts Center. Also sponsor University of Wisconsin-Superior On-Of Paper Exhibition, High School Art Scholarship Competition ($300-$500 for study at University of Wisconsin-Superior).

VISUAL ARTS ASSISTANTSHIPS: **Graduate Program.** Assistantships of about $4200 each to bachelor degree graduates from accredited institutions, accepted by University of Wisconsin Graduate Division as full-time students. Submit slide portfolio for entry review. Competition includes all media.

JUDGING: By University visual arts faculty.

ENTRY FEE: None (possible application fee to University of Wisconsin Graduate Division).

DEADLINES: Entry, March.

239

Virginia Museum Fellowships

Virginia Museum of Fine Arts
Boulevard & Grove Avenue
Richmond, Virginia 23221 U.S.A.
Tel: (804) 257-0824

Entry March

State; **entry open to Virginia;** annual; established 1978. Purpose: to provide financial aid for education and experience in the arts. Sponsored by Virginia Museum of Fine Arts. Supported by Woman's Council of the Virginia Museum, Virigina Commission for the Arts (VCA), NEA.

VISUAL ARTS FELLOWSHIPS: **Painting, Printmaking, Sculpture, Art History Study.**

Student Scholarships: Up to $2000 to students who attend or will attend recognized undergraduate art school. Paid over 10-12 months. Submit work samples (1 original, 10 slides; if 3D, 1 additional detail slide per item), 3 professional recommendations, most recent academic transcript. Require monthly reports and assigned work aiding the Museum. Competition includes photography, crafts, design, film.

Graduate Student Fellowships: Up to $4000 to students who attend or will attend graduate school at recognized college or university. Requirements same as for scholarships.

VISUAL ARTS GRANTS: **Painting, Printmaking, Sculpture Professional Work.**

Professional Grants: Up to $2500 to professional artists to aid in work or assist in project benefiting Virginians. Paid over 10-12 months. Requirements same as for scholarships.

VCA Professional Grants: 4 $8000 stipends to professionals for work on project. Paid in lump sum. Requirements same as for scholarships.

ELIGIBILITY: Born in or resident of Virginia for 5 of last 10 years.

JUDGING: Entry review and awards judging by committee of board members, artists; finalists interviewed at museum. Based on artistic merit, financial need. Partial awards at judges' discretion. May be terminated at any time for lack of diligence, sincerity, failure to submit monthly reports. Not responsible for loss or damage.

DEADLINES: Application, March. Notification, May.

240

Women's Graphic Center New Moves Scholarships

Sue Maberry, Administrative Director
Women's Building
1727 North Spring Street
Los Angeles, California 90012 U.S.A.
Tel: (213) 222-2477, 221-6161

Entry Quarterly

International; **entry open to low-income women age 50 and over;** quarterly; established 1973. Purpose: to further recognition, development of women artists through workshops, exhibitions. Sponsored by and held at Women's Building in Los Angeles. Supported by NEA, CAC, Women's Building. Have gallery, slide library, type and design service, access to printing equipment, studios. Also sponsor Publication Project.

GRAPHICS SCHOLARSHIPS: **Workshops, Special Projects.** Limited scholarships to low-income women age 50 and over for classes in graphics, in-depth consultations on publishing, promoting art work. Competition includes writing.

ELIGIBILITY: Low-income women who are Pacific-Asian, Latina, Black, Native American, or other minority; age 50 and over; disabled; single mother; participants in drug or alcohol programs.

JUDGING: Not specified.

DEADLINES: Application, quarterly, 2 weeks prior to commencement of workshop.

241

Anabel Mack Taylor Tuition Scholarhips
Rosary College Graduate School of Fine Arts
Mary Ewens, Dean
Via Boccaccio 123
50133 Florence, ITALY

Continuous

International; entry open to all; continuous; established 1960. Purpose: to help graduate-study artists with tuition costs. Sponsored by Rosary College (River Forest, Illinois). Supported by Anabel and Myron Taylor Trust Fund. Average statistics (all sections): 40 entrants, 5 countries, 10 scholarships. Held at Rosary College in Florence, Italy. Have studios, classrooms, library, reception rooms. Also sponsor special summer courses open to part-time or graduate students. Second contact: Sister Lenore Joyce, Admissions Office, Rosary College, River Forest, Illinois 60305; tel: (312) 366-2490.

VISUAL ART FELLOWSHIPS: Painting, Printmaking, Sculpture, Art History Graduate Study. Partial 1-year tuition grants to students for full-time Master's degree study.

JUDGING: By admissions committee. Based on applications from students wishing full-time degree study.

DEADLINES: Open.

242

International Center for the Teaching of Mosaic (CISIM) Scholarships
Lawyer Giovanni Amadei, Chair
Azienda Autonoma Soggiorno e Turismo
Via San Vitale, 2
48100 Ravenna, ITALY Tel: (0544) 35755

Entry April

International; **entry open to non-Italians ages 14-50;** annual in June-September; established 1966. Purpose: to encourage cultural exchange, spread knowledge of art and technical methods in mosaic making. Sponsored by CISIM. Supported by Tourist Office of Ravenna. Recognized by Academy of Fine Arts. Have field trips.

MOSAIC SCHOLARSHIPS: Summer Study in Ravenna. Small number of 100,000L grants (given at end of course) available to students to cover fees for 15-day summer course at CISIM. Submit curriculum vitae, other relevant information.

ELIGIBILITY: Entrants may not professionally practice art of mosaic, or have diplomas from institutes specializing in mosaic.

JUDGING: Preference to those supported by declarations from individuals, institutes that confirm interest in mosaic.

ENTRY FEE: 100,000L (Beginners section); 130,000L (Advanced section).

DEADLINES: Application, April. Courses, June-September.

SCULPTURE

Sculpture in any medium. Includes FREE-STANDING, STONE DESIGN. (Also see other SCULPTURE CATEGORIES.)

243

Butler Institute of American Art Ohio Ceramic, Sculpture and Craft Show
Joan Chopler, Public Relations Coordinator
524 Wick Avenue
Youngstown, Ohio 44502 U.S.A.
Tel: (216) 743-1107, 743-1711

Entry December

State; **entry open to Ohio residents, former residents;** annual in January-February; established 1947. Purpose: to provide annual representation of contemporary visual art. Sponsored and supported by Butler Institute of American Art. Average statistics (all sections): 350 entries, 110 finalists, 6 awards, 3400 attendance. Held at Butler Institute of American Art in Youngstown for 6 weeks. Have galleries, cases, stands. Also sponsor national midyear show. Area Artists' Annual.

SCULPTURE CONTEST: **General,** limit 3 per entrant (pair, set considered 1 work). Competition includes ceramics, crafts.

AWARDS: $1500 Butler Institute Purchase Prizes. Friends of American Art Purchase Prize. $100 Sidney S. Moyer Award to sculpture. $50 Cash Award.

JUDGING: By 1 nationally known ceramic artist, Institute staff. May withhold awards. Not responsible for loss or damage.

SALES TERMS: Work need not be for sale. 10% commission charge.

ENTRY FEE: $1 per item plus $3 per mailed container. Entrant pays return postage.

DEADLINES: Entry, judging, December. Event, January-February.

244

Foothills Art Center North American Sculpture Exhibition
Marian J. Metsopoulos, Executive Director
809 15th Street
Golden, Colorado 80401 U.S.A.
Tel: (303) 279-3922

Entry March

International; **entry open to U.S., Canada, Mexico;** annual in Spring; established 1979. Purpose: to give exposure to best works from eligible countries. Sponsored by Foothills Art Center. Supported by private organizations. Average statistics: 600 entries, 3 countries, 69 finalists, 8 awards, 4000 attendance; $900 total sales. Held at Foothills Art Center in Golden for 5 weeks. Also sponsor Energy Art Exhibition, Rocky Mountain National Watermedia Exhibition; workshops.

SCULPTURE CONTEST: **General,** in permanent medium (bronze, glass, polyresin, stone, wood), original; maximum 125 cubic feet, 500 pounds (sculpture); maximum 24x36 inches, 100 pounds, ready for hanging (bas relief); limit 3 per entrant. Artist responsible for assembly. Submit maximum 3 8x10-inch glossy black and white photographs per sculpture for entry review. Request resumes of accepted artists. No classwork.

AWARDS: $6000 in 8 Cash Awards.

JUDGING: Entry review and

awards judging by 2 prominent jurors. Sponsor keeps photographs of accepted works for permanent exhibition collection, catalog, publicity purposes; insures works during exhibition.

SALES TERMS: All work must be for sale. 30% commission charge.

ENTRY FEE: $10 each plus shipping and handling.

DEADLINES: Entry, judging, March. Notification, April. Event, May-June.

245

Marietta College Crafts National (MCCN) Exhibition

Arthur Howard Winner, Director
Marietta College Art Department
Marietta, Ohio 45750 U.S.A.
Tel: (614) 373-4643, ext. 275

Entry September

National; **entry open to U.S. amateurs, students:** annual in November; established 1972. Formerly called MARIETTA COLLEGE CRAFTS REGION EXHIBITION (1972-1973). Purpose: to display and reward artists throughout U.S. Sponsored and supported by Marietta College. Average statistics (all section): 2840 entries, 1100 entrants; $5500 in awards. Held at Marietta College for 1 month. Also sponsor Marietta National Painting and Sculpture Exhibition (April).

SCULPTURE CONTEST: **Any Medium General,** original; limit 3 per entrant (1 set constitutes 1 entry). Submit 4 35mm slides for entry review and awards judging. No molds, class work. Competition includes photography, crafts.

AWARDS: $2500 Judges' Award. $1000 Judges' Award of Craftmanship. $1500 in Puchase Awards. The Hand and the Spirit Crafts Gallery Award.

JUDGING: By 3 national judges. Based on merit. Purchase Prizes selected by Marietta College Art Department. Sponsor insures during exhibition only; not responsible for loss or damage.

SALES TERMS: Work need not be for sale. 25% commission charge (including purchase prizes).

ENTRY FEE: $15 plus return postage.

DEADLINES: Entry, judging, September. Notification, October. Event, awards, November. Materials returned, January.

246

National Sculpture Society Annual Exhibition

Claire A. Stein, Executive Director
15 East 26th Street
New York, New York 10010 U.S.A.
Tel: (212) 889-6960

Entry February

National; **entry open to U.S.;** annual in April-May; established 1933. Purpose: to promote art of figurative sculpture in the U.S. Sponsored and supported by National Sculpture Society. Average statistics: 800 entries, 95 finalists. Held in New York City for 25 days. Publish *National Sculpture Review.*

SCULPTURE CONTEST: **Any Medium Free-Standing,** any size; limit 1 per entrant. Submit 8x10 monochrome glossy photographs for entry review.

Medal, Relief, 20x24 inches maximum, mounted on wood or other suitable material, ready for hanging; limit 1 per entrant. Submit 8x10-inch monochrome glossy photographs for entry review.

AWARDS: Gold, Silver, Bronze Medals. $1000 Chilmark Award miniature metal sculpture. $500 Dr. Maurice B. Hexter Prize to creative free-standing sculpture. $500 Kalos Kagathos Foundation Sculpture Prize to representational nude or figures depicting sport. 1 $350, 2 $300, 2 $250, 2 $200, 1 $150, 2 $100, 1 $50 Cash Awards. Life-size head cast in bronze to meritorious work.

JUDGING: By 5 sculptors (free standing), 3 sculptors (relief). Not responsible for loss or damage.

SALES TERMS: 20% commission charge. Work need not be for sale.

ENTRY FEE: $5 plus return postage.

DEADLINES: Entry, February. Event, judging, April-May.

247

Pen and Brush Annual Sculpture Exhibition

Mrs. Marion Roller, Sculpture Section Co-Chair
16 East 10th Street
New York, New York 10003 U.S.A.
Tel: (212) 475-3669

Entry February

International; **entry open to women;** annual in March. Sponsored by The Pen and Brush (founded 1893). Average statistics: 40 entries, 10 awards. Held in New York City for 3 weeks. Have music, writing workshops.

SCULPTURE CONTEST: By Women Any Medium General (except plastilene), maximum 300 pounds, 6 feet; limit 1 (in the round), 1 (relief) per entrant. Submit 8x10-inch monochrome photographs for entry review. Also have watercolor, oil, print, poetry, writing sections.

AWARDS: $250 Roman Bronze Works Award. $200 Tallix Foundry Cast Award. $150, 3 $100, 2 $50 Cash Awards. Solo Award (free one-man show for 2 weeks at Pen and Brush). $25, $50 sculpture certificate. 50-pound Clay Award.

JUDGING: Entry review and awards judging by 3 jurors. Not responsible for loss or damage.

ENTRY FEE: $10 plus return postage.

DEADLINES: Entry, February. Event, judging, March. Materials removed, April.

248

San Jose Art League 3-Dimensional Art Regional Exhibition

482 South Second Street
San Jose, California 95113 U.S.A.
Tel: (408) 294-4545

Entry May

State; **entry open to California residents over age 18;** annual in May-June; established 1970. Formerly called ART REGIONAL to 1976. Purpose: to give recognition to emerging artists. Sponsored by San Jose Art League (nonprofit). Supported by Santa Clara Valley Music and Arts Foundation, Fine Arts Commission, City of San Jose. Average statistics: 200 entries, 100 entrants. Held at San Jose Art League Galleries for 1 month. Also sponsor 2-D Art Regional, monthly Art Festival.

SCULPTURE CONTEST: All Media General (except plaster, other perishable materials), original, maximum 50 inches wide, 150 pounds, bas-relief minimum 3-inch projection, prepared for exhibition; unlimited entry. Require hand-delivery. No class work, fragile entries. Competition includes crafts.

AWARDS: $1000 in Cash Awards.

JUDGING: By 2 art professionals. Not responsible for loss or damage.

SALES TERMS: Work need not be for sale. 25% commission charge.

ENTRY FEE: $5 each work (set equals 1).

DEADLINES: Entry, May. Event, May-June.

249

City of Marino International Biennial of Stone Sculpture
Comune di Marino
Franco Campegiani
Via Leone Ciprelli 16
00047 Marino (Rome), ITALY

Entry June

International; entry open to all; biennial (even years) in September-October; established 1977. Purpose: to utilize and promote local stone (Lapis Albanus), related handcrafts. Sponsored by Regione Lazio, Ministero Turismo e Spettacolo, Provincia di Roma, Ministero Pubblica Istruzione. Supported by public and private corporations. Recognized by Pro Local Marino-E.P.T. Roma. Average statistics: 70 entries, 15 countries, 2 finalists, 1 winner, 6000 attendance. Held in Marino for 1 month. Have noncompetitive exhibition. Second contact: Presso Associazione Pro Loco, Piazza Matteotti, 1, 00047 Marina (Rome), Italy.

SCULPTURE SKETCH CONTEST: Stone Design General, sketch on paper, 40-60cm high (excluding base); 20-40cm high (foreign); limit 1 per entrant. Submit technical relation with works less than 30cm. Require winner to direct the execution of sculpting his sketch.

AWARDS: 1,000,000L Purchase-Bonus to winning sketch. Up to 3,000,000L compensation and travel, living expenses (maximum of 2 months) to winners for directing the sculpting of their work in Italy. Other minor prizes.

JUDGING: By local commission chosen by organization. Based on simple, aesthetic criteria (initial selection). Not responsible for loss or damage.

ENTRY FEE: None.

DEADLINES: Entry, judging, January. Event, September-October.

250

Jacinto Higueras International Sculpture Contest
Jacinto Higueras Museum Foundation
Marcial Medina, President
Plaza del Generalisimo, 1
Santisteban del Puerto
Jaen, SPAIN Tel: 47-00-07

Entry October

International; entry open to all; annual in November; established 1975. Purpose: to honor memory of distinguished Spanish sculptor, Jacinto Higueras (1877-1954), born in Santisteban del Puerto. Sponsored and supported by Jacinto Higueras Museum Foundation, Ministry of Foreign Affairs, Ministry of Culture, Diputacion Provincial de Jaen, Instituto de Estudios Jiennenses. Average statistics: 40 entries, 5 countries, 2 awards. Held at Museo Jacinto Higueras for 1 week. Second contact: Luis Higueras, Farmacia San Juan, Santisteban del Puerto (Jaen), Spain.

SCULPTURE CONTEST: General. Dimensions, weight unspecified; unlimited entry.

AWARDS: 125,000 Pts., and Trophy First Place. 60,000 Pts., and Medal, Second Place.

JUDGING: By prominent art critics, writers, First Prize winner of previous year. Sponsor keeps winning entries for permanent museum exhibition; may withhold awards. Not responsible for loss or damage.

SALES TERMS: Work need not be for sale. No commission charge.

ENTRY FEE: None. Entrant pays return postage.

DEADLINES: Entry, October. Event, November.

SMALL WORKS

Small Drawing, Painting, Prints, Sculpture, Visual Arts, and Mixed Media, including AMERICAN WEST and SOUTHWEST. Small Art Works are usually larger than Miniatures, ranging in size from 12x12 to 15x15 inches maximum framed (12x12x12 to 15x15x15 inches for sculpture). However, these sizes may vary. (Also see MINIATURE.)

251

Bosque Art Gallery National Western Small Painting Show
L. M. Shinn, Director
655 South Bosque Loop
Bosque Farms, New Mexico 87068
U.S.A. Tel: (505) 869-2762

Entry May

National; **open to U.S.;** annual in June-July; established 1977. Purpose: to promote, encourage Western art from all artists known and unknown. Sponsored and supported by Bosque Art Gallery. Recognized by Albuquerque Gallery Association. Average statistics: 250 entries, 185 entrants, 60 winners, $1500 in total sales. Held at Bosque Art Gallery in Bosque Farms for 1 month.

VISUAL ARTS CONTEST: **American West-Southwest Small Works,** 12x16 inches maximum, framed, ready for hanging; limit 3 per entrant. No copies; sculpture, crafts, seascapes.

AWARDS: Purchase and Cash Awards. First, Second, Third Place Ribbons. Plaques.

JUDGING: Entry review by gallery director and 1 artist; awards judging by artist alone. Sponsor may photograph entries for publicity, catalog. Not responsible for loss or damage.

SALES TERMS: All work must be for sale. 20% commission charge.

ENTRY FEE: $10 per work (refundable if not accepted). Entrant pays return postage.

DEADLINES: Entry, May. Judging, June. Event, June-July.

252

Mullaly-Matisse Galleries National Small Painting Exhibition
1025 Haynes
Birmingham, Michigan 48011 U.S.A.
Tel: (313) 645-2741

Entry not Specified

National; **entry open to U.S. residents over age 18;** biennial (odd years) in February; established 1974. Purpose: to bring national competitive show to Michigan. Sponsored by Mullaly-Matisse Gallery. Average statistics: 500 entries, 300 entrants, 100 finalists, 8 awards. Held at Mullaly-Matisse Gallery for 1 month.

PAINTING CONTEST: **Small**

Works, maximum 10x10 inches (14x14 inches including frame); limit 2 per entrant.

AWARDS: $1000 in Cash Awards.

JUDGING: Entry review, awards judging by 1 art professional. Sponsor may photograph entries for publicity, catalog.

SALES TERMS: Prefer all work be for sale. 33-1/3% commission charge.

ENTRY FEE: Not specified. Entrant pays return postage.

DEADLINES: Entry, not specified. Event, February.

253

New York University Small Works Competition

Robert J. Coad, Assistant Director
80 Washington Square East Galleries
New York, New York 10003 U.S.A.
Tel: (212) 598-3369

Entry January

International; entry open to all; annual in January-February; established 1977. Purpose: to provide exposure for artists. Sponsored by New York University. Average statistics: 4000 entries, 2200 entrants, $4000 total sales. Held at New York University for 4 weeks.

VISUAL ARTS CONTEST: All Media Small Works, 12 inches maximum any dimension including matting, frame, base, ready for hanging or prepared for exhibition; limit 3 per entrant. No works under glass, valued over $2000. Competition includes photography.

AWARDS: $350 best of show. $50 juror's awards. Honorable Mention.

JUDGING: By 1 prominent museum curator. Not responsible for loss or damage.

SALES TERMS: Work need not be for sale. 20% commission charge.

ENTRY FEE: $5 per work plus return postage.

DEADLINES: Entry, January. Event, January-February.

254

Purdue University Small Print Exhibition (60 Square Inches)

Purdue University Galleries
Mona Berg, Gallery Director
Department of Creative Arts
West Lafayette, Indiana 47907
U.S.A. Tel: (317) 494-3061

Entry February

National; **entry open to U.S.;** biennial in April; established 1977. Purpose: to give exposure to small, intimate, quality prints. Sponsored by Purdue University Galleries. Average statistics (all sections): 400 entries, 200 entrants, 55 finalists, 5 awards, 5000 attendance. Held at Stewart Center Gallery for 1 month. Also sponsor National Cone Box Show (open to U.S. ceramics artists).

PRINT CONTEST: Any Type Small Works, original, 60 square inches maximum, mounted with firm backing, matted in clean, hinged mats; limit 2 per entrant. Produced in previous 3 years. No frames, glass, photography.

AWARDS: Minimum 4 Purchase Prizes for Purdue Galleries Collection.

JUDGING: By print media jurors. Sponsor may photograph entries for publicity; not responsible for loss or damage.

SALES TERMS: Work need not be for sale. No commission charge.

ENTRY FEE: $8.

DEADLINES: Entry, February. Event, April.

255

Zaner Gallery Small Works National Competition

John Haldoupis, Director
100 Alexander Street
Rochester, New York 14620 U.S.A.
Tel: (716) 232-7578

Entry August

National; **entry open to U.S. residents over age 18;** annual in November-December; established 1981. Average statistics: 3000 entries, 1800 entrants, 120 finalists, 13 awards, 1000 attendance. Held at Zaner Gallery in Rochester for 1-2 months. Also sponsor National Watermedia Biennial, exhibitions of nationally exhibited artists.

DRAWING CONTEST: **Small Works,** original, 15 inches maximum any dimension including matting, framing, ready for hanging; limit 2 per entrant. Executed in previous 2 years. Submit 1 2x2-inch cardboard or plastic-mounted slide each entry.

PAINTING CONTEST: **Small Works,** including watercolor. Requirements, restrictions same as for Drawing.

PRINT CONTEST: **Small Works.** Requirements, restrictions same as for Drawing.

SCULPTURE CONTEST:**Small Works,** original, 15 inches maximum any dimension (including base); prepared for exhibition; limit 2 per entrant. Submit 2 2x2-inch cardboard or plastic-mounted slides each entry.

MIXED MEDIA CONTEST: **Small Works.** Requirements, restrictions same as for Drawing.

AWARDS: (all sections): $500 Zaner Corporation Purchase Award. 12 $50 Juror's Awards.

JUDGING: Entry review and awards judging by 1 artworld personage. Accepted slides remain in gallery for documentation. Sponsor may reproduce entries for publicity, catalog. Not responsible for loss or damage.

SALES TERMS: Work need not be for sale. 30% commission charge.

ENTRY FEE: $8 first, $10 second work plus return postage.

DEADLINES: Entry, August. Notification, September. Event, November-December. Materials returned, January.

VISUAL ARTS (General)

General Visual Arts in all media, including ART FAIR. (Also see other VISUAL ARTS.)

256

Bridgton Arts Show

Bridgton Town Hall
Bridgton, Maine 04009 U.S.A.

Entry September

International; entry open to all; annual in October; established 1970. Held at Bridgton Town Hall for 3 days.

VISUAL ARTS CONTEST: **General,** original, 25 square feet maximum; limit 2 per entrant. No previously sold work.

AWARDS: $1000 Best in Show. $500 First Honorable Mention. $350

Second Honorable Mention. $200 Popular Choice Prize. $200 Artists' and Patrons' Choice Prize.

JUDGING: By 3 professional judges (except Popular and Patrons' Choice Prizes).

SALES TERMS: Work need not be for sale. 20% commission charge.

ENTRY FEE: $20.

DEADLINES: Entry, September. Event, October.

257

Brownsville Art League International Art Show
Tencha Sloss, Chair
P. O. Box 3404
Brownsville, Texas 78520 U.S.A.
Tel: (512) 546-1356, 542-0941

Entry February

International; **entry open to adults and students;** annual in March; established 1971. Sponsored by Brownsville Art League. Held at International Friendship Garden Pavillion, Fort Brown, Brownsville.

VISUAL ARTS CONTEST: General, original, maximum 6 feet width (paintings), 4 feet in greatest dimension, 200 pounds (sculpture); paintings framed, matted, ready for hanging. Divisions: Adult, Junior (High School, Intermediate, Elementary). Adult categories: Acrylic Under Glass and Watercolor, Acrylic-Oil, Drawing-Pastel, Graphics (including etchings, woodcuts, monographs), Sculpture. Junior categories: Acrylic-Oil, Watercolor, Graphics (including drawing, sketches, etchings, woodcuts, monographs), Sculpture. Also have photography and marquetry sections.

AWARDS: Adults: $500 Best of Show. $100 First, $50 Second, Third Prizes to each of 5 categories. First National Bank Purchase Award. $150 Clara Ely Award to acrylic under glass, watercolors and oils, acrylics. Grumbacher Silver Medallion, Bronze Medallion to paintings in any medium (except collage). Honorable Mentions. Ribbons. Juniors: First ($25 to High School, $15 to Intermediate, $10 to Elementary), Second, Third Prizes to each of 4 categories. Honorable Mentions. Ribbons.

JUDGING: By 1 juror. Purchase Award by League Fine Arts Selection Committee and Bank Representatives. Not Responsible for loss or damage.

SALES TERMS: Work need not be for sale. 30% commission charge.

ENTRY FEE: Adults: $5, $3 each additional. Juniors: $1, 50¢ each additional. Entrant pays return postage.

DEADLINES: Entry, February. Judging, event, March.

258

College of the Mainland National Art Competition
College of the Mainland Art Gallery
Jean Wetta, Director
8001 Palmer Highway
Texas City, Texas 77591 U.S.A.
Tel: (713) 938-1211, ext. 348

Entry January

National; **entry open to U.S.;** annual in March-April; established 1981. Sponsored and supported by and held in Texas City for 3 weeks. Average statistics: 300 entries, 100 entrants. Also sponsor artists-speakers program and exhibition.

VISUAL ARTS CONTEST: General (media alternate yearly, including drawing-prints and painting), 3x4 feet maximum including matting or heavy mounting, smearable surfaces under acetate; limit 3 per entrant. Submit 35mm slides for entry review.

AWARDS: $500 First, $300 Second, $200 Third Place Purchase Awards.

JUDGING: Entry review and awards judging by 1 judge. Sponsor retains slides of accepted work, may reproduce entries for publicity. Not responsible for loss or damage.

SALES TERMS: Work need not be for sale. 10% commission charge.

ENTRY FEE: $3 per work plus return shipping.

DEADLINES: Entry, January. Acceptance, February. Event, March-April. Materials returned, May.

259

Faber Birren Color Award Show
Stamford Art Association
39 Franklin Street
Stamford, Connecticut 06905 U.S.A.

Entry October

International; entry open to all; annual in November; established 1981. Purpose: to inspire people to pursue interest in color. Sponsored by and held at Stamford Art Association Galleries for 23 days. Supported by Faber Birren endowment. Have demonstrations, panel discussions, scholarships.

VISUAL ARTS CONTEST: All Media Color, original, maximum 40x72 inches (wxh), framed, ready for hanging; 3D work 60 pounds maximum; limit 1 per entrant. Require hand-delivery. Competition includes photography, textiles, ceramics, illumination.

AWARDS: $500, Certificate, Plaque or Medal to best of show.

JUDGING: By 1 prominent gallery curator. Sponsor insures entries (up to $1000) while on premises. Not responsible for loss or damage.

ENTRY FEE: $10.

DEADLINES: Entry, October. Event, November. Materials returned, December.

260

Felician College Art Festival
Iris G. Klein, Director
P. O. Box 546105
Surfside, Florida 33154 U.S.A.
Tel: (305) 868-6870

Entry January

International; **entry open to professionals;** annual in July; established 1972. Purpose: to raise money for Felician College. Sponsored by Patrons of Felician College and Sisters of the College. Average statistics (all sections): 112 entrants, 10,000 attendance. Held at 3800 West Peterson Avenue, Chicago for 1 day.

VISUAL ARTS CONTEST: All Media General. Submit slides or prints for entry review. Competition includes photography, crafts.

AWARDS: $250 in Purchase Awards.

JUDGING: Entry review by art fair director. Awards judging by panel. Not responsible for loss or damage.

ENTRY FEE: Not specified.

DEADLINES: Entry, January. Acceptance, June. Judging, event, July.

261

Fountain Festival of Arts and Crafts
Fountain Hills Chamber of Commerce
John D. Taska, Manager

P. O. Box 17598
Fountain Hills, Arizona 85268 U.S.A.
Tel: (602) 837-1654

Entry November

International; **entry open to U.S., Canada, Mexico;** annual in November; established 1975. Started as local craft show for area artists. Purpose: to attract artists, craftspeople. Sponsored and supported by Fountain Hills Chamber of Commerce. Average statistics (all sections): 200 entrants, 15,000 attendance. Held in Fountain Hills for 3 days. Have entertainment, food, camping.

VISUAL ARTS CONTEST: General (including drawing, painting, sculpture), limit 3 per entrant. Competition for some awards includes crafts.

AWARDS: $500 Best of Show (includes all sections). $100 to drawing or painting. $100 to sculpture.

JUDGING: By 3 professionals.

ENTRY FEE: $5 per work. $75 (optional) for booth space. All work must be for sale.

DEADLINES: Entry, event, November.

262

Galerie Triangle National Exhibition

Averille and Charles Jacobs, Directors
1206 Carrollburg Place S. W.
Washington, DC 20024 U.S.A.
Tel: (202) 554-7700

Entry July

National; **entry open to U.S.;** annual in September; established 1980. Purpose: to display high-quality, marketable works from artists of all races. Sponsored by and held at Galerie Triangle, Washington, D.C. for 1 month. Average statistics (all sections): 40 entrants, 50 entries, 13 finalists, 4 awards, 100 attendance. Also sponsor East Coast Regional Exhibition, monthly contests. Second contact: P. O. Box 8232, SW Station, Washington, D.C. 20024.

VISUAL ARTS CONTEST: All Media General, 40x40 inches maximum including frame, ready for hanging; limit 4 per entrant. Submit 4 slides (not glass) or photos for entry review. Competition includes photography.

AWARDS: $100 First, $50 Second, $25 Third Place Prize.

JUDGING: Entry review and awards judging by 2 gallery directors.

SALES TERMS: All work must be for sale. 30% commission charge.

ENTRY FEE: $30 (refundable if not accepted). Sponsor pays return postage.

DEADLINES: Entry, July. Judging, August. Event, September.

263

GALEX Annual Competitive Art Exhibition

Galesburg Civic Art Center
Sue Anne Fones, Director
14 East Main Street
P. O. Box 258
Galesburg, Illinois 61401 U.S.A.
Tel: (309) 342-7415

Entry January

International; **entry open to age 18 and over;** annual in March-April; established 1966. Purpose: to provide international show where quality works represent contemporary trends in visual arts. Sponsored and supported by Galesburg Civic Art Center, local business. Average statistics: 2000 entries, 1000 entrants, 70 semifinalists, 12 finalists. Held for 4-6 weeks. Have sculpture stands. Publish *The Artifacts, New Art Examiner.* Also sponsor year-round Sales Rental Gallery.

VISUAL ARTS CONTEST: **All Media General,** maximum 5x5 feet, 9 feet high (for 3D), framed, ready for hanging; limit 2 per entrant. Completed in previous 3 years. Submit slide for entry review (3 slides for each 3D entry). No works exhibited in other Civic Art Center shows, items requiring suspension from ceiling.

AWARDS: $1200 in 3 Cash Awards. Purchase Prizes. Kent Leasure Memorial Award. Patron Award. Best Print Award.

JUDGING: Entry review and awards judging by 1 artist. Sponsor insures during exhibition.

SALES TERMS: Work need not be for sale. 30% commission charge.

ENTRY FEE: $5 plus return postage.

DEADLINES: Entry, January. Notification, February. Judging, event, March-April.

264

Greater Hazleton Creative Arts Festival

Arts Council of Greater Hazleton
Alice Laputka, President
Mezzanine, Northeastern Building
Hazleton, Pennsylvania 18201 U.S.A.
Tel: (717) 459-2975

Entry April

National; **entry open to U.S.;** annual in May; established 1966. Sponsored and supported by Arts Council of Greater Hazleton. Supported and recognized by Pennsylvania Council on the Arts. Average statistics (all sections): 14 awards, 20,000 attendance. Held at Highacres, Hazleton Campus of Pennsylvania State University for 3 days. Have nonjuried indoor Open Art Show; performances, displays, workshops, demonstrations, children's events.

VISUAL ARTS CONTEST: **General** (drawing, painting, prints, sculpture, mixed-media), 4x5 feet maximum, framed, ready for hanging (except sculpture); limit 5 per entrant. Completed in previous 18 months. Also have photography, crafts sections.

ART FAIR: **Visual Arts.** Entrants provide and attend sales displays.

AWARDS: $300 Purchase Award. $150 First, $100 Second, $75 Third Place Award (contest). Ribbons (art fair).

JUDGING: By 2 jurors from Philadelphia Arts College. Not responsible for loss or damage.

SALES TERMS: 10% commission charge. Work need not be for sale (contest). No commission charge (art fair).

ENTRY FEE: $3 per work (contest). $5 (1 day), $9 (2 days) for 10-foot space (art fair).

DEADLINES: Entry, April. Judging, event, May.

265

Hill Country Arts Foundation Juried Arts Exhibition

Jeanne Bowman
P. O. Box 176
Ingram, Texas 78025 U.S.A.
Tel: (512) 367-5121

Entry March

National; **entry open to U.S.;** annual in April; established 1972. Purpose: to promote art interests. Sponsored by and held at Hill Country Arts

Foundation in Ingram for 2 weeks. Average statistics (all sections): 170 entries, 5 awards, $800 total sales. Also sponsor Hill Country Arts Foundation Photography-Graphics Exhibition, Summer Art Classes, Summer Theater.

VISUAL ARTS CONTEST: **All Media General** (except collage), original, 60x60 inches maximum, 2D framed, ready for hanging; limit 3 per entrant. Produced in previous year. No supervised work.

AWARDS: $1000 in Awards.

JUDGING: By 1 juror. Not responsible for loss or damage.

SALES TERMS: Work need not be for sale. 20% commission charge.

ENTRY FEE: $5 per work plus return postage.

DEADLINES: Entry, March. Event, April.

266

Middletown Fine Arts Center American Art Exhibition
Edith Kohler, President
130 North Verity Parkway
Middletown, Ohio 45042 U.S.A.
Tel: (513) 424-2416

Entry August

National; **entry open to U.S.;** annual in September-October; established 1975. Formerly area art show, became national 1981. Sponsored by Middletown Fine Arts Center. Average statistics (all sections): 300 entries, 200 entrants, 1500 attendance, $200 average sales per entrant. Held in Middletown for 4 weeks. Also sponsor Mario Cooper Watercolor Workshop (October).

VISUAL ARTS CONTEST: **All Media General,** maximum 60x72 inches, 100 pounds including frame, ready for hanging. Submit 35mm mounted slides for entry review. Categories: Oil and Acrylics; Acrylics and Watercolor; Pastel, Charcoal, Pencil, Pen and Ink; Prints; Other. Also have photography section.

AWARDS: $1000 to best of show (all media). $100 First Place each category.

JUDGING: Entry review by 5-member committee. Awards judging by 2 art professionals. Not responsible for loss or damage.

SALES TERMS: Prefer all art be for sale. 33-1/3% commission charge.

ENTRY FEE: $7 per work plus return postage.

DEADLINES: Entry, August. Event, awards, September-October.

267

North Dakota Art Exhibition
Minot Art Gallery
Shelly Ellstrom, Director
P. O. Box 325
North Dakota State Fairgrounds
Minot, North Dakota 58701 U.S.A.
Tel: (701) 838-4445

Entry February

National; **entry open to U.S.;** annual in March; established 1970. Purpose: to provide opportunity for children and adults to participate in visual arts. Sponsored by Minot Art Gallery and Association. Supported by North Dakota Council of the Arts and Humanities, NEA. Held at Minot Art Gallery for 3 weeks. Also sponsor annual outdoor Art Fair, regular exhibitions.

VISUAL ARTS CONTEST: **All Media General.** Sculpture maximum 6 feet, 100 pounds; 2D framed or matted with acetate, ready for hanging;

limit 2 per entrant. No wet entries, plaster or excessively fragile sculpture. Competition includes photography, crafts.

AWARDS: $1000 in Cash, Purchase Prizes. Public Opinion Award.

JUDGING: By art professional. Sponsor may reproduce entries for publicity, insures accepted works. Not responsible for loss or damage of works not accepted for exhibition.

ENTRY FEE: $6. No sales commission charge.

DEADLINES: Entry, February. Event, March.

268

Paper in Particular National Exhibition of Works On-Of Paper
Columbia College Art Department
Columbia, Missouri 65216 U.S.A.

Entry November

National; **entry open to U.S.;** annual in January-February; established 1980. Sponsored by Columbia College and Missouri Arts Council. Held at Columbia College for 4 weeks.

VISUAL ARTS CONTEST: General, on-of paper. Submit maximum 3 slides for entry review.

AWARDS: 1-person show at Columbia College.

JUDGING: By 1 art professor. Sponsor reserves right to reproduce entries in catalog and press; retains slides as permanent collection of Columbia College. Not responsible for loss or damage.

ENTRY FEE: None.

DEADLINES: Entry, November. Event, January-February.

269

Paula Insel Annual Art Exhibition
Galerie Paula Insel
987 Third Avenue
New York, New York 10022 U.S.A.
Tel: (212) 355-5740

Entry July

International; entry open to all; annual in September; established 1955. Sponsored by Galerie Paula Insel, United Mutual Banks. Average up to 100 entrants. Held at varying locations for 2 weeks. Also sponsor Paula Insel Puerto Rican Art Exhibition (March), 20 bank shows, "This is My City" annual event.

VISUAL ARTS CONTEST: All Media General (including painting, sculpture, collage), 20x24 inches maximum including frame (larger accepted as more than 1 entry), may be unframed, ready for hanging.

AWARDS: Merchandise Prizes. Ribbons.

JUDGING: By critics. Sponsor not responsible for loss or damage.

SALES TERMS: All work must be for sale. 40% commission charge.

ENTRY FEE: $8 per work plus return postage.

DEADLINES: Entry, July. Judging, event, September.

270

Paula Insel Puerto Rican Art Exhibition
Galerie Paula Insel
39 Los Meros
Box 7271
Playa Ponce, Puerto Rico 00731
U.S.A. Tel: (809) 844-8478

Entry January

International; entry open to all; annual in March; established 1975. Sponsored by Galerie Paula Insel. Average statistics (all sections): 40 entries, 10 entrants. Held at airports for 2 weeks. Also sponsor Paula Insel Art Exhibition (September), bank shows.

VISUAL ARTS CONTEST: **All Media General** (including painting, sculpture, collage) 20x24 inches maximum (larger accepted as more than 1 entry), may be framed, ready for hanging.

AWARDS: Merchandise Prizes.

JUDGING: Not Specified. Not responsible for loss or damage.

SALES TERMS: All work must be for sale. 40% commission charge.

ENTRY FEE: $8 per work plus return postage.

DEADLINES: Entry, January. Judging, event, March.

271

Pensacola National Art Exhibition

Pensacola Junior College
Allan Peterson, Gallery Director
Visual Arts Gallery
1000 College Blvd.
Pensacola, Florida 32504 U.S.A.
Tel: (904) 476-5410, ext. 2254

Entry December

National; **entry open to U.S.;** annual in March; established 1976. Purpose: to sample contemporary American works in various media. Sponsored by and held at Pensacola Junior College for 3 weeks. Average statistics: 1200 entries, 400 entrants.

VISUAL ARTS CONTEST: **General** (media change each year), original. Submit 35mm slides for entry review.

AWARDS: $1200 Purchase Awards. Show Invitations.

JUDGING: Sponsor retains slides of accepted work; insures work during exhibition.

ENTRY FEE: $8 plus return postage. No sales commission charge.

DEADLINES: Entry, December. Awards, event, March.

272

West Michigan Seaway Festival Juried Art Show

Gilbert P. Buckley, Executive Director
470 West Western Avenue
Muskegon, Michigan 49440 U.S.A.
Tel: (616) 722-6520

Entry March

International; entry open to all; annual in July; established 1961. Purpose: to promote artists in Muskegon area. Sponsored by West Michigan Seaway Festival, Inc. Average statistics (all sections): 250 entrants, 20,000 attendance, 35 maximum works displayed. Held at Muskegon Museum of Art for 3 weeks. Also sponsor Outdoor Art Fair and Village Market. Have contest, races, games; historical, artistic, musical attractions; concerts, parade, fireworks display.

VISUAL ARTS CONTEST: **General** (including drawing, graphics, painting, and works in clay, metal, and wood), size and weight limited to hand-carriable; dry, completely assembled; framed, matted or mounted, ready for hanging (wall work); limit 2 per entrant. Original, completed in previous 2 years. Submit 1 slide per work for entry review. Require hand-delivery of accepted works. Competition includes graphics.

AWARDS: $500 First, $300 Second, $200 Third, Best of Show. $100 Award each category. $100 People's Choice Award. Cash and Purchase Awards.

JUDGING: By panel of judges. Not responsible for loss or damage.

SALES TERMS: 25% commission charge.

ENTRY FEE: $5 1 work, $7.50 2 works, plus return postage.

DEADLINES: Entry, March. Event, judging, July.

VISUAL ARTS (Regional-State)

Limited to specific region, state. Visual Arts in all media. (Also see other VISUAL ARTS.)

273

Arrowhead Biennial Art Exhibition
Duluth Art Institute
Robert A. Dearmond
506 West Michigan Street
Duluth, Minnesota 55802 U.S.A.
Tel: (218) 727-8013

Entry February

Regional; **entry open to Midwest U.S. and Canada adults;** biennial (even years) in May-June; established early 1900s. Alternates with Lake Superior National Crafts Exhibit (odd years). Purpose: to encourage excellence in regional fine arts. Sponsored and supported by Duluth Art Institute. Held in Duluth for 6 weeks. Also sponsor regular exhibits, shows, lectures, classrooms, workshops, theatrical performances.

VISUAL ARTS CONTEST: **General** (including drawing, painting, prints, sculpture, mixed media), limit 3 per entrant. Submit slides for entry review.

ELIGIBILITY: Open to Minnesota, Michigan, Wisconsin, North Dakota, Ontario (Canada) residents age 18 and over.

AWARDS: $300 First, $150 Second, $100 Third Place, $50 Honorable Mention to each medium.

JUDGING: By 1 academic.

SALES TERMS: 25% commission charge.

ENTRY FEE: $3 per work.

DEADLINES: Entry, February. Acceptance, March. Materials due, April. Notification, May. Event, May-June.

274

Boulder Center for the Visual Arts Annual Exhibition
Janis Stahlhut, Assistant Director
1750 13th Street
Boulder, Colorado 80302 U.S.A.
Tel: (202) 443-2122

Entry October

State; **entry open to Colorado;** annual (month varies); established 1976. Purpose: to promote Colorado artists. Formerly called BOULDER ARTS 1976-1979, ARTS to 1981. Supported by City of Boulder, Boulder business community. Average statistics (all sections): 500 entries, 400 entrants, 3000 attendance. Held at Boulder Center for the Visual Arts for 6 weeks. Have community gallery, educational events.

VISUAL ARTS CONTEST: **All Media General,** framed (no exposed glass edges), under glass (no acetate), ready for hanging; limit 2 per entrant. Completed in previous 2 years. Original design and execution. Require hand-delivery. No work valued over

$2000. Competition includes prints.

AWARDS: Grumbacher Award (painting); minimum $1500 Cash Prizes.

JUDGING: By 2 judges. Sponsor may reproduce entries for catalog, publicity, records. Accepted entries insured during exhibition.

SALES TERMS: All work must be for sale. 20% commission charge.

ENTRY FEE: Not specified.

DEADLINES: Entry, October. Event, varies.

275

Connecticut Artists Annual Exhibition

Slater Memorial Museum--Norwich Free Academy
J. P. Gualtieri, Director
108 Crescent Street
Norwich, Connecticut 06360 U.S.A.
Tel: (203) 887-2505

Entry Various

State; **entry open to Connecticut;** annual in Spring; established 1944. Purpose: to provide opportunity for artists to exhibit work. Average statistics (all sections): 375 entries, 250 entrants, 150 finalists, 4 awards, 5000 attendance. Held at Slater Museum in Norwich for 5-6 weeks.

VISUAL ARTS CONTEST: General (drawing, painting, prints, sculpture); limit 2 per entrant. Require hand-delivery.

AWARDS: $250 First, $100 Second, $75 Third, $50 Fourth Prizes.

JUDGING: By 1 juror.

SALES TERMS: 20% commission charge.

ENTRY FEE: $5.

DEADLINES: Entry, various. Event, Spring.

276

Erie Art Center Annual Spring Show

John Vanco, Director
338 West Sixth Street
Erie, Pennsylvania 16507 U.S.A.
Tel: (814) 459-5477

Entry March

Regional; **entry open to Erie-area residents;** annual in April-May; established 1923. Sponsored by Erie Art Center (nonprofit, founded 1898). Average statistics (all sections): 495 entries, 219 entrants, 8 awards, 300 attendance. Held at Erie Art Center Galleries for 1-1/2 months.

VISUAL ARTS CONTEST: All Media General, maximum 72x72 inches, 100 pounds maximum, framed, ready for hanging; limit 3 per entrant. Residents within 250 miles of Erie. No Crafts. Competition includes fine arts (all media), photography.

AWARDS: $2000 in cash (minimum of $250 per winner). $2500 in patron purchases. Juror's Mentions.

JUDGING: By professional artist. Sponsor may reproduce entries for publicity, educational purposes. Not responsible for loss or damage.

SALES TERMS: Sales encouraged but not mandatory. 25% commission charge (including patron purchases).

ENTRY FEE: $5 plus $5 handling charge.

DEADLINES: Entry, March. Judging, April. Event, April-May.

277

Exhibition 280
Huntington Galleries
Don Silosky, Curatorial Assistant
Park Hills
Huntington, West Virginia 25701
U.S.A. Tel: (304) 529-2701

Entry January

Regional; **entry open to age 18 and over within 280 miles of Huntington;** annual in March-April; established 1952. Works On Walls (even years) alternates with Works Off Walls (odd years). Supported by Huntington Galleries (nonprofit organization accredited by American Association of Museums), Arts and Humanities Commission of West Virginia Department of Culture and History, NEA. Average 1000 entries (all sections). Have 300-seat auditorium, studio workshops, library.

VISUAL ARTS CONTEST: **General;** limit 2 per entrant. Produced in previous 3 years. Competition includes photography, crafts.

AWARDS: $3000 in Purchase Awards. 3 $2000 Excellence Awards.

JUDGING: By 3 art professionals. Based on excellence and creativity. Sponsor insures during exhibition only; not responsible for in-transit loss or damage.

ENTRY FEE: $10 plus return postage. No sales commission charge.

DEADLINES: Entry, January. Judging, February. Awards, event, March-April.

278

Galerie Triangle East Coast Regional Exhibition
Averille and Charles Jacobs, Directors
1206 Carrollburg Place S. W.
Washington, DC 20024 U.S.A.
Tel: (202) 554-7700

Entry September

Regional; **entry open to U.S. East Coast;** annual in December-January. Purpose: to recognize East Coast artists in visual arts. Sponsored by and held at Galerie Triangle in Washington D.C. for 1 month. Average statistics (all sections): 30 entries, 15 entrants, 3 awards, 100 attendance. Also sponsor National Exhibition, monthly contests. Second contact: P. O. Box 8232, SW Station, Washington, D.C. 20024.

VISUAL ARTS CONTEST: **All Media General,** 40x40 inches maximum including frame, ready for hanging; limit 4 per entrant. Competition includes photography.

AWARDS: $100 First, $50 Second, $25 Third Place Prize.

JUDGING: Entry review and awards judging by gallery staff.

SALES TERMS: All work must be for sale. 30% commission charge.

ENTRY FEE: $30 (refundable if not accepted) plus return postage on slides and photos.

DEADLINES: Entry, September. Judging, October. Event, December-January.

279

Graduate School for Community Development (GSCD) All Media Juried Exhibition
568 Fifth Avenue
San Diego, California 92101 U.S.A.
Tel: (714) 236-1521

Entry September

Regional; **entry open to San Diego;** annual in October; established 1977.

Purpose: to promote local artists. Sponsored by GSCD. Average statistics: 250 entries, 3 awards, 1000 attendance, $1500 total sales. Held at Multiculture Arts Institute Gallery in San Diego for 1 month. Also sponsor Annual Festival of the Arts, Photography Juried Art Exhibition, various art shows.

VISUAL ARTS CONTEST: All Media General, maximum 6 feet (height or width), 300 pounds (larger requires gallery staff approval), paintings framed and wired for display, watercolors framed under glass (or other protective surface); limit 3 per entrant. Completed in previous year. No wet paintings.

AWARDS: $200 First, $100 Second and Third Prize and three-person show.

JUDGING: By 3 established local artists or art administrators.

SALES TERMS: 25% commission charge.

ENTRY FEE: $5 per work.

DEADLINES: Entry, September. Event, October.

280

Island Arts Council Choochokam Art Exhibition

Richard Proctor, President
120 First Street
P.O. Box One
Langley, Washington 98260 U.S.A.
Tel: (206) 321-5240

Entry June

State; **entry open to Washington;** annual in July; established 1976. Named after Choochokam, The Langley Arts and Pleasure Fair. Purpose: to provide community with quality exhibition, artists with opportunity to express talents. Sponsored and supported by Island Arts Council. Average statistics (all sections): 600 entries, 300 entrants, 10 awards. Held on Widbey Island, Langley, for 2-4 days. Also sponsor Choochokam Arts and Pleasure Fair.

VISUAL ARTS CONTEST: General (drawing, painting, prints, sculpture) original, ready for hanging; limit 2 per entrant. Require hand-delivery. No kits, molds, ring blanks. Competition includes photography, crafts, graphics.

AWARDS: $1000 minimum Cash Prizes.

JUDGING: By 3 professional artists, art educators. Based on quality, content. Sponsor may photograph works for publicity, archival purposes. Not responsible for loss or damage.

SALES TERMS: 10% commission charge. Sold works may be replaced with reserve pieces.

ENTRY FEE: $5.

DEADLINES: Entry, June. Judging, event, July.

281

Long Beach Art Association (LBAA) Open Juried Exhibition

Gerald Spencer, Chair
325 Golden Shore
Long Beach, California 90802 U.S.A.
Tel: (213) 435-5995

Entry January, October

State; **entry open to Southern California;** semiannual in February, October; established 1924. Purpose: to promote visual arts; enrich cultural life of community. Sponsored by LBAA, Long Beach Recreation Department. Supported by LBAA membership. Recognized by City of Long Beach. Average statistics (all sections): 300 entries, 100 entrants, 3 awards. Held at Long Beach Gallery, Golden Shore for 1 month. Also sponsor workshops, competitions, membership exhibits.

VISUAL ARTS CONTEST: All Media General, original, 18-65 inches in any direction (including frame). Require hand-delivery. No unframed glass pieces, photography, crafts.

AWARDS: $250 First, $150 Second, $100 Third Prize. Honorable Mentions.

JUDGING: By 1 noted Southern California artist.

SALES TERMS: 20% commission charge.

ENTRY FEE: $5 per work.

DEADLINES: Entry, January, October. Event, February, October-November.

282

Marin County Fair Fine Art Competition

Yolanda F. Sullivan, Manager
Marin Center Fairgrounds
San Rafael, California 94903 U.S.A.
Tel: (415) 499-6400

Entry May

State; **entry open to California;** annual in July; established 1945. Sponsored by Marin County Fairs and Expositions. Average statistics: 350 entries, 13 awards. Held at San Rafael. Have entertainment. Also have photography, music, film, crafts contests.

VISUAL ARTS CONTEST: General, limit 2 per entrant. Other requirements, restrictions not specified.

AWARDS: $1300 Prize Awards, Ribbons.

JUDGING: By 3 artists.

SALES TERMS: Work need not be for sale. 20% commission charge.

ENTRY FEE: $3.

DEADLINES: Entry, May. Judging, June. Event, July.

283

Maryland Biennial Exhibition

Baltimore Museum of Art
Robin Greene, Coordinator
Art Museum Drive
Baltimore, Maryland 21218 U.S.A.
Tel: (301) 369-6310, 396-6308

Entry September

State; **entry open to Maryland residents;** biennial (odd years) in December-January; established 1933. Formerly called MARYLAND ANNUAL to 1974. Purpose: to provide exposure for local artists. Sponsored and supported by Baltimore Museum of Art. Average statistics (all sections): 2000 entries, 1800 entrants, 140 finalists, 27 awards. Held at museum for 6 weeks.

VISUAL ARTS CONTEST: General, on paper, original, 144 inches maximum length plus width including frame; watercolors, pastels, graphics framed under glass or plexiglass; limit 2 per entrant. Some biennials (in future) may include sculpture, other works not on paper (3D work maximum 16 feet in all directions, 500 pounds). Produced in previous 2 years. Require hand-delivery. Competition includes photography.

AWARDS: $3000 in Cash Awards (all sections).

JUDGING: By 2 judges (noted artist, and curator, gallery dealer). Sponsor may reproduce entries for catalog, publicity. Entries insured during exhibition only.

ENTRY FEE: None.

DEADLINES: Entry, September. Judging, awards, October. Event, December-January.

284

New Orleans Triennial
New Orleans Museum of Art
William A. Fagaly, Curator
P.O. Box 19123
New Orleans, Louisiana 70179
U.S.A. Tel: (504) 488-2631

Entry Spring

Regional; **entry open to Southeastern U.S.;** triennial in Spring; established 1887. Formerly called ARTISTS BIENNIAL to 1980. Purpose: to give Southeastern U.S. artists opportunity for review and exposure. Sponsored by Art Association of New Orleans (annual to 1960, 1969 became biennial, 1980 triennial). Average statistics (all sections): 3700 entries, 1300 entrants. Held at New Orleans Museum of Art for 1-1/2 months.

VISUAL ARTS CONTEST: **All Media General,** unlimited dimensions; limit 3 per entrant. Submit 2x2-inch slide of each work (2-dimensional), 3 2x2-inch slides (3-dimensional), cardboard mounted for entry review. Require paper documentation, type-written proposal and-or 8x10-inch black and white photographs for conceptual pieces. Competition includes crafts, film, photography, video.

ELIGIBILITY: Residents of Kentucky, Tennessee, West Virginia, North Carolina, South Carolina, Georgia, Alabama, Mississippi, Arkansas, Louisiana, Texas.

AWARDS: Purchase Awards. 1-person exhibit at museum.

JUDGING: By nationally prominent authority in contemporary art . Entries insured during exhibition. Not responsible for in-transit loss or damage.

ENTRY FEE: None. No sales commission charge.

DEADLINES: Entry, event, Spring.

285

Richmond Art Center Spring Exhibition
Clayton Pinkerton, Curator
Civic Center Plaza
25th and Barret
Richmond, California 94804 U.S.A.
Tel: (415) 231-2163

Entry February

State; **entry open to California;** annual in Spring; established 1951. Alternates painting, sculpture, photography on rotating basis. Purpose: to present rich and varied arts to San Francisco Bay Area public. Sponsored by and held at Richmond Art Center for 4 weeks. Average statistics (all sections): 300 entries, 200 entrants, 100 finalists, 10 awards, 1500 attendance, 7 total sales. Also sponsor Annual Exhibition: Designer-Craftsman.

VISUAL ARTS CONTEST: **General, Varying Media** (including painting, sculpture, small format) on rotating schedule, dimensions, requirements may vary yearly with media; painting, small format wall mounted, framed for hanging (sculpture unspecified); limit 2 per entrant. Produced in previous 2 years. No supervised, overly fragile, breakable work. Submit 5 slides maximum (1 per work) for entry review. Require work hand-delivered. Also have crafts section.

AWARDS: Up to $500 in Cash Awards.

JUDGING: By 1-3 curators. Based on artistic merit. May photograph entries for publicity, catalog, records. Sponsor insures accepted entries.

SALES TERMS: 25% commission charge.

ENTRY FEE: $10 plus return postage.

DEADLINES: Entry, February. Judging, March. Event, March-April.

286

Roseville Art Center Annual Open Show

Phyllis Kozlen, Director
424 Oak Street
Roseville, California 95678 U.S.A.
Tel: (916) 783-4117

Entry March

Regional; **entry open to Sacramento and surrounding counties;** annual in April; established 1974. Purpose: to provide meaningful showcase for artists. Sponsored by and held at Roseville Art Center for 3 weeks. Average statistics (all sections): 200 entries, 75 entrants, 12-15 awards.

VISUAL ARTS CONTEST: **All Media General,** original, 2D or 3D art, 48x48 inches maximum, ready for hanging or presentation; limit 3 per entrant. Require hand-delivery. No photography, jewelery.

AWARDS: $250 Best of Show. $50 High Merit Award. $25 Merit Award. Honorable Mentions.

JUDGING: By 1 artworld personage.

SALES TERMS: Work need not be for sale. 30% commission charge.

ENTRY FEE: $4 per work.

DEADLINES: Entry, March. Event, April.

287

Triton Museum of Art Competitive Exhibition

Jo Farb Hernandez, Director
1505 Warburton Avenue
Santa Clara, California 95050 U.S.A.
Tel: (408) 248-4585

Entry March

Regional; **entry open to San Francisco Bay Area;** biennial (odd years) in April; established 1980. Media rotate on 4- or 5-year cycle. Purpose: to provide Bay Area artists with exhibition opportunity. Average statistics (all sections): 850 entries, 425 entrants, 29 finalists, 6 awards. Held at Linn Pavilion, Triton Museum of Art for 3-4 weeks.

VISUAL ARTS CONTEST: **General,** drawings, paintings (acrylic, oil, watercolor), and prints, 6x6 feet maximum, framed or ready to hang (requirements for other media not specified); limit 2 per entrant. Completed in previous 2 years. Require hand-delivery. No glassed, rolled or improperly framed work.

AWARDS: $200 First, $150 Second, $100 Third Place. Honorable Mentions. 1-year Museum membership to winners.

JUDGING: By 3 judges. Sponsor insures works from time of receipt to designated pick-up.

SALES TERMS: 25% commission charge.

ENTRY FEE: $5 each item.

DEADLINES: Entry, March. Event, awards, April.

288

West Michigan Juried Art Competition

Muskegon Museum of Art
Mary Riordan, Director
296 West Webster Avenue
Muskegon, Michigan 49440 U.S.A.
Tel: (616) 722-2600

Entry March

State; **entry open to West Michigan adults;** annual in March-April; established 1926. Purpose: to encourage regional artists to produce work of exhibition caliber. Sponsored by Muskegon Museum of Art (formerly Hackley Art Gallery). Supported by local businesses and individuals. Average statistics (all sections): 400 entries, 125 finalists, 10 awards, 3000 attendance. Held at Muskegon Art Gallery for 5-6 weeks.

VISUAL ARTS CONTEST: **General,** including drawing, painting, prints, and works in clay, metal, wood; original, size limited to that which can be carried by one man, dry, wall works framed, matted, or mounted, ready for hanging; limit 2 per medium. Completed in previous 2 years. Competition includes photography.

AWARDS: (all sections): $1000 in Cash Awards.

JUDGING: By 1 art professional. Sponsor may photograph entries for publicity. Not responsible for loss or damage.

SALES TERMS: Work need not be for sale. 25% commission charge.

ENTRY FEE: $5 first, $2.50 second entry. Entrant pays return shipping costs if not hand-delivered.

DEADLINES: Entry, March. Event, March-April. Material returned, May.

OTHER, THEME

Painting, Sculpture, and Visual Arts, including BUSINESS ART PROJECT SUPPORT, CHRISTMAS, HUMOR-SATIRE, THEME.

289

Business in the Arts Awards

Business Committee for the Arts (BCA)
Edwin C. Stone, Awards Administrator
Suite 2600, 1501 Broadway
New York, New York 10036 U.S.A.
Tel: (212) 921-0700

Entry March

International; **entry open to business firms, tax-exempt arts organizations;** annual in June; established 1966. Purpose: to encourage greater business support of arts; honor business firms for cultural efforts. Sponsored and supported by *Forbes Magazine,* BCA (founded 1967). Average statistics: 500 entrants, 50 awards. Held in various cities for 2 days.

ART PROJECT SUPPORT CONTEST: **Business Sponsorship, Participation, Financial Aid.** Undertaken, continued, completed during previous calendar year. Submit 1 detailed typewritten letter of nomination (3 pages maximum); films, slides, tape displays may accompany but not considered for awards. Categories: First-Time, Return (winners from previous years). Competition includes all media.

ELIGIBILITY: Business firms, business groups (shared sponsorship), business service associations, nonprofit, tax-exempt arts organizations operating on yearly budget under $1 million

AWARDS: Up to $25 Awards each to First-Time, Return. Fine art print to winners. Cash Grant Awards to winning American Arts organizations.

JUDGING: By 12 judges from arts, business, government. Based on value of companys' projects in fostering arts; degree of active company personnel involvement; impact on, importance to arts groups, community, general public. Special consideration to programs conceived and supported by company. Materials not returned.

ENTRY FEE: None.

DEADLINES: Entry, March. Judging, April. Notification, awards, June.

290

Courage Center Christmas Card Competition
Fran Bloomfield, Coordinator
3915 Golden Valley Road
Golden Valley, Minnesota 55422
U.S.A. Tel: (612) 588-0811, ext. 216

Entry February

National; **entry open to U.S.;** annual in December-March; established 1970. Purpose: to encourage Christmas card sales to aid handicapped persons. Sponsored by Courage Center. Average statistics: 1000 entries, 200 entrants, 30 semifinalists, 14 finalists, over 700,000 reproductions of original art used last year. Held at Courage Center in Golden Valley for 4 months. Publish *Courage News* (5 times yearly).

VISUAL ARTS CONTEST: All Media Christmas Theme (including acrylic, oil, watercolor, sculpture, collage), suitable for reproduction, reduction to 4-3/4x6-1/4 or 5-3/8x7-7/8 inches; limit 10 per entrant. Submit slides or prints for entry review; entrant background information; special-unusual conditions of production. Competition includes photography, crafts.

AWARDS: Media Exposure, Credit on Cards.

JUDGING: By art selection committee. Based on artistic merit, suitability of subject, reproduction quality. Artist donates 1-year exclusive reproduction rights (full credit to artist). Sponsor insures while in possession.

ENTRY FEE: None.

DEADLINES: Entry, February. Event, December-March. Awards, April.

291

Galerie Triangle Monthly Contests
Averille and Charles Jacobs, Directors
1206 Carrollburg Place S.W.
Washington, DC 20024 U.S.A.
Tel: (202) 554-7700

Monthly

National; **entry open to U.S.;** monthly (except January, February); established 1980. Purpose: to honor quality artists. Sponsored by and held at Galerie Triangle in Washington, D.C. Average statistics (all sections): 6 entries, 2 awards. Also sponsor National and East Coast Exhibitions. Second contact: P.O. Box 8232, SW Station, Washington, D.C. 20024.

VISUAL ARTS CONTEST: All Media Theme. Submit 1 or more slides or photographic prints, biography or resume. Competition includes photography.

AWARDS: 2 $50 Awards.

JUDGING: By 2 gallery directors. All entries viewed in entirety.

ENTRY FEE: $2 each work plus return postage.

DEADLINES: Monthly.

292

Louisville Art Center Association Juried Exhibition
James S. Adams, Administration
The Water Tower
3005 Upper River Road
Louisville, Kentucky 40207 U.S.A.
Tel: (502) 896-2146

Entry August

Regional; **entry open to residents age 18 and over living within 250-mile radius of Louisville;** annual in September-October; established 1981. Purpose: to expose work of regional artists. Sponsored by Art Center Association (founded 1909), oldest visual arts organization in Louisville. Average statistics (all sections): 100 entrants, 24 finalists. Held at Art Center Association, Old Louisville Pumping Station #1 (national historic landmark), Louisville for 1 month. Also sponsor annual showcase exhibition. Have lectures, studio tours, workshops; other exhibitions, productions, performances (10 per year). Second contact: Jan Arnow, Art Center Association, The Water Tower, 3005 Upper River Road, Louisville, Kentucky 40207.

VISUAL ARTS CONTEST: All Media Theme, rotating theme in 4-year cycle (Water, Earth, Air, Fire); framed or otherwise ready for exhibit, able to fit through 6-foot 8-inch by 6-foot door (2D only); limit 2 per entrant. Submit 2 slides of work for entry review. Require hand-delivery. Entrants provide sales displays. Categories: 2D, 3D. Competition includes special theme category (varies each year).

AWARDS: Purchase and Merit Awards.

JUDGING: By nationally known professional artist. Based on thematical, technical relation to theme. Purchase Awards become property of award sponsor. Sponsor insures work during exhibition only; not responsible for in-transit loss or damage.

SALES TERMS: Work need not be for sale. 30% commission charge.

ENTRY FEE: $10 plus return postage.

DEADLINES: Entry, August. Judging, September. Event, September-October.

293

Gabrovo International Biennial of Cartoon and Satirical Sculpture
House of Humor and Satire
Stefan Furtounov, Director
P. O. Box 104
5300 Gabrovo
BULGARIA Tel: (066) 27228, 27229

Entry January

International; entry open to all; biennial (odd years) in May-September; established 1973. Purpose: to stimulate artistic presentation of humor and satire. Theme: Laughter has Enabled the World to Survive. Sponsored by and held at House of Humor and Satire in Gabrovo for 5 months. Supported by Union of Bulgarian Artists, Bulgarian Journalists Union, National Commission for UNESCO. Average statistics (all sections): 2200 entries, 1000 entrants, 51 countries, 460 semifinalists. Tickets: 40 Stotinki. Publish *Apropos* magazine. Also sponsor International Biennial of Humor and Satire in Painting, International Photo Jokes Competition, Hitar Petar (Artful Peter) Prize for Humor and Satire in Literature.

SCULPTURE CONTEST: Humorous-Satirical, limit 2 per entrant. Submit brief biography, photograph. Competition for some awards includes cartoons. Also have painting, photography, writing sections.

AWARDS: Gabrovo Necklace, 750 levs to sculpture. (Includes cartoons) Golden Aesop, Sculpture, 1500 levs Grand Prize. 2 Second Prizes (Gabrovo Necklace and 500 levs), 3 Third Prizes (250 levs). Ten 100 levs Cash Prizes. Special Prizes.

JUDGING: By international jury. All works remain in sponsor's possession for Humor of Nations Fund. Not responsible for loss or damage.

ENTRY FEE: None. Sponsor pays shipping up to 300 levs.

DEADLINES: Entry, January. Judging, May. Event, May September.

294

Gabrovo International Biennial of Humor and Satire in Painting

House of Humor and Satire
Stefan Furtounov, Director
P. O. Box 104
5300 Gabrovo, BULGARIA Tel: (066) 2-72-29, 2-93-00

Entry February

International; entry open to all; biennial (odd years) in May-September; established 1977. Purpose: to stimulate humor and satire in painting. Sponsored by and held at House of Humor and Satire in Gabrovo for 5 months. Supported by Committee of Arts and Culture, Bulgarian Artists Union, Gabrovo Municipality. Average statistics: 200 entries, 24 countries, 74 semifinalists. Tickets: 40 Stotinki. Publish *Apropos* magazine. Also sponsor Hitar Petar (Artful Peter) Prize for Humor and Satire in Literature, International Photo Jokes Competition, International Biennial of Cartoon and Satirical Sculpture.

PAINTING CONTEST: Humorous-Satirical, mixed-media. Submit 18x24cm monochrome photograph for entry review. Also have sculpture, cartoon, writing sections.

AWARDS: 1000 Levs Union of Bulgarian Artists Prize. 3 1000 Levs Prizes. Purchase Prizes. Group of artists chosen for 4-day visit as guests of festivial.

JUDGING: By jury. Not responsible for loss or damage.

ENTRY FEE: None. Sponsor pays return postage.

DEADLINES: Entry, February. Judging, May. Event, May-September.

ART FAIRS, FESTIVALS (All Media)

Arts & Crafts Fairs, Festivals, Shows, Sales, Exhibitions, and Auctions accepting ALL FINE ARTS MEDIA (Listed alphabetically by state). Attendance usually required.

295

Tucson Festival Arts and Crafts Fair

Tucson Festival Society
Jarvis Harriman, Executive Director
8 West Paseo Redondo
Tucson, Arizona 85705 U.S.A.
Tel: (602) 622-6911

Entry February

Regional; **entry open to Southwest U.S., Mexico professionals;** annual in April; established 1951. Purpose: to celebrate Tucson cultural heritage and contemporary activity. Sponsored by Tucson Festival Society. Recognized by International Festivals Association. Average statistics (all sections): 100 entrants, 50,000 attendance. Held in Reid Park in Tucson for 3 days. Have security, refreshments, entertainment, display booths.

ART FAIR: All Media. Submit 5 35mm slides for entry review. Entrants provide and attend sales displays. No commercial reproductions. Competition includes photography, crafts.

AWARDS: Cash Awards. Ribbons to best of show, most attractive booths.

JUDGING: Entry review by jury. Awards judging by regional juror.

ENTRY FEE: $75 for 8x8-foot booth (refundable if not accepted).

DEADLINES: Entry, February. Judging, event, April.

296

Sacramento Festival of the Arts Outdoor Arts Show

Sacramento Regional Arts Council (SRAC)
Ennan West, Coordinator
562-A Downtown Plaza Mall
Sacramento, California 95814 U.S.A.
Tel: (916) 441-1044, 446-2885

Entry September-October

International; entry open to all; annual in September-October; established 1962. Purpose: to provide opportunity for artists to display, sell work; showcase performing artists. Sponsored and supported by SRAC, City of Sacramento, Downtown Association. Average statistics (all sections): 250 entrants, 15 awards, 15,000 attendance. Held at K Street Mall in Sacramento for 2 days.

ART FAIR: All Media, original, by individual, gallery, or organization. Entrants provide and attend sales displays. No kits, mass-produced work. Competition includes crafts and photography.

AWARDS: $1200 in Cash Awards.

JUDGING: Entry review based on originality, professionalism. Awards judging by 3 judges. Based on technique, originality, overall excellence. Not responsible for loss or damage.

SALES TERMS: Work need not be for sale. No commission charge.

ENTRY FEE: $20 for 5x15-foot space.

DEADLINES: Entry, event, September-October.

297

Fourth Street Festival of the Arts and Crafts

Ruth Conway, Linda Knudsen, Chairs
P. O. Box 1257
Bloomington, Indiana 47402 U.S.A.
Tel: (812) 824-4217

Entry June

International; entry open to all; annual in September; established 1977. Purpose: to provide quality art and craft fair to south-central Indiana. Sponsored by Bloomington Committee for the Arts, Area Arts Council, Business Committee for the Arts. Recognized by Bloomington Mayor's Office. Average statistics (all sections): 180 entrants, 80 exhibitors, 10 awards, 30,000 attendance. Held at Fourth and Grant Streets, Bloomington during Labor Day weekend. Have musicians, performances.

ART FAIR: All Media. Entrants provide and attend sales displays. Submit 4 photographs or 2x2-inch slides for entry review. No guilds, cooperatives, commercially made entries. Competition includes crafts, photography.

AWARDS: Purchase Prizes from local organizations.

JUDGING: Entry review by 6 community artists. Not responsible for loss or damage.

SALES TERMS: All work must be for sale. No commission charge.

ENTRY FEE: $35 for 10x10-foot space (1 space per entrant; partnership is 1 entrant).

DEADLINES: Entry, notification, June. Event, September.

298

Washington Park Art Fair
Michigan City Art League (MCAL)
Toni Clem, Director
P. O. Box 923
Michigan City, Indiana 46360 U.S.A.
Tel: (219) 874-6047

Entry July

International; entry open to all; annual in August; established 1960. Formerly called MICHIGAN CITY ART FAIR to 1980. Purpose: to promote art, artists, art appreciation in area. Sponsored and supported by MCAL (nonprofit, founded 1932). Held in Washington Park on the lakefront, Michigan City for 2 days. Have water boat show, demonstrations. Also sponsor workshops. Second contact: Henrietta Kominairec, First Bank, Fifth and Franklin, Michigan City, Indiana 46360.

ART FAIR: All Media, original. Entrants provide and attend sales displays. Submit 4 slides of work for entry review and 1 of display, resume, explanation of technique. No copies, reproductions. Competition includes photography, crafts.

AWARDS: $500 in Cash Awards.

JUDGING: By 1 judge. Entries viewed in entirety. Not responsible for loss or damage.

SALES TERMS: Work need not be for sale. No commission charge.

ENTRY FEE: $35 for 15x30-foot space. $25 for 15x20-foot space (2 artists maximum).

DEADLINES: Entry, July. Notification, event, August.

299

DubuqueFest Art Fair
Dubuque Fine Arts Society
Ruth Nash, Co-Chair
422 Loras Boulevard
Dubuque, Iowa 52001 U.S.A.
Tel: (319) 583-6201, 588-9751

Entry March

International; entry open to all; annual in May; established 1979. Considered largest Iowa arts and crafts festival. Purpose: to create new art audience, sell juried arts and crafts. Sponsored by DubuqueFest, nonprofit corporation under auspices of Dubuque Fine Arts Society; Dubuque Artists Guild. Supported by government, private grants. Average statistics: 250 entries, 100 finalists, 45,000 attendance. Held in Washington Park, Dubuque for 2 days (indoor location available in case of rain). Have food, demonstrations, entertainment.

ART FAIR: All Media, original. Entrants provide sales displays. Submit 3 slides or color prints for entry review. Competition includes crafts.

AWARDS: $100 to best of show. Purchase Awards.

JUDGING: Entry review and awards judging by college art faculty.

Based on aesthetic quality. Not responsible for loss or damage.

ENTRY FEE: $35 (2 days), $20 (1 day) per 10x10-foot space. No sales commission charge.

DEADLINES: Entry, March. Event, May.

300

Red River Revel Arts and Crafts Festival

Barnett Lipman, Executive Director
520 Spring Street
Shreveport, Louisiana 71101 U.S.A.
Tel: (318) 424-4000

Entry May

International; entry open to all; annual in October; established 1976. Purpose: to celebrate fine art and crafts in fun atmosphere. Sponsored by Junior League of Shreveport, Louisiana Bank & Trust Company, City of Shreveport. Supported by Aetna Life & Casualty Foundation, Louisiana State Arts Council, NEA. Average statistics (all sections): 100 entrants, 200,000 attendance, $150,000 total sales, $1500 average sale. Held along Red River in downtown Shreveport for 1 week. Have international food, entertainment, demonstrations, nonjuried show on last day of festival, 24-hour security. Also sponsor Red River Revel Run, Children's Art Education Program, workshops. Second contact: 800 Snow Street, Shreveport, Louisiana 71101.

ART FAIR: All Media, original. Entrants attend sales displays. Submit 4 35mm slides for entry review. Competition includes photography, crafts.

AWARDS: Over $2000 in Purchase Awards.

JUDGING: By 3 professional jurors. Not responsible for loss or damage.

SALES TERMS: 20% commission charge (no charge for nonjuried show).

ENTRY FEE: $25 ($35 shared) 1/2 week, $50 ($70 shared) 1 week for 2 8x4-foot panels in triangular tent (2D work), 8-foot table in 10x10-foot tent (3D work). $25 for nonjuried show (no sharing).

DEADLINES: Entry, May (nonjuried show, June). Event, October.

301

Fell's Point Fun Festival

Society for the Preservation of Fell's Point and Federal Hill, Inc.
Margaret E. Mach, Executive Director
804 South Broadway
Baltimore, Maryland 21231 U.S.A.
Tel: (301) 675-6750

Entry October

International; entry open to all; annual in October; established 1967. Purpose: to raise funds to preserve historic houses, districts. Sponsored by Society for the Preservation of Fell's Point. Average statistics (all sections): 300 entries, 250,000 attendance. Held in Fell's Point, Baltimore for 2 days. Have dance performances, music, children's entertainment, food, theater, lectures, flea market. Also sponsor Historic Harbor House Tour, conferences, preservation projects, other tours.

ART FAIR: All Media. Entrants provide and attend sales displays. Divisions: Professional, Amateur.

AWARDS: Cash Prizes to first, second place, each division.

JUDGING: By 3 professionals.

ENTRY FEE: Not specified.

DEADLINES: Entry, event, October.

302

Kalamazoo Institute of Arts Art Fair

Thomas A. Kayser, Director
314 South Park Street
Kalamazoo, Michigan 49007 U.S.A.
Tel: (616) 349-7775

Entry March

International; entry open to all; annual in June; established 1951. Formerly called CLOTHESLINE ART FAIR. Sponsored by Kalamazoo Institute of Arts. Average statistics (all sections): 125 entrants, 2 awards, 20,000 attendance. Held in Bronson Park, Kalamazoo for 1 day. Have refreshments, entertainment, silent auction, children's art fair.

ART FAIR: All Media, original. Entrants provide and attend sales displays. Submit 6 35mm slides, cardboard mounted for entry review. Competition includes photography, crafts.

AWARDS: $100 Best of Show. $100 Directors' Choice.

JUDGING: By jury of artists, art educators, Art Fair Chair.

ENTRY FEE: $5 jury fee plus $20 (refundable) booth fee.

DEADLINES: Entry, March. Judging, April. Event, June.

303

Saginaw West Side Art Festival

West Saginaw Civic Association (WSCA)
Patricia Becker, Coordinator
114 South Michigan, Room 14
Saginaw, Michigan 48602 U.S.A.
Tel: (517) 790-0266

Entry March

International; entry open to all; annual in June; established 1964. Purpose: to expose area residents to many art forms. Sponsored by WSCA. Supported by WSCA, Saginaw Public Schools, Saginaw Symphony. Average statistics (all sections): 100 entrants, 2 countries, 3 awards, 10,000 attendance. Held in Saginaw's Courthouse Square for 2 days. Have musical entertainment, overnight security. Second contact: Ruth Frieling, 2011 Carman, Saginaw, Michigan 48602.

ART FAIR: All Media, original. Entrants provide and attend sales displays. Submit 3 slides for entry review. No commercially made entries. Competition includes photography, crafts.

AWARDS: $75 First, $50 Second, $25 Third Prize.

JUDGING: By 3 local artists-celebrities.

ENTRY FEE: $5 plus $20 (refundable) for 10x6-foot space (2 spaces maximum). No sales commission charge.

DEADLINES: Entry, March. Notification, April. Event, June.

304

Edina Art Festival

50th & France Business & Professional Association
P. O. Box 24122
Edina, Minnesota 55424 U.S.A.

Entry April

International; entry open to all; annual in June; established 1965. Purpose: to provide opportunity for artists to display, sell work. Sponsored by 50th & France Business & Professional Association. Average 185 entrants (all sections). Held in Edina for 3 days.

ART FAIR: All Media, original, recently completed. Entrants provide and attend sales displays. Require hand-delivery. Submit 3 slides for entry review. No photographs, dealers, agents, imports, commercial molds, patterns, kits. Competition includes crafts.

AWARDS: $2000 in Purchase Awards.

JUDGING: Not specified.

ENTRY FEE: $40 for 10x12-foot booth. No sales commission charge.

DEADLINES: Entry, April. Event, June.

305

Meridian Art in the Park Arts and Crafts Festival

Greater Meridian Chamber of Commerce (GMCC)
2000 Ninth Street
P. O. Box 790
Meridian, Mississippi 39301 U.S.A.
Tel: (601) 693-1306

Entry March

International; **entry open to artists age 18 and over;** annual in April; established 1977. Purpose: to bring community closer together, educate in fine arts. Sponsored by GMCC, Meridian Junior Auxiliary. Supported by GMCC, Mississippi Arts Commission, private donations. Average statistics: 68 entrants, 40 countries, 30,000 attendance. Held in Highland Park for 1 day during 2-week Lively Arts Festival (indoor location available in case of rain). Have food, entertainment, demonstrations, antique car show, races. Second contact: Randy Shoults, Meridian Jr. College, 5500 Highway 19 North, Meridian, Mississippi 39301; tel: (601) 483-8241, ext. 147.

ART FAIR: All Media, original. Entrants provide and attend sales displays (limit 100). No commercial molds, kits. Competition includes crafts.

AWARDS: $500 Purchase Award to best of show. 3 $100 Juror Awards. 3 $50 Merit Awards. $750 in Purchase Awards.

SALES TERMS: All work must be priced and for sale. No commission charge.

ENTRY FEE: $25 per 10x10-foot booth.

DEADLINES: Entry, March. Event, April.

306

Kalispell Art in the Park Art and Crafts Fair

Festival Chair
Second Avenue East and Third Street
P. O. Box 83
Kalispell, Montana 59901 U.S.A.
Tel: (406) 755-5268

Entry May

International; entry open to all; annual in July; established 1968. Purpose: to provide marketplace for artists and craftsmen. Sponsored and supported by Hockaday Center for the Arts. Average statistics: 75 entrants, 1 award, 7000 attendance. Held in County Courthouse Park, Kalispell for 3 days. Have food, children's activities, entertainment, overnight security.

ART FAIR: All Media, original. Entrants provide and attend sales displays. Submit 5 35mm slides for entry review. No kits, commercial patterns. Competition includes crafts.

AWARDS: Cash Prize to most attractive booth.

JUDGING: Entry review and awards judging by committee. Based on overall merit of booth. Not responsible for loss or damage.

ENTRY FEE: $5 (with slides) plus $50 per 10x12-foot booth (may be shared by 2 or more artists; 50 available).

DEADLINES: Entry, May. Acceptance, June. Event, July.

307

Downtown Syracuse Arts and Crafts Fair
Downtown Committee of Syracuse
Laurie Reed, Public Information Department
1900 State Tower Building
Syracuse, New York 13202 U.S.A.
Tel: (315) 422-8284

Entry May

International; entry open to all; annual in July; established 1971 as nonprofit show. Sponsored by Downtown Committee of Syracuse. Supported by area businesses. Average statistics (all sections): 150 entrants, 2 countries, 40 awards, 25,000 attendance, $500 average sale. Held at Columbus Circle, downtown Syracuse for 3 days.

ART FAIR: All Media, original. Entrants provide and attend sales displays. Submit 5 2x2-inch 35mm slides (4 of work, 1 of display) for entry review (no glass or metal mounts). No agents, dealers, commercially processed work. Also have photography, crafts sections.

AWARDS: $2500 Cash Awards. Honorable Mentions. Purchase Awards, additional prizes as available.

JUDGING: Entry review by screening committee. Awards judging by 3 judges. Not responsible for loss or damage.

ENTRY FEE: $5. $45 for 8x10-foot space (maximum 2 per entrant). Tables and panels, $6 each.

DEADLINES: Entry, May. Notification, June. Event, July.

308

City Stage Celebration
United Arts Council of Greensboro
Helen Snow, Executive Director
200 North Davie Street
Greensboro, North Carolina 27401
U.S.A. Tel: (919) 373-4510

Entry August

International; entry open to all; annual in October; established 1980. Purpose: to spotlight arts in the community. Sponsored by United Arts Council of Greensboro, Miller Brewing Company. Supported by Miller Brewing Company, private donations. Held in downtown Greensboro for 2 days; attendance 200,000. Have special exhibits, demonstrations, displays, nonjuried crafts sale, visual and performing arts, entertainment, recreation, ethnic food, refreshments. Also sponsor City Stage Photography Competition.

ART FAIR: All Media, original; unlimited entry. Submit 3 slides or photographs, resume for entry review (except invited artists, group exhibitors), publicity. No imports, kits, commercial molds. Competition includes crafts.

AWARDS: Minimum $1000 in Purchase, Cash Awards.

JUDGING: Entry review by committee. Sponsor may reproduce entries for publicity. Not responsible for loss or damage.

ENTRY FEE: $35 for 12-foot-square

space ($45 for 2 exhibitors, $55 3 exhibitors per space). $100 for 12x30-foot space for group exhibitors. No sales commission charge.

DEADLINES: Entry, August. Event, October.

309

Westerville Music and Arts Festival
Westerville Area Chamber of Commerce
Sharon Martin, Executive Secretary
5 West College Avenue
Westerville, Ohio 43081 U.S.A.
Tel: (614) 882-8917

Entry May

International; entry open to all; annual in July; established 1974. Purpose: to provide outlet for artists as community service. Sponsored by Westerville Area Chamber of Commerce. Average statistics (all sections): 150 entrants, 20 awards, 30,000 attendance. Held at Otterbein College for 2 days. Have art auction, demonstrations, entertainment, refreshments.

ART FAIR: All Media, original. Submit 5 prints or slides for entry review. Entrants provide and attend sales displays. Divisions: Professional, Amateur. Competition includes photography. Also have crafts section.

AWARDS: $200 Best in Show. 4 $100 Arts Awards to professionals, 4 $75 Arts Awards to amateurs (including photography).

JUDGING: By 2 judges. Based on quality, appearance, creativity. Not responsible for loss or damage.

SALES TERMS: All work must be for sale. No commission charge.

ENTRY FEE $50 for 12 linear foot booths.

DEADLINES: Entry, May. Event, July.

310

Mount Hope Outdoor Art Show
Mount Hope Estate and Winery
R. Keith McNally, Director of Public Relations
P. O. Box 685
Cornwall, Pennsylvania 17016 U.S.A.
Tel: (717) 665-7021

Entry May, August

International; entry open to all; semiannual in June, September; established 1980. Purpose: to allow mixture of arts to be presented in new surroundings. Sponsored and supported by and held for 2 days at Mount Hope Estate and Winery. Average statistics (all sections): 200 entrants, 6 awards, 5000 attendance. Have Victorian mansion, winery, music, food. Tickets: $2. Also sponsor music dance, multicultural events.

ART FAIR: All Media, original, maximum 10x5 feet (lxw). Entrants provide and attend sales displays. Submit 2 slides or photographs for entry review. No commercially produced work.

AWARDS: $200 Best of Show (to be reproduced on wine label). $200 Center of Lebanon Association Award. 5 Judges' Merit Awards. Purchase Prizes.

JUDGING: By 3 outside judges. Not responsible for loss or damage.

SALES TERMS: All work must be for sale. No commission charge.

ENTRY FEE: $50 for 1 space, $85 for 2. For both shows: $75 for 1, $135 for 2 (refundable). Spaces may be shared.

DEADLINES: Entry, May, August. Event, June, September.

311

Western Art Association (WAA) Art Show and Auction
Jacqueline Leinbach, Coordinator
100 North Ruby Street
P. O. Box 893
Ellensburg, Washington 98926
U.S.A. Tel: (509) 962-2934

Entry March

International; **entry open to U.S., Canadian artists and dealers;** annual in May; established 1972. Proceeds go to Elmsview Center for handicapped adults. Purpose: to promote Western art and heritage. Sponsored and supported by WAA. Average statistics (all sections): 2000 entries, 100 entrants, 7 awards, $16,000 total sales. Held at Holiday Inn in Ellensburg for 3 days. Have champagne reception, banquet, security, accommodations. Tickets: $15 (auction). Also sponsor Art Show at Ellensburg Rodeo, scholarships. Second contact: Dr. Darwin J. Goocky, President, 509 North Willow, Ellensburg, Washington 98926; tel: (509) 925-4666.

ART FAIR-AUCTION: All Media Western Theme (including painting and sculpture). Art Fair: Limit 3 artists-dealers per room. Entrants provide and attend sales displays. Auction: original, framed art, (bronze sculptures mounted), ready for hanging, presentation; limit 3 per entrant (1 selected entry eligible for purchase award). Submit authentication of contemporary-deceased artists' work; works for entry review. Entrant may place minimum reserve price on entries. Also have small auction, silent auctions.

AWARDS: Best of Show in oil, watercolor, sculpture, other media. Main Auction: $1000 Purchase Award. ACC Powell Award. Judge's Award. $100 Kittitas County CowBelles and Cattlemen's Association Award, Plaque, WAA Ribbon to best portraying beef industry.

JUDGING: Entry review by 5-person committee. Awards judging by honorary chair. Sponsor may withhold awards. Not responsible for loss or damage.

SALES TERMS: All work must be for sale. Sales commission charge: 10%-20% on bronzes, 20%-30% other media. $25 charge on works of deceased if not sold.

ENTRY FEE: $200-$300 for room, functions (refundable). Entrant pays return postage on entries not accepted for auction.

DEADLINES: Entry, March. Event, May.

312

Monument Square Art Fair
Mrs. John R. Hackl,
Secretary-Treasurer
223 Sixth Street
Racine, Wisconsin 53403 U.S.A.
Tel: (414) 637-7706, 633-3215

Entry January

National; **entry open to U.S.;** annual in June; established 1963. Purpose: to seek out, encourage new talent through competition. Sponsored by American Association of University Women, Racine Branch; Downtown Association of Racine; Racine Art Association. Average statistics (all sections): 140 entrants (limit), $1500 total prizes, $14,000 total purchase awards, 9000 attendance, $71,000 total sales. Held at YMCA in Racine for 2 days. Have entertainment, music, bus tours, children's activities.

ART FAIR: All Media, original. Entrants provide and attend sales displays. Submit 3 pieces of work or 10 slides for entry review. Demonstrations encouraged. Competition includes photography, crafts.

AWARDS: $400 First, $300 Second, $200 Third Prize. 8 $75 Excellence Awards. $14,000 in Purchase Awards.

JUDGING: Entry review by Art Fair Board of Directors (at Wustum Museum). Awards judging by 2 art professionals. Not responsible for loss or damage.

ENTRY FEE: $5 plus $40 for 12x15-foot space.

DEADLINES: Entry, January. Acceptance, February. Event, June.

ART FAIRS, FESTIVALS (Specific Media)

Arts & Crafts Fairs, Festivals, Shows, Sales, and Exhibitions accepting DRAWING, GRAPHICS, PAINTING, PRINTS, SCULPTURE, MIXED MEDIA and COLLAGE (listed alphabetically by state). Attendance usually required.

313

Fine Arts Museum of the South Outdoor Arts and Crafts Fair

Greta Massing
P. O. Box 8404
Mobile, Alabama 36608 U.S.A.
Tel: (205) 343-2667

Entry September

National; **entry open to U.S.;** annual in September; established 1964. Purpose: to offer community opportunity to aquire fine original art works. Sponsored by Fine Arts Museum of the South. Average statistics: 200 entrants, 20 awards, 40,000 attendance, $85,000 total sales. Held at Fine Arts Museum at Langan Park, Mobile for 2 days. Have entertainment, food, children's activities. Tickets: 50¢.

ART FAIR: Drawing, Painting, Prints, Sculpture, Mixed Media, original. Painting media: acrylic, oil, tempera; watercolor. Drawing includes pastel. Submit slides of work for entry review. Entrant attendance required. Competition includes photography, crafts.

AWARDS: $3000 total Purchase Prize Awards; 5 $200 Awards of Distinction; 10 Merit Award Ribbons (all sections).

JUDGING: By jury. All cash will be awarded, combined, or divided at judges' discretion.

ENTRY FEE: $35 exhibition fee. $5 jury fee.

DEADLINES: Event, September.

314

Helen Keller Festival Art-Craft Show

Tennessee Valley Art Association
Ann McCutchen, Chair
511 North Water Street
P. O. Box 474
Tuscumbia, Alabama 35674 U.S.A.
Tel: (205) 383-0533

Entry June

International; entry open to all; annual in June; established 1964. Purpose: to commemorate Helen Keller's birthdate, birthplace. Sponsored and supported by Tennessee Valley Art Association. Average statistics (all sections): 135 entrants, 40,000 attendance. Held in Spring Park, Tuscumbia for 2 days. Have booth assistants, camping, security.

ART FAIR: **Graphics, Painting, Sculpture** (and other fine arts media), original. Entrants provide and attend sales displays both days. Submit 3 photographs or slides for entry review; include 8x10-inch glossies, other promotional material for publicity. No commercial kits. Divisions: Adult, Junior (grades 1-12). Also have crafts section.

AWARDS: $100 Best in Show, $100 Best Display. $100 First, $75 Second, $50 Third Prize. 3 $25 Merit Awards.

JUDGING: By 3-member jury. Not responsible for loss or damage.

ENTRY FEE: $30 for 12x10-foot booth, $2.50 for electricity. Juniors, $5. No sales commission charge.

DEADLINES: Entry, event, June.

315

Grand Prairie Festival of Arts

Grand Prairie Arts Council
Mrs. Neil Maynard, President
P. O. Box 65
Stuttgart, Arkansas 72160 U.S.A.
Tel: (501) 673-7278

Entry September

International; entry open to all; annual in September; established 1957. Purpose: to encourage cultural development in Grand Prairie area. Theme: Yesterday, Today, and Tomorrow. Sponsored and supported by Grand Prairie Art Council. Held at Grand Prairie War Memorial, Stuttgart for 3 days. Have talent demonstrations, entertainment. Also sponsor One Man Shows, special exhibits, Madelene Jones Oliver Memorial Scholarship.

ART FAIR: **Drawing, Painting, Prints, Sculpture,** original, 4x4 feet maximum including frame (paintings), framed or matted, under plastic or glass, ready for hanging, dry. Produced in previous 2 years (adult), 1 year (youth). Entrants provide and attend sales displays. Divisions: Adult, Youth (Grand Prairie students only). Adult categories: Graphics (any medium), Painting (any medium abstract, animal, landscape, portrait, religious, rice and duck capital, still life, novice), Sculpture (any medium), Theme (any medium). Youth Categories: Drawing (black and white, color), Painting (any medium). Also have crafts, photography, creative writing sections.

AWARDS: Adults: 2 $250 Best of Show; 3 $100 Best of Show Realistic, 2 $100 Best Theme; 2 $75 Popular Vote Awards; Ribbons. Children, Youth: Special Awards. Clothesline Show: Best of Show Trophies; Cash Awards.

JUDGING: By 1 juror and popular vote. Sponsor may reproduce entries for catalogs, publicity. Not responsible for loss or damage.

SALES TERMS: 10% commission charge (except Clothesline Show).

ENTRY FEE: $3 per adult entry (youth free). Clothesline Show, $10 per entrant. Late registration, $5 additional.

DEADLINES: Entry, event, September.

316

Affaire in the Gardens Arts and Crafts Fair

Beverly Hills Recreation and Parks Department
Michele Merrill
450 North Crescent Drive
Beverly Hills, California 90210 U.S.A.
Tel: (213) 550-4864

Entry February, July

International; **entry open to professionals;** semiannual in April, September; established 1974. Purpose: to bring appreciation of fine arts and crafts to Beverly Hills and vicinity. Sponsored by Beverly Hills Recreation and Parks Department. Average statistics (all sections): 200 entrants, 3 countries, 50 awards, 30,000 attendance. Held at Beverly Gardens Park in Beverly Hills for 1 weekend.

ART FAIR: Drawing, Painting, Prints, Sculpture. Entrants provide and attend sales displays. Submit 5 photos (preferred) or slides of work; photos of complete display, entrant, work demonstration; press photos, resume. Require seller's permit. No clothing arts. Categories: Drawing-Graphics-Prints, Acrylic-Oil, Watercolor, Sculpture. Competition includes crafts, photography.

AWARDS (all sections): $500 Vernors Purchase Award. $100 Mayor's Award. $100 to best of show. Each category: $100 First. Ribbons to first, second, third place. 2 Honorable Mentions.

JUDGING: Entry review by jury. Awards judging by professional. Based on quality, originality. Not responsible for loss or damage.

SALES TERMS: 10% commission charge (except Clothesline Show).

ENTRY FEE: $5 plus $70 (refundable if not accepted) for 9x12-foot display area. Entrant pays return postage.

DEADLINES: Entry, February, July. Acceptance, March, August. Judging, event, April, September.

317

Westwood Sidewalk Art and Craft Show

Western Los Angeles Regional
Chamber of Commerce
Wayne Erickson, General Manager
10880 Wilshire Boulevard
Los Angeles, California 90024 U.S.A.
Tel: (213) 475-4577

Entry February, July

International; entry open to all; semiannual in May, October; established 1969. Sponsored by Western Los Angeles Regional Chamber of Commerce. Average statistics: 600 entrants, 2 countries, 40 awards, 125,000 attendance. Held in 3 Los Angeles locations for 2 days.

ART FAIR: Drawing, Painting, Prints, Sculpture. Entrants provide and attend sales displays. Submit 3 photographs (minimum) of current work. Categories: Drawing, Graphics, Prints; Oil; Watercolor; Sculpture. Also have photography, crafts sections.

AWARDS: 4 $150 First, 4 $100 Second, 4 $50 Third Prizes each to oils, sculpture, watercolors, graphics. 4 $150 Awards to mixed media.

JUDGING: By museum exhibitors. Based on quality, originality. Not responsible for loss or damage.

ENTRY FEE: $95. $200 for booth space according to location (may be shared).

DEADLINES: Entry, February, July. Judging, events, May, October.

318

Grand Junction Art Festival

Michael Shannon, Chair
P. O. Box 1774
Grand Junction, Colorado 81501
U.S.A. Tel: (303) 243-2411

Entry August

International; **entry open to professional artists;** annual in September; established 1976. Purpose: to display and market professional art work. Sponsored by Grand Junction Art Festival Ltd. Supported by local banks and businesses. Average statistics (all sections): 100 entrants, 25 awards, 10,000 attendance, $8500 sales. Held in Grand Junction for 2 days. Have live street entertainment.

ART FAIR: Painting, Prints, Sculpture, Mixed Media, handmade, 2D work framed or unframed. Entrants provide and attend sales displays. Submit 5 slides of sculpture for entry review. No items assembled from commercial parts. Competition includes photography.

AWARDS: Cash, Merit, Purchase Awards.

JUDGING: By 2 judges.

SALES TERMS: All work must be for sale. No commission charge.

ENTRY FEE: $35 for unlimited space (on first-come basis).

DEADLINES: Entry, August. Event, September.

319

Mystic Outdoor Art Festival
Mystic Chamber of Commerce
Marion Tetlow, Director
P. O. Box 300
Mystic, Connecticut 06355 U.S.A.
Tel: (203) 536-8559

Entry April

International; entry open to all; annual in August; established 1957. Sponsored by Mystic Chamber of Commerce. Average statistics (all sections): 800 entrants, 400 finalists, 22 awards, 80,000 attendance. Held in Mystic for 1 weekend.

ART FAIR: Drawing, Painting, Prints, Sculpture, Mixed Media. Entrants provide and attend sales displays. Submit 3 slides of work for entry review. No imports, dealers, gimmicks, crafts. Divisions: Adult, 17 and over; Junior, 17 and under. Competition for Best in Show includes photography, graphics.

AWARDS: $300 Best in Show all sections and media. $100 First, $50 Second, Ribbons Third Place Awards to oils, watercolor, pastels, sculpture, mixed media, drawing (including graphics).

JUDGING: Entry review by 5 judges. Sponsor may withhold awards. Not responsible for loss or damage.

ENTRY FEE: $10 plus $15 for 4x12-foot booth. Juniors free.

DEADLINES: Entry, April. Notification, June. Event, August.

320

Old Saybrook Outdoor Art Exhibit
Old Saybrook Chamber of Commerce
Rupert W. Thomas, Executive Director
61 Main Street
P. O. Box 625
Old Saybrook, Connecticut 06475
U.S.A. Tel: (203) 388-3266

Entry July

International; entry open to all; annual in July; established 1963. Purpose: to provide opportunity for artists to show work in community. Sponsored and supported by Old Saybrook Chamber of Commerce, business community. Average statistics (all sections): 110 entrants, 16 awards, 3500 attendance, $12,000 total sales. Held on Main Street schoolgrounds of Old Saybrook for 2 days.

ART FAIR: Drawing, Painting, Prints, Sculpture, original. Entrants provide and attend sales displays. Submit 1 entry (wired for hanging) for entry review. No crafts. Categories: Drawing-Prints, Pastel, Acrylic, Oil, Watercolor, Sculpture, Portrait. Competition includes graphics, photography.

AWARDS: $250 First, $150 Second, $100 Third Place Awards. 3 $50, 6 $25 Prizes. First, Second, Third Place Ribbons.

JUDGING: By 1 or more judges. Not responsible for loss or damage.

ENTRY FEE: $25. No sales commission charge.

DEADLINES: Entry, event, July.

321

Art in the Sun Festival
Greater Pompano Beach Chamber of Commerce
Susan Hatcher, Director of Special Projects
2200 East Atlantic Boulevard
Pompano Beach, Florida 33062
U.S.A. Tel: (305) 941-2940

Entry January

International; entry open to all; annual in March; established 1972. Purpose: to encourage acquaintance with the arts through juried show. Sponsored by Greater Pompano Beach Chamber of Commerce. Supported by local business. Held at Jay-Cee Park, Pompano Beach for 2 days. Have food, free parking, security during festival.

ART FAIR: Drawing, Painting, Prints, Sculpture, original. Entrants provide and attend sales displays. Submit 3 2x2-inch 35mm slides of work, 1 of display for entry review. No frames, copies, reproductions, trade-processed prints unless under direct supervision of reputable service. Categories: Drawing, Painting (acrylic, oil, watercolor, mixed media), Sculpture (including clay, metal, stone, wood). Competition for some awards include crafts, photography.

AWARDS: $600 Best of Show (all sections). $300 First, $200 Second, $100 Third, 3 Honorable Mentions to each category. Merit Ribbons, Artist Ribbons, Purchase Money Awards (all sections).

JUDGING: Entry review by Selection Committee. Awards judging by 1 judge each category. Also have peer judging. Sponsor not responsible for loss or damage.

ENTRY FEE: $50 for 15x15-foot booth space (maximum 200 booths) plus return postage. Work need not be for sale.

DEADLINES: Entry, January. Judging, event, March.

322

City of Miami Beach Outdoor Festival of the Arts
Miami Beach Fine Arts Board
P. O. Box "O"
Miami Beach, Florida 33119 U.S.A.
Tel: (305) 673-7733

Entry November

International; entry open to all; annual in February; established 1975. Purpose: to foster appreciation of, interest in creative and performing arts. Sponsored and supported by City of Miami Beach. Average statistics (all sections): 200 entrants, 200,000 attendance, $15,000 sales. Held outside Convention Center, Miami Beach for 2 days. Have children's corner, international foods, performing arts programs.

ART FAIR: Drawing, Painting, Prints, Sculpture, original (no copies), family oriented; 4-piece display minimum. Entrants provide and attend sales displays. Submit 3 2x2-inch slides of work for entry review. No kits, molds, jointly created work, dealers (except foreign). Categories: Drawing-Graphics, Painting, Sculpture. Also have photography, crafts sections.

AWARDS: $500 First, $250 Second, $100 Third Prize, each category. $1000 Purchase Award to best of show; $100 to best display; Merit Ribbons (all sections).

JUDGING: Entry review by screening committee. Awards judging by 3 national judges. Not responsible for loss or damage.

ENTRY FEE: $85 for 10x10-foot space (each category). All work must be for sale.

DEADLINES: Entry, November. Notification, January. Event, February.

323

Gainesville Spring Arts Festival

Lona Stein, Coordinator
Santa Fe Community College
P. O. Box 1530
Gainesville, Florida 32602 U.S.A.
Tel: (904) 377-5161, ext. 383;
372-1976

Entry January

International; entry open to all; annual in April; established 1970. Sponsored by Santa Fe Community College (SFCC), SFCC Endowment Corporation. Supported by NEA, Fine Arts Council of Florida. Recognized by Gainesville Area Chamber of Commerce. Average statistics (all sections): 225 maximum participants, 63,000 attendance. Held on N.E. First Street in historic Gainesville for 2 days. Have children's arts-crafts display, instruction areas; entertainment.

ART FAIR: **Drawing, Painting, Prints, Sculpture,** original, appropriate for family viewing. Entrants provide and attend sales displays. Submit 3 2x2-inch slides, each category, for entry review (winning entrants in previous year automatically accepted). No kits, molds, mass-produced work. 2D categories: Drawing, Graphics, and Prints; Acrylic, Oil, Mixed Media; Watercolor. Sculpture categories (include other 3D media): Clay, Glass, Metal, Wood. Competition includes photography, crafts.

AWARDS: (all sections): $500 Best of Show; 5 $200 Distinction Awards; 5 $100 Merit Awards; 5 $50 Honorable Mention Awards to 2D and 3D, each. 10 $250 Excellence Awards (1 per category).

JUDGING: By 2 nationally prominent judges.

ENTRY FEE: $5 (application fee), each category. $35 for 15x10-foot minimum space.

DEADLINES: Entry, January. Notification, February. Event, April.

324

Gasparilla Sidewalk Art Festival

Leslie Osterweil, Board President
P. O. Box 10591
Tampa, Florida 33679 U.S.A.
Tel: (813) 253-3292

Entry November

International; entry open to all; annual in March; established 1971. Named after Jose Gaspar, legendary pirate. Purpose: to bring quality art to Tampa; provide funds for artists to continue work. Sponsored by Gasparilla Sidewalk Art Festival Board. Supported by art patrons, local businesses. Average statistics (all sections): 300 maximum participants. Held by river on Doyle Carlton Drive in Tampa for 2 days.

ART FAIR: Drawing, Painting, Prints (may accept other media), original, framed or mounted (except watercolors, drawings, prints not framed must be in portfolio). Completed in previous 3 years. Entrants provide and attend sales displays. Submit 3 2x2-inch 35mm slides for entry review (winning entrants in previous 3 years automatically accepted). No crafts, glass or metal slides, commercially reproduced entries, dealers. Competition includes photography.

AWARDS: (includes all sections): $3000 Best of Show. $2000 Gasparilla Award. 3 $1000 Merit Awards. 10 $400 Honorable Mentions. 10 $300 Juror Awards.

JUDGING: Entry review by selection committee. Awards judging by internationally known artist. Not responsible for loss or damage.

ENTRY FEE: $10 (processing fee), $25 (refundable if not accepted) for 8x12-foot space. Entrant pays return postage. All work must be for sale.

DEADLINES: Entry, November. Notification, January. Event, March.

325

Great Gulfcoast Arts Festival

Pensacola Arts Council
Art Show Chair
P. O. Box 731
Pensacola, Florida 32594 U.S.A.

Entry July

National; **entry open to U.S.;** annual in November; established 1973. Formerly called FESTIVAL FEVER DAYS to 1975. Purpose: to bring quality visual and performing arts to Pensacola. Sponsored by Pensacola Arts Council, *Pensacola News-Journal.* Average statistics (all sections): 300 entrants, 200 maximum participants, 40 winners, 60,000 attendance, $100,000 total sales, $500 average sale. Held in Pensacola for 2 days. Have food, entertainment, children's arts-theater, workshops, special museum exhibits.

ART FAIR: Drawing, Painting, Prints, Sculpture, Mixed Media, original, framed. Drawing media: charcoal, ink wash, pastel, pen and ink, pencil. Painting media (considered 2 categories): acrylic or oil; watercolor. Print media include etchings, serigraphs, woodcuts. Sculpture media include clay, metal, plastic, wood. Submit 3 2x2-inch 35mm slides of work (no glass or metal mounts) for entry review. Require display of minimum 4 works. Entrants provide and attend sales displays. Team entries acceptable. No proxy exhibitors, portfolios, commercial entries. Competition includes photography, crafts.

AWARDS: $500 to best of show. $200 First, $100 Second, $75 Third Prize. $25 Merit Award Prizes. Over $2000 in purchase awards (all sections).

JUDGING: Entry review by jury. Awards judging by 3 out-of-town artists, teachers. May withhold awards. Not responsible for loss or damage.

ENTRY FEE: $5 for entry review. $40 for 100-square-foot space.

DEADLINES: Entry, July. Notification, September. Event, November.

326

Halifax Art Festival

Museum of Arts and Sciences Guild
Art Festival Chair
P. O. Box 504
Ormond Beach, Florida 32074
U.S.A. Tel: (904) 255-0285

Entry August

International; entry open to all; annual in November; established 1972. Formerly called HALIFAX SIDEWALK ART SHOW to 1972. Sponsored and supported by Museum of Arts and Sciences Guild, business leaders. Average statistics (all sections): 175 maximum participants, 60,000 attendance. Held at Old Ormond Hotel (founded 1888), Ormond Beach for 2 days. Have concessions, entertainment. Second contact: 1040 Museum Blvd., Daytona Beach, Florida 32074.

ART FAIR: **Drawing, Painting, Prints, Sculpture,** framed. Completed in previous 2 years. Submit 3 slides of work in each category for entry review. Entrants provide and attend sales displays. Require display of minimum 4 works. No partner or group entrants, commercial reproductions. Painting categories: Acrylic-Oil, Watercolor. Drawings and prints considered 1 category. Competition includes photography, crafts.

AWARDS (all sections): $500 Judges' Choice Award. 8 $300 Distinction Awards. 30 $100 Merit Awards. $800 Museum Purchase Award. Museum Acquisition Award. ($6700 total prize money.)

JUDGING: By 2 art professionals. Not responsible for loss or damage.

ENTRY FEE: $35 for 10x10-foot covered or 12x12-foot uncovered space.

DEADLINES: Entry, August. Acceptance, September. Event, November.

327

Indian River Festival Arts and Crafts Fair
Titusville Area Chamber of Commerce
2000 Washington Avenue
P. O. Box 880
Titusville, Florida 32780 U.S.A.
Tel: (305) 267-3036

Entry April

International; entry open to all; annual in April; established 1976. Sponsored by Titusville Area Chamber of Commerce. Average statistics (all sections): 120 entries, 50,000 attendance. Held in Sandpoint (adjacent to Indian River) for 3 days. Have food, musical performances, sporting events, carnival rides, children's activities, auction, races.

ART FAIR: **Drawing, Painting, Prints, Sculpture,** original, framed. Entrants provide and attend sales displays. No commercial kits, mass produced, nudes, copies. Divisions: General, Student (includes all media). Categories: Drawings-Graphics (including etching, lithography, serigraphy); Acrylic, Oil, Mixed Media, Pastel; Watercolor; Sculpture. Also have photography, crafts sections.

AWARDS: $150 to best, 2 $25 Merit Awards to general, each category. $50 to best, 10 $10 Merit Awards to student (junior high, senior high). $50 People's Choice Award (all sections). Purchase Awards.

JUDGING: By qualified judges. May withhold awards.

ENTRY FEE: $25 (general), $2 (student) per entrant for 10x10-foot space.

DEADLINES: Event, awards, April.

328

Mainsail Arts Festival
City of St. Petersburg
Phill Whitehouse, Coordinator
P. O. Box 2842
St. Petersburg, Florida 33731 U.S.A.
Tel: (813) 893-7732

Entry February

International; entry open to all; annual in March; established 1976. Formerly called MAINSAIL SIDEWALK ARTS FESTIVAL. Purpose: to present outstanding art to St. Petersburg area in informal atmosphere. Sponsored by City of St. Petersburg, St. Petersburg Art Commission, Junior League Art Center. Average statistics (all sections): 150 entrants, 30 awards, 20,000 attendance. Held in St. Petersburg for 2 days. Also sponsor Performing Arts Festival same weekend. Second contact: Glenn Anderson, St. Petersburg Arts Commission, 1450 16th Street North, St. Petersburg, Florida 33704.

ART FAIR: **Drawing, Painting, Prints, Sculpture,** original; minimum 4 items displayed. Entrants provide and attend sales display. Submit 3 35mm slides in standard mounts, for entry review. No copies, velvet paintings, commercially produced entries. Categories: Drawing-Graphics, Painting, Sculpture, Vanguard. Also have photography, craft sections.

AWARDS: $9000 in Cash Awards. $1500 Best of Show (all sections). Each category: $500 First, $250 Second Place. 15 $150 Merit Awards (all sections).

JUDGING: Entry review and awards judging by 2 judges. Based on quality. Not responsible for loss or damage.

SALES TERMS: Work need not be for sale. No commission charge.

ENTRY FEE: $7.50 jury fee. $25 (refundable) for 12x12-foot space.

DEADLINES: Entry, February. Event, March.

329

Mount Dora Art Festival

Harlow C. Middleton
P. O. Box 916
Mount Dora, Florida 32757 U.S.A.
Tel: (904) 383-8105

Entry December

International; entry open to all; annual in February; established 1975. Known as New England Festival of the South. Purpose: to promote participation, education in the arts. Sponsored and supported by private donations, artists' registration fees. Average statistics (all sections): 240 entrants, 5 countries, 70 awards, 40,000 attendance. Held in downtown Mount Dora for 1 weekend.

ART FAIR: **Drawing, Painting, Prints, Sculpture, Mixed Media,** original, framed for hanging, minimum 4 per category. Entrants provide and attend sales displays. Submit 3 slides of work, 1 of display; resume for entry review. No copies, pornography, commercially produced entries. Categories: Drawing-Graphics, Acrylic-Oil, Watercolor, Sculpture, Mixed Media. Also have photography, craft, youth-student sections.

AWARDS: $1000 Best of Show Award (all sections). Each category: $300 First, $200 Second, $100 Third Prize. $50 Alderman Award. $50 Merit Award.

JUDGING: By committee of teachers, artists. Not responsible for loss or damage.

ENTRY FEE: $5 handling charge plus $25 (refundable) per category for 8x14-foot space. No sales commission charge.

DEADLINES: Entry, December. Notification, January. Event, February.

330

River City Arts Festival Street Artist Market

Arts Assembly of Jacksonville
632 May Street
Jacksonville, Florida 32204 U.S.A.
Tel: (904) 633-3748

Entry January

National; **entry open to U.S. residents age 18 and over;** annual in April; established 1972. Formerly called JACKSONVILLE ARTS FESTIVAL. Purpose: to provide opportunity for artists to display, sell their work. Sponsored by Arts Assembly of Jacksonville, Fine Arts Council of Florida. Supported by NEA. Held in downtown Jacksonville for 2 days. Have artists' demonstrations. Also sponsor concurrent Visual Arts Competition, Film-Video Contest, Poetry Contest.

ART FAIR: **Drawing, Painting, Prints, Other,** original, unframed; limit 5 per entrant (maximum 100 juried, 50 nonjuried entrants). Submit 5 35mm slides for entry review (none for nonjuried section). Entrants provide and attend sales displays. No frames, velvet paintings, commercial displays. Categories: Drawing-Painting (including watercolor), Prints (including photography), Clay-Glass, Fiber-Metal-Wood.

AWARDS: $100 Judges' Award. $500 First, $300 Second Prizes to each category. 2 $100 Merit Awards to each category.

JUDGING: By artists, artist-teachers (3 for entry review, 2 for awards judging). Not responsible for loss or damage.

ENTRY FEE: $5 per category plus $40 for 10x10-foot exhibit area (refundable) plus return postage (juried section). $40 (nonjuried section). Work need not be for sale.

DEADLINES: Entry, January. Judging, event, April.

331

Space Coast Art Festival

Gloria Farinella, Registration Chair
P. O. Box 135
Cocoa Beach, Florida 32931 U.S.A.
Tel: (305) 783-4371

Entry August

International; entry open to all; annual in November; established 1964. Purpose: to promote furtherance of cultural development. Sponsored by Space Coast Festival, Cocoa Beach Women's Club, City of Cocoa Beach. Average statistics (all sections): 275 accepted entrants, 100,000 attendance. Held in Cocoa Beach (south of Kennedy Space Center) for 2 days.

ART FAIR: **Drawing, Painting, Prints, Sculpture,** original, framed or in portfolio. Produced in previous 2 years. Entrants provide and attend sales displays. Submit 2x2-inch slides each section for entry review. No commercially produced entries. Categories: Drawing-Graphics-Pastel, Paintings (acrylic, oil, mixed media), Watercolor, Sculpture. Competition for some awards includes crafts, photography.

AWARDS: $1000 to best display (all sections). $500 to best of show all categories. $100 Merit Awards (3 to painting, 2 watercolor, 2 drawing-graphics-pastel, 1 sculpture). Purchase Awards. Honorable Mentions.

JUDGING: Entry review by jury. Awards judging by 2 art educators. Not responsible for loss or damage.

SALES TERMS: Work need not be for sale. No commission charge.

ENTRY FEE: $35 per 12-foot space. Entrant pays return postage.

DEADLINES: Entry, August. Notification, September. Event, November.

332

Tarpon Springs Arts and Crafts Festival

Tarpon Springs Chamber of Commerce
Scottie Gemmell
914 South Pinellas Avenue
Tarpon Springs, Florida 33589
U.S.A. Tel: (813) 937-6109

Entry February

International; entry open to all; annual in April; established 1975. Sponsored by Tarpon Springs Chamber of Commerce. Average statistics: 200 entrants, 2 countries, 37 awards, 50,000 attendance. Held at Craig Park, Tarpon Springs for 2 days. Have performing arts, food, refreshments. Second contact: Kaye Cotton, 112 South Pinellas Avenue, Tarpon Springs, Florida 33589.

ART FAIR: **Drawing, Painting, Prints, Sculpture,** original. Entrants provide and attend sales displays. Submit 3 2x2-inch 35mm slides of work each category, 1 of display stand. No photographs, brochures, work samples, frames, velvet paintings, commercial molds or displays. Competition includes crafts, photography.

AWARDS: $1000 Best of Show. $375 First Prize each category. 30 $100 Awards of Distinction. $4000 in Purchase Awards (all sections).

JUDGING: By noted authorities and recognized judges.

ENTRY FEE: $5 jury fee. $45 (refundable) for 10x12-foot booth space.

DEADLINES: Entry, February. Judging, event, April.

333

Walt Disney World Festival of the Masters

Pat Phaneuf, Coordinator
P. O. Box 35
Lake Buena Vista, Florida 32830
U.S.A. Tel: (305) 824-5635

Entry July

International; **entry open to previous prize winners;** annual in November; established 1975. Formerly called ART FESTIVAL IN THE VILLAGE to 1979. Purpose: to provide opportunity for public to purchase originals by award-winning artists; promote visual arts. Sponsored by Lake Buena Vista Communities Inc. Average statistics (all sections): 200 entrants, 27 states, 45 awards, 100,000 attendance. Held at Walt Disney World Village, Florida for 3 days.

ART FAIR: **Drawing, Painting, Prints, Sculpture, Mixed Media,** original, framed, under glass or plexiglass; limit 4 per entrant in each of 2 categories. Entrants provide and attend sales displays. Submit 3 2x2-inch 35mm slides of work for entry review. No glass or metal-mounted slides, copies, commercial reproductions, picture frames, velvet paintings. Competition includes photography, crafts.

ELIGIBILITY: Entrant must have won best of show, first 3 places, merit awards, public or exhibitors awards in a recognized art show, festival or fair in previous 3 years ending in May.

AWARDS: $700 First, $350 Second, $175 Third Prize each category. 19 $100 Merit Awards (all sections). Judges' Selection Ribbons. Purchase Awards for Disney World Permanent Collection.

JUDGING: By several experts. Sponsor may reproduce entries for publicity. Not responsible for loss or damage.

ENTRY FEE: $100 (refundable) for 120-square-foot booth space. Entrant pays return postage. Work need not be for sale.

DEADLINES: Entry, judging, July. Event, November.

334

Affair on the Square Sidewalk Art Show
Chattahoochee Valley Art Association (CVAA)
William B. Gay, Director
112 Hines Street
P. O. Box 921
LaGrange, Georgia 30241 U.S.A.
Tel: (404) 882-3267

Entry April

International; **entry open to professional artists;** annual in May; established 1963. Sponsored by CVAA. Held outdoors in LaGrange for 2 days. Have auditorium space in case of rain. Also sponsor LaGrange National Competition, Harvest Heyday Arts and Crafts Show.

ART FAIR: Drawing, Painting, Prints, Sculpture. Entrants provide and attend sales displays. Submit 4 works. Competition for some awards includes photography, crafts.

AWARDS: Up to $1000 in Purchase Awards (all sections). $75 Merit Award and Blue Ribbon to best, each section. 1 exhibitor chosen for 1-person show at CVAA gallery (all sections). 10 Honorable Mention Ribbons.

JUDGING: By art professional. Not responsible for loss or damage.

ENTRY FEE: $25 (individual), $40 (group) for maximum 10 linear feet (5x5- or 5x10-foot hanging panel) or equivalent table space. No sales commission charge.

DEADLINES: Entry, April. Event, judging, May.

335

Chiaha Harvest Fair
Chiaha Guild of Arts and Crafts (CGAC)
Nancy L. Smith, Publicity Director
P. O. Box 1282
Rome, Georgia 30161 U.S.A.
Tel: (404) 295-4828

Entry October

National; **entry open to U.S.;** annual in October; established 1965. Considered one of South's oldest arts and crafts fairs. Named after Cherokee Indian word "meeting of the hills and waters." Purpose: to provide public with opportunity to buy quality art work. Sponsored and supported by CGAC. Annual statistics: 70 entrants, 12 awards, 10,000 attendance. Held during Heritage Holidays Festival at Heritage Park, Rome for 2 days. Have food booths, plant sales, children's activities, entertainment. Tickets: 50¢-$1. Second contact: Bambi Berry, Exhibits Chair, Rt. 10, Horseleg Creek Road, Rome, Georgia 30161.

ART FAIR: Drawing, Painting, Prints, Sculpture, original; unlimited entry. Entrants provide and attend sales displays. Submit slides (or photos) and description of each work for entry review. No reproductions, decoupage, hobby kits, unlimited prints. Competition includes photography, crafts.

AWARDS: All Sections: $100 Best of Show; 10 $50 Merit Awards. $500 in Purchase Awards; CGAC Purchase Award.

JUDGING: By 1 art professional. CGAC Purchase Award by Harvest

Fair Committee. Not responsible for loss or damage.

ENTRY FEE: $30 for 8x15-foot booth (2 or more may share). No sales commission charge.

DEADLINES: Entry, event, October.

336

Golden Isles Arts and Crafts Festival

Glynn Art Association
Mrs. William C. Hendrix, Associate Director
Island Art Center, 2012 Demere Road
P. O. Box 673
St. Simons Island, Georgia 31522
U.S.A. Tel: (912) 638-8770

Entry July

International; entry open to all; annual in October; established 1969. Purpose: to bring quality artwork to public in fun atmosphere. Sponsored and supported by Glynn Art Association, Glynn County Department of Leisure Services. Average statistics (all sections): 500 entrants, 165 acceptances, 10 awards, 50,000 attendance. Held in Neptune Park, St. Simons Island for 2 days. Have food, entertainment. Also sponsor Island Art Center offering complete art training.

ART FAIR: **Drawing, Painting, Prints, Sculpture,** original. Painting media: acrylic, oil, watercolor, mixed media. Entrants provide and attend sales displays. Submit slides or photos for entry review. Request publicity information. No decoupage, kits, molds, commercial work. Also have photography, crafts sections.

AWARDS: $300 to best of show (all sections). $150 to best painting. 2 $100 Equal Merit Awards to best prints-drawings. $100 to best sculpture. Honorable Mentions at judges' discretion. Option for special 1-person exhibits to winners.

JUDGING: Entry review by jury committee. Awards judging by 1-2 judges. Not responsible for loss or damage.

ENTRY FEE: $45 per 6x8-foot panel or minimum 100-square-foot space (no sharing). No sales commission charge.

DEADLINES: Entry, July. Acceptance, August. Event, October.

337

57th Street Art Fair

Sue Goldhammer, Committee Head
5555 South Everett Avenue
Chicago, Illinois 60637 U.S.A.
Tel: (312) 644-5800

Entry March

International; **entry open to age 18 and over;** annual in June; established 1948. Evolved from turn-of-century artists' colony, now oldest outdoor art fair in Midwest. Sponsored by 57th Street Art Fair Committee. Average statistics: 300 entrants, 10 awards, 20,000 attendance. Held in Chicago's Hyde Park for 2 days. Second contact: 400 North Michigan Avenue, Suite 904, Chicago, Illinois 60611.

ART FAIR: **Drawing, Painting, Prints, Sculpture,** original. Entrants provide and attend sales displays. Submit 1 work sample (Chicago-area residents), 2 35mm slides (outside Chicago) for entry review. Competition includes photography, crafts.

AWARDS: $500 Best of Fair. 3 $200 Awards. 3 $75 Newcomer Awards. Ribbons.

JUDGING: By panel of artists, critics. Not responsible for loss or damage.

SALES TERMS: All work must be for sale. No commission charge.

ENTRY FEE: $2 screening fee. $20 for maximum 12-foot space.

DEADLINES: Entry, March. Notification, April. Event, June.

338

Greenwich Village Art Fair
Rockford Art Association
Burpee Art Museum
737 North Main Street
Rockford, Illinois 61103 U.S.A.
Tel: (815) 965-3131

Entry May

National; **entry open to U.S. residents age 18 and over;** annual in September; established 1948. Purpose: to raise funds for Burpee Art Museum. Sponsored by Rockford Art Association. Average statistics: 200 entrants, 25,000 attendance. Held in Burpee Museum, Rockford for 2 days. Tickets: 50¢-$2. Also sponsor annual watercolor competition (national), art exhibition, small sculpture competition (local).

ART FAIR: Drawing, Painting, Prints, Sculpture, Collage, original; maximum 200 entrants. Entrants provide and attend sales displays. Submit 5 35mm slides for entry review. No commercial kits. Competition includes photography, crafts.

AWARDS: All Sections: $500 Best of Show. $300 Two Dimensional Award. $300 Three Dimensional Award. $50 Merit Awards. Purchase Awards.

JUDGING: By 1 judge.

SALES TERMS: All work must be for sale. No commission charge.

ENTRY FEE: $5 plus return postage. $50 for 10x15-foot space.

DEADLINES: Entry, May. Notification, June. Awards, event, September.

339

Park Forest Art Fair
Park Forest Art Center
Eugene R. Dooley
410 Lakewood Boulevard
Park Forest, Illinois 60466 U.S.A.

Entry June

International; **entry open to age 18 and over;** annual in September; established 1955. Sponsored by Park Forest Art Center, Park Forest Plaza Merchants' Association, shopping center owners and managers. Average 180 entrants (all sections). Held at Park Forest Shopping Plaza for 2 days.

ART FAIR: Drawing, Painting, Prints, Sculpture, original. Entrants provide and attend sales displays. Submit 5 slides for entry review. No group displays. Competition includes photography, crafts.

AWARDS: $600 First, $400 Second, $200 Third, $100 Fourth Prizes. $100 Municipal Art League Award. $1600 in Purchase Awards.

JUDGING: Not responsible for loss or damage.

SALES TERMS: All work must be for sale. No commission charge.

ENTRY FEE: $5 jury fee with application, $20 registration fee for minimum 12-foot space.

DEADLINES: Entry, June. Registration, August. Event, September.

340

Lafayesta
Lafayette Art Center
Sharon Theobald, Executive Director
101 South 9th Street
Lafayette, Indiana 47901 U.S.A.
Tel: (317) 742-1128

Entry June

National; **entry open to U.S.;** annual in September; established 1974. Formerly called FIESTA, INTERNATIONAL FESTIVAL OF ARTS AND CRAFTS to 1980. Purpose: to expose area residents to outstanding artists. Theme: International Folk Arts Festival. Sponsored and supported by Lafayette Art Center. Held at Indiana Veterans Home in West Lafayette for 2 days. Have ethnic food, children's arts and crafts area, demonstrations, entertainment. Tickets: $1-$5. Also sponsor Tippecanoe Biennial.

ART FAIR: Graphics, Painting, Sculpture. Entrants provide and attend sales displays. Submit 4 35mm slides for entry review (no glass mounts). Competition includes photography, crafts.

AWARDS: $5000 in Excellence, Merit, Purchase, Commission Awards.

JUDGING: Entry review by jury headed by University Art Coordinator. Awards judging by 2 art professionals. Not responsible for loss or damage.

ENTRY FEE: $30 (refundable) for 8x10-foot booth (2 artists maximum) plus return postage.

DEADLINES: Entry, June. Notification, July. Event, September.

341

Fort Dodge Art in the Park
Fort Dodge Area Fine Arts Council
Visual Arts Committee
Blanden Memorial Art Gallery
920 Third Avenue South
Fort Dodge, Iowa 50501 U.S.A.
Tel: (515) 573-2801, 573-2316

Entry July

International; entry open to all; annual in August; established 1974. Purpose: to give exposure to artists, educate public; encourage community support of arts. Sponsored by Fort Dodge Area Fine Arts Council; Fort Dodge Department of Parks, Recreation, Forestry; Riverfront Commission. Supported by local businesses, organizations. Average statistics (all sections): 90 entrants maximum, 21 awards, 10,000 attendance. Held at Alson Park, Fort Dodge for 1 day. Have entertainment, food service, demonstrations. Also sponsor Artist-in-Schools; drama, puppet presentations.

ART FAIR: Drawing, Painting, Print, Sculpture. Painting media: acrylic, oil, watercolor. Entrants provide and attend sales displays. Submit 5 slides or photos of work for entry review. Competition includes photography, crafts.

AWARDS: $8000 in Purchase Awards (all sections).

JUDGING: Entry review by screening board. Awards judging by 3-5 art professionals. Based on originality, creativity. Not responsible for loss or damage.

ENTRY FEE: $15. No sales commission charge.

DEADLINES: Entry, July. Event, August.

342

Parsons Kansas Outdoor Arts and Crafts Fair

Art Fair Board
Anne Maloney
P. O. Box 995
Parsons, Kansas 67357 U.S.A.
Tel: (316) 421-4294

Entry July

International; entry open to all; annual in July; established 1961. Purpose: to provide Parsons residents opportunity to see, buy arts and crafts. Sponsored by Art Fair Board. Average statistics (all sections): 1000 entries, 120 entrants, 28 awards. Held at Parsons Plaza for 2 days. Have entertainment.

ART FAIR: **Painting, Prints, Sculpture** (and other fine arts media), original, 2D work matted and-or framed, ready for hanging; unlimited entry. Entrants provide and attend sales displays. No manufactured items, commercially processed prints. Divisions: Adults, Sunday Painters (2D media only), Junior-Senior High, Children. Competition for some awards includes photography, crafts.

AWARDS: $100 to best of show (all sections). Arts: $60 First, $30 Second, $15 Third to adult. $30 First, $15 Second, $10 Third to Sunday painters. $20 First, $10 Second, $5 Third to junior-senior high.

JUDGING: By 3 art professionals. Works receive public critique.

ENTRY FEE: $15 (junior-senior high school students and children free) plus $5 per table or 4x8-foot pegboard.

DEADLINES: Entry, event, July.

343

River Bend Art Fair

Atchison Art Association
Marilyn Buehler
P. O. Box 308
Atchison, Kansas 66002 U.S.A.
Tel: (913) 367-7337

Entry May

International; entry open to all; annual in May; established 1964. Sponsored by Atchison Art Association. Average statistics (all sections): 130 entrants, 10 awards. Held at Atchison Mall for 2 days. Have featured artist, demonstrations, entertainment.

ART FAIR: **Drawing, Painting, Prints, Sculpture;** limit 1 entry for competition, unlimited for display. Entrants provide and attend sales displays. No commercially processed prints. Competition includes photography, crafts.

AWARDS: $150 First, $100 Second, $50 Third Prize. 3 $25 Judges' Awards. $25 Best Display Award. 6 Honorable Mentions.

JUDGING: By 2 judges. Not responsible for loss or damage.

ENTRY FEE: $20 for space or table, $12 for 4x8-foot panel. No sales commission charge.

DEADLINES: Entry, event, May.

ALPHABETICAL EVENT/SPONSOR/AWARD INDEX

Alphabetical index to each EVENT, SPONSOR, and AWARD (followed by identifying CODE NUMBER of the event).

A

AAO Gallery International All on Paper Exhibition: 84
Academic Artists Association National Exhibition of Contemporary Realism in Art: 51
Adolph and Esther Gottlieb Foundation Grants for Visual Artists: 119
Affair on the Square: 58
Affair on the Square Sidewalk Art Show: 334
Affaire in the Gardens Arts and Crafts Fair: 316
Alameda County Agricultural Fair Association: 52
Alameda County Fair Exhibition of Fine Arts: 52
Alan Rothenberg Scholarship: 227
Alaska State Fair Art Competition: 53
Albright-Knox Art Gallery (AKAG): 82
Alden B. Dow Creativity Center: 219
Alice Lloyd College (ALC) Works on Paper Art Exhibition: 45
All Oregon Art Exhibition: 93
Allied Artists of America (AAA) Annual Open Exhibition: 105
American Academy in Rome: 220
American Academy in Rome-NEH Fellowships: 17
American Annual at Newport Exhibition: 46
American Art Exhibition: 266
American Association of University Women, Racine Branch: 312
American Exhibition: 85
Anabel Mack Taylor Tuition Scholarhips: 241
Anacortes Arts and Crafts Festival Nonprofessional Competition: 1
Anne Giles Kimbrough Award: 137
Apeiron Workshops Artist-in-Residence Program: 205
Appalachian National Drawing Competition: 28
Appalachian State University Art Department: 28
Arati Artists Gallery: 158
Arkansas Annual Art Exhibition: 54
Arkansas Artists Exhibition: 54
Arkansas Arts Center Delta Art Exhibition: 189
Arkansas Arts Center Prints, Drawings and Crafts Exhibition: 109
Arkansas Wildlife Federation (AWF) Art Exhibition: 12
Arrowhead Biennial Art Exhibition: 273
Arrowmont School of Arts and Crafts Spring and Summer Assistantships: 206
Art Association of Harrisburg: 191
Art Association of New Orleans: 284

Art Association of Newport (AAN): 46
Art Association of Newport (AAN) American Exhibition: 85
Art Fair Board: 342
Art Festival in the Village: 333
Art in New State Building Program: 132
Art in Public Places Program: 132
Art in the Park: 305
Art in the Sun Festival: 321
Art on the Green Juried Show: 190
Art Regional: 248
Art Show of the Ozarks: 170
Arteder International Graphic Arts Exhibition: 115
Artforms Open Juried Exhibit: 83
Artists Biennial: 284
Artists' Days at Vizcaya International Competition: 36
Artists for Environment Foundation Artists-in-Residence Program: 207
Arts Assembly of Jacksonville: 330
Arts Council of Great Britain: 30, 134
Arts Council of Greater Hazleton: 264
Arts Council of Northern Ireland: 226
Arts NW Student Juried Fine Art Show: 2
Arts on the Line Program: 126
Associated Art Organizations (AAO) of Western New York: 84
Associated Students: UC Santa Barbara (UCSB): 145
Atchison Art Association: 343
Atlanta Playhouse Theatre Ltd.: 48
Atlanta Womens Chamber of Commerce: 48
AWF Painting of the Year: 12

B

Ball State University (BSU) Drawing and Small Sculpture Show: 116
Baltimore Museum of Art: 283
Bath Country Art Festival: 163
Baycrafters Annual Juried Art Show: 68
Baycrafters, Inc.: 155
Bellevue Art Museum: 182
Beloit and Vicinity Exhibition: 69
Berks Art Alliance Regional Juried Show: 70
Betty Brazil Memorial Fund Woman Sculptor Grant: 120
Beverly Art Center and Vanderpoel Art Association: 147
Beverly Art Center Art Fair and Festival: 147
Beverly Hills Recreation and Parks Department: 316
Bosque Art Gallery National Western Small Painting Show: 251
Boston Printmakers National Exhibition: 195
Boulder Arts: 274
Boulder Center for the Visual Arts Annual Exhibition: 274
Bridgton Arts Show: 256
Brooklyn Museum Art School Painting and Sculpture Scholarships: 227
Brown University: 19
Brownsville Art League International Art Show: 257
Brush and Palette Club National Art Exhibition: 31
BSU Art Gallery: 116
BSU Drawing and Small Sculpture Show: 116
Burbank Fine Arts Federation Multimedia Juried Show: 71
Bureau of Indian Affairs: 215
Burleson Annual Open Juried Art Exhibition: 86
Burleson Area Chamber of Commerce: 86
Bush Foundation Fellowships for Artists: 135
Business Committee for the Arts (BCA): 289
Business in the Arts Awards: 289
Butler Institute of American Art Ohio Ceramic, Sculpture and Craft Show: 243

C

Cal Poly Ink and Clay Exhibition: 75
California Exposition and State Fair Art Show: 94
California State Fair: 94
California State Polytechnic University (Cal Poly) Art Department: 75
California Survey of Watercolor and Drawing Competition: 32
Callaway Gardens Art Festival: 58
Cambridge Arts Council: 126, 126
Cameo Art Gallery National Miniature Show: 162
Canada Council Grants: 142
Canaday Award: 104
CAPS Program Fellowship Grants: 136
Carnegie Institute: 103
Central South Art Exhibition: 72
Change Inc. Emergency Assistance Grants: 121
Charles and Emma Frye Art Museum: 34
Chattahoochee Valley Art Association (CVAA): 58, 334
Chautauqua Art Association Galleries: 47
Chautauqua National Exhibition of American Art: 47
Chiaha Guild of Arts and Crafts (CGAC): 335
Chiaha Harvest Fair: 335
Chilmark Award: 246
Choochokam Arts and Pleasure Fair: 280
Christmas Card Competition: 290
Chrysler Museum: 97
Cintas Fellowship Program: 122
Citizens Council for the Arts: 190
City of Marino International Biennial of Stone Sculpture: 249
City of Mesa Cultural Activities Department: 80
City of Miami Beach Outdoor Festival of the Arts: 322
City of St. Petersburg: 328
City of Walnut Creek Purchase Award: 177
City Stage Celebration: 308
Civil War Round Table of New York Awards: 154
Clare Hart DeGloyer Award: 137
Cleveland County Council: 30
Cleveland (U.K.) International Drawing Biennale: 30
Coca-Cola Bottling Company (CCBC) of Elizabethtown Art Show: 55
Cocoa Beach Women's Club: 331
College of the Mainland Art Gallery: 258
College of the Mainland National Art Competition: 258
Colorado Graphic Arts Center: 201
Columbia College: 268
Community Arts Section: 76
Comune di Marino: 249
Connecticut Artists Annual Exhibition: 275
Connecticut Women Artists Annual Exhibition: 95
Cooper Union for the Advancement of Science and Art Scholarships: 228
Cooperstown Art Association (CAA) Art Exhibition: 87
Council for International Exchange of Scholars: 27
Council for International Exchange of Scholars (CIES): 212
Country Art Festival: 163
Courage Center Christmas Card Competition: 290
Cracow International Print Biennale: 204
Crafton Hills Watercolor College Seminar Award: 186
Craftsman Press Award: 182
Creative Artists Program Service: 136
Creative Artists Public Service (CAPS) Program Fellowship Grants: 136
Creative Arts Center: 71
Cummington Community of the Arts Artist in Residence Scholarships: 208

D

Dakota Center for the Arts Midwest Miniature Show: 164
Dale Fellowship: 23
Dale Fellowships: 20
Dale Warren Wildlife Award: 153
Dallas Museum of Fine Arts (DMFA) Awards to Artists: 137
DeGloyer Award: 137
Del Mar College National Drawing and Small Sculpture Show: 117
Demarest Trust Fund Grants: 123
Dogwood Festival International Art Show: 48
D'Orlando Memorial Art Scholarship: 235
Downtown Committee of Syracuse: 307
Downtown Syracuse Arts and Crafts Fair: 307
Dubuque Fine Arts Society: 299
DubuqueFest Art Fair: 299
Ducks Unlimited National Wildlife Art Show: 13
Dulin Gallery of Art: 110
Dulin National Print and Drawing Competition: 110
Duluth Art Institute: 273
Dumond Memorial Award: 106

E

Early American Culture Fellowships: 26
Eastbay Watercolor Society (EWS) Annual Exhibition: 177
Eastman Kodak Company: 6
Eben Demarest Trust Fund Grants: 123
Edina Art Festival: 304
Edward MacDowell Medal: 216
Edward Maverick Fund: 210
Edwin Austin Abbey Memorial Scholarship for Mural Painting: 229
El Paso Museum of Art: 167
El Paso National Sun Carnival Art Exhibition: 167
Electrum Juried Art Show: 56
Elizabethtown-White Lake Chamber of Commerce: 44
Emerald Necklace Juried Art Competition: 155
Emile Gruppe Award: 41
Energy Art Exhibition: 14
Environmental Art & Sculpture Competition: 138
Erhman Mansion Art Show and Crafts Fair: 92
Erie Art Center Annual Spring Show: 276
Evansville Museum of Arts and Science Art Committee: 99
Exhibition 280: 277
Exhibition of Contemporary and Older Art: 175

F

Faber Birren Color Award Show: 259
Fairfax County Council of the Arts (FCCA): 146
Fairfield Art Show Oak Room Exhibition: 57
Fairfield Chamber of Commerce: 57
Falkirk Annual Juried Art Exhibition: 96
Felician College Art Festival: 260
Fell's Point Fun Festival: 301
Feria Internacional de Muestras de Bilbao: 115
Festival Fever Days: 325
Fine Arts Council of Florida: 330
Fine Arts Institute: 100
Fine Arts League National Spring Show: 88
Fine Arts Museum of the South Outdoor Arts and Crafts Fair: 313
Fine Arts Work Center in Provincetown Fellowships: 209
Finley Fellowship: 23
First Eastern National Bank: 33
Fisher Award: 182
Flanagan Center for Creative Persons Residencies: 223

Fondation des Etats-Unis: 225
Fontainebleau Fine Arts and Music Schools Association Residence Scholarships: 210
Foothills Art Center: 14, 183
Foothills Art Center North American Sculpture Exhibition: 244
Forecast Outdoor Art Projects Competition: 138
Forecast Public Artspace Productions: 138
Fort Dodge Area Fine Arts Council: 341
Fort Dodge Art in the Park: 341
Fort Hays State University Art Department: 37
Fountain Festival of Arts and Crafts: 261
Fountain Hills Chamber of Commerce: 261
Four State Student Drawing Competition: 3
Fourth Street Festival of the Arts and Crafts: 297
Fremont County Library Award: 153
Friends of American Art Award: 243
Friends of the Meadows Museum of Art: 63
Fulbright Awards for University Teaching and Advanced Research Abroad: 212
Fulbright-Hays Grants: 211

G

Gabrovo International Biennial of Cartoon and Satirical Sculpture: 293
Gabrovo International Biennial of Humor and Satire in Painting: 294
Gainesville Spring Arts Festival: 323
Galerie Paula Insel: 269
Galerie Triangle East Coast Regional Exhibition: 278
Galerie Triangle Monthly Contests: 291
Galerie Triangle National Exhibition: 262
Galesburg Civic Art Center: 263
GALEX Annual Competitive Art Exhibition: 263
Galleon World Travel Prize: 161
Gasparilla Sidewalk Art Festival: 324
George Pinca Award: 184
Gilpin County Arts Association Annual Exhibition: 73
Glynn Art Association: 336
Golden Isles Arts and Crafts Festival: 336
Gottlieb Foundation Grants for Visual Artists: 119
Graduate School for Community Development (GSCD) All Media Juried Exhibition: 279
Grand Central Art Galleries Award: 105
Grand Junction Art Festival: 318
Grand Junction Chamber of Commerce: 31
Grand Prairie Arts Council: 315
Grand Prairie Festival of Arts: 315
Great Gulfcoast Arts Festival: 325
Greater Hazleton Creative Arts Festival: 264
Greater Kingsport Competitive Art Show: 33
Greater London Arts Association: 224
Greater London Council (GLC): 161
Greater Meridian Chamber of Commerce (GMCC): 305
Greater Pompano Beach Chamber of Commerce: 321
Greenwich Village Art Fair: 338
Grumbacher Award: 51, 54, 85, 180
Guggenheim Memorial Fellowships: 124

H

Halifax Art Festival: 326
Harness Tracks of America Annual Art Competition and Auction: 15
Harriet Hale Woolley Scholarships: 225
Harrisburg Art Association Juried Exhibition: 191

Hartland Art Council: 74
Hartland Art Show: 74
Harvest Heyday Arts and Crafts Show: 58
Haystack Mountain Residence Grants: 213
Haystack Mountain School of Crafts: 213
Helen Keller Festival Art-Craft Show: 314
Helena Arts Council: 56
Helene Wurlitzer Foundation of New Mexico Residencies: 214
Heritage Holidays Festival: 335
Hill Country Arts Foundation Juried Arts Exhibition: 265
Hill Country Arts Foundation Photography-Graphics Exhibition: 143
Hirshhorn Museum and Sculpture Garden Summer Internships: 18
Hockaday Center for the Arts: 306
House of Humor and Satire: 293, 294
Houston Watercolor Art Society Spring Open Exhibition: 178
Hudson Valley Art Association (HVAA) Annual Exhibition: 106
Humboldt Cultural Center: 32
Humboldt State University Art Department: 32
Hunterdon Art Center Annual Print Exhibition: 196
Huntington Galleries: 277

I

Imperial Tobacco Portrait Award: 11
Indian River Festival Arts and Crafts Fair: 327
Ink and Clay Exhibition: 75
Institute of American Indian Arts Residence Scholarships: 215
Institute of International Education: 122
Institute of International Education (IIE): 211
Inter-Arts of Marin Public Art Competition: 139
International Center for the Teaching of Mosaic (CISIM) Scholarships: 242
International Grand Prix of Contemporary Art: 67
Inveresk International Artists in Watercolor Competition: 35
Inveresk Paper Company Ltd.: 35
Irene Leache Memorial Art Exhibition: 97
Island Arts Council Choochokam Art Exhibition: 280

J

J. K. Ralston Museum and Art Center: 59
Jacinto Higueras International Sculpture Contest: 250
Jacinto Higueras Museum Foundation: 250
Jacksonville Arts Festival: 152, 330
Jacobson Memorial Award: 107
Japan-United States Friendship Commission: 221
John Carter Brown Library Research Fellowships: 19
John F. and Anna Lee Stacey Scholarship Fund: 230
John Gregory Prize: 10
John Laing Limited: 176
John Moores Liverpool Art Exhibition: 175
Johnson Atelier Sculpture Apprenticeship Program Tuition Scholarships: 231
Johnson Atelier Technical Institute of Sculpture: 231
Joseph Cain Memorial Purchase Award: 117
Judith Selkowitz Fine Arts Annual Competition for Representational Painters: 168

K

Kalamazoo Institute of Arts Art Fair: 302
Kalispell Art in the Park Art and Crafts Fair: 306
Kalos Kagathos Foundation Sculpture Prize: 246
Kansas National Small Painting, Drawing and Print Exhibition: 37
Kate Neal Kinley Memorial Fellowship: 232
Kearney State College Art Department: 233
Kearney State College Special Activities Grants Scholarships in Art: 233
Kent Leasure Memorial Award: 263
Kiamichi Owa-Chito Art Show: 16
Kimbrough Award: 137
Kinley Memorial Fellowship: 232
Kitchener-Waterloo Art Gallery: 83
Kress Fellowship: 23

L

La Junta Fine Arts League National Art Show: 88
La Mirada Festival of Arts Art Competition and Exhibition: 148
Lafayesta: 340
Lafayette Art Center: 340
LaGrange College: 58
LaGrange National Competition: 58
Laing Painting Competition: 176
Lake Superior National Crafts Exhibit: 273
Lake Tahoe State Parks Advisory Committee: 92
Laramie Art Guild American National Miniature Show: 165
Lincoln Days Celebration Annual Tri-State Art Show: 156
Lively Arts Festival: 305
Lodi Art Center (LAC) Annual Show: 149
London Silver Vaults Prize: 161
Long Beach Art Association (LBAA) Open Juried Exhibition: 281
Louisville Art Center Association Juried Exhibition: 292
Lowick House Printmaking Workshops Equipment and Facilities Loans: 134
Lowick House Printmaking Workshops Residencies: 224
Ludwig Vogelstein Foundation Grants: 125

M

MacDowell Colony Residence Fellowships: 216
MacDowell Corporate Award: 216
Mainsail Arts Festival: 328
Mamaroneck Artists Guild Open Juried Exhibition: 150
Marietta College Art Department: 192
Marietta College Crafts National (MCCN) Exhibition: 245
Marietta National Painting and Sculpture Exhibition: 192
Marin County Fair Fine Art Competition: 282
Maritime International Art Awards Show: 157
Maryland Biennial Exhibition: 283
Massachusetts Bay Transportation Authority (MBTA) Arts on the Line Program: 126
Massachusetts Council on the Arts and Humanities: 195
Maurice Hexter Prize: 246
Max Beckmann Memorial Scholarships: 227
MBTA Arts on the Line Program: 126
McCurtain County Art Club: 16
Mellon Fellowships: 20
Meridian Art in the Park Arts and Crafts Festival: 305
Metropolitan Museum of Art Residence Fellowships: 20
Miami Art Center Helpers (Mach I): 197
Miami Beach Fine Arts Board: 322

Miami Graphics Biennial: 197
Miami International Print Biennial: 197
Michigan City Art Fair: 298
Michigan City Art League (MCAL): 298
Michigan Department of Natural Resources: 76
Michigan State Fair Fine Arts Exhibit: 76
Mid America Biennial Art Exhibition: 38
Middletown Fine Arts Center American Art Exhibition: 266
Mid-Michigan Art Exhibition: 98
Mid-States Art Exhibition: 99
Midwest Miniature Show: 164
Midwest Watercolor Society Open Juried Show: 179
Mills Scholarship: 20
Minot Art Gallery: 267
Mint Museum Biennial Exhibition of Piedmont Painting and Sculpture: 193
Missouri Arts Council: 268
Monaco National Museum: 67
Mondak Historical and Arts Society Annual Art Show: 59
Montalvo Artist-in-Residence Program: 217
Montalvo Center for the Arts: 217
Montana Miniature Art Society International Show: 166
Monte-Carlo International Grand Prix of Contemporary Art: 67
Monument Square Art Fair: 312
Mount Dora Art Festival: 329
Mount Hope Estate and Winery: 310
Mount Hope Outdoor Art Show: 310
Mt. Hood Community College Art Mall Gallery: 198
Mullaly-Matisse Galleries National Small Painting Exhibition: 252
Museum of African Art Academic Internships: 21
Museum of Arts and Sciences Guild: 326
Muskegon Museum of Art: 288
Mystic Chamber of Commerce: 319
Mystic Outdoor Art Festival: 319
Mystic Seaport Museum Store: 157

N

National Academy of Design: 229
National Academy of Design Annual Exhibition: 60
National Arts Club Award: 105
National Arts Club (NAC) Open Watercolor Exhibition: 180
National Collection of Fine Arts (NCFA) Summer Internships: 22
National Endowment for the Arts (NEA) Visual Arts Fellowships and Grants to Individuals and Organizations: 127
National Endowment for the Arts (NEA) Visual Arts Grants to Organizations: 128
National Endowment for the Humanities (NEH) Grants: 129
National Gallery of Art Center for Advanced Study in the Visual Arts Predoctoral Fellowship Program: 23
National Gallery of Art Center for Advanced Study in the Visual Arts Senior Fellow Program: 24
National League of American Pen Women Scholarships for Mature Women: 234
National Portrait Gallery (London): 11
National Sculpture Society: 10
National Sculpture Society Annual Exhibition: 246
National Small Sculpture and Drawing Exhibition: 118
National Watercolor Society Award: 186
National Watermedia Biennial: 255
National Western Small Painting Show: 251
National Wildlife Art Show: 13
NEA Visual Arts Fellowships and Grants: 127
NEA Visual Arts Grants to Organizations: 128

NEH Grants: 129
New England Exhibition of Painting, Drawing and Sculpture: 107
New Jersey Painters and Sculptors Society National Exhibition: 89
New Jersey Water Color Society Open Exhibition: 181
New Moves Scholarships: 240
New Orleans Museum of Art: 284
New Orleans Triennial: 284
New York Graphic Society Award: 107
New York State Education Department: 218
New York State Summer School of the Arts School of Visual Arts Scholarships: 218
New York University Small Works Competition: 253
North American Sculpture Exhibition: 14
North Carolina Arts Council: 44
North Dakota Annual Print and Drawing Show: 111
North Dakota Art Exhibition: 267
North Idaho College Presidents Purchase Award: 190
North Kitsap Annual Open Art Show: 39
North Kitsap Arts and Crafts Committee: 39
North Tahoe Fine Arts Council: 92
Northern Arts: 134
Northwest Watercolor Society: 182
Northwest Watercolors Annual Exhibition: 182
Northwood Institute Creativity Fellowships: 219

O

Ogunquit Art Center National Exhibition of Paintings: 169
Ohio Arts Council Aid to Individual Artists: 140
Ohio Ceramic, Sculpture and Craft Show: 243
Oklahoma Watercolor Association: 185
Old Colorado City Historic Juried Art Show: 158
Old Saybrook Chamber of Commerce: 320
Old Saybrook Outdoor Art Exhibit: 320
Ontario Arts Council: 83
Open Paintings on Canvas Exhibition: 173
Orange County Art Association (OCAA) All Media Juried Exhibition: 151
Oregon Arts Commission: 93
Oregon Printmakers Annual Juried Show: 198
Oregon State Fair: 93
Owensboro Museum of Fine Art (OMFA): 38
Ozark Writers and Artists Guild Art Show: 144
Ozarks Annual Painting Exhibit: 170

P

Palm Beach Art Galleries: 108
Palm Beach International Art Competition: 108
Paper in Particular National Exhibition of Works On-Of Paper: 268
Park Forest Art Center: 339
Park Forest Art Fair: 339
Parkersburg Art Center (PAC) Print, Painting, and Drawing Exhibition: 40
Parsons Kansas Outdoor Arts and Crafts Fair: 342
Pastel Society of America Award: 105, 106
Paula Insel Annual Art Exhibition: 269
Paula Insel Puerto Rican Art Exhibition: 270
Pauly D'Orlando Memorial Art Scholarship: 235
Pen and Brush Annual Sculpture Exhibition: 247
Pensacola Arts Council: 325

Pensacola Junior College: 271
Pensacola National Art Exhibition: 271
Percy R. Baker Award: 180
Peters Valley Craftsmen Internship Program: 236
Playhouse in the Hills: 208
Polish Artists' Union: 204
Potsdam National Drawing Exhibition: 29
Potsdam National Print Exhibition: 199
Prince Rainier Medal: 67
Print Club International Competition: 200
Prix de la Ville de Monaco: 67
Puerto Rican Art Exhibition: 270
Puget Sound Area Painting Exhibition: 34
Puget Sound Group of Painters Award: 182
Purdue University Galleries: 254
Purdue University Small Print Exhibition (60 Square Inches): 254

Q

Quinebaug Valley Council for the Arts and Humanities (QVCAH) All Arts Festival: 61

R

Readers Digest Award: 107
Reading Public Museum: 70
Red River Revel Arts and Crafts Festival: 300
Religious Art Guild: 235
Renaissance Guild: 36
Richmond Art Center Spring Exhibition: 285
Ridge Art Association Annual Fine Arts Competition: 90
River Bend Art Fair: 343
River City Arts Festival Street Artist Market: 330
River City Arts Festival Visual Arts Competition: 152
Robert Smithson Scholarships: 227
Rockford Art Association: 338
Rockport Chamber of Commerce: 4
Rockport National Amateur Festival: 4
Rocky Mountain National Watermedia Exhibition: 14, 183
Rocky Mountain Regional Print Show: 201
Rocky Mountain School of Art Annual Scholarship Competition: 5
Rome Prize Fellowships: 220
Rosary College Graduate School of Fine Arts: 241
Roseville Art Center Annual Open Show: 286
Roulet Medal: 104
Rousseau Fellowships: 20

S

Sacramento Festival of the Arts Outdoor Arts Show: 296
Sacramento Regional Arts Council (SRAC): 296
Saginaw West Side Art Festival: 303
Salmagundi Club Open Juried Nonmember Exhibition: 41
San Bernardino County Museum Association Traditional Artists Exhibition: 100
San Diego Art Institute (SDAI) Annual Exhibition: 101
San Diego Watercolor Society Award: 186
San Francisco Foundation: 139
San Jose Art League 2-Dimensional Art Regional Exhibition: 49, 248
San Mateo County Fair Arts Committee: 62
San Mateo County Fair International Visual Arts Competition: 62
San Rafael Recreation Department: 96
Santa Clara County Fair Art Exhibit: 77

Santa Fe Community College: 323
Santa Rosa Annual Statewide Art Show: 42
Santa Rosa Art Guild (SRAG): 42
Schaefer Maritime Art Award: 157
Scholastic Art Awards: 6
Scholastic, Inc.: 6
School of the Ozarks Art Department: 170
Sculpture Associates Certificate Award: 106
Sculpture Space Facilities Loans for Professional Sculptors: 130
SECCA Grants: 141
SECCA Southeastern Competition: 112
Second Street Gallery National Juried Exhibition: 113
Sekretariat Miedzynarodowego Biennale Grafiki: 204
Seventeen Magazine: 7
Seventeen's Annual Art Contest: 7
Sheldon Swope Art Gallery: 81
Shreveport Art Guild National Exhibition: 63
Silvermine Guild Center for the Arts: 107
Sister Kenny Institute (SKI) International Art Show by Disabled Artists: 64
Slater Memorial Museum--Norwich Free Academy: 275
Smith Fellowship: 23
Smithsonian Institution: 18, 21, 22
Smithsonian Institution Office of Fellowships & Grants: 25
Smithsonian Institution Research Fellowships: 25
Society for the Preservation of Fell's Point and Federal Hill, Inc.: 301
Society of Colonial Wars Awards: 159
South Carolina State Fair: 102
South Carolina State Fair Fine Arts Juried Show: 102
Southeast Arkansas Art and Science Center: 12
Southeast Arkansas Art and Science Center (SEAASC): 54
Southeastern Arts Council: 44
Southeastern Center for Contemporary Art (SECCA): 112
Southeastern Center for Contemporary Art (SECCA) Grants: 141
Southern California Exposition Art in All Media Exhibition: 78
Space Coast Art Festival: 331
Spectrum Magazine Art Contest: 145
Spirit of London Painting Competition: 161
Spokane Falls Community College (SFCC): 3
Springville Museum of Art National April Salon: 65
St. Petersburg Art Commission: 328
Stacey Scholarship Fund: 230
Stamford Art Association: 259
State University of New York (SUNY)-Potsdam: 29, 199
Sterling Guards Limited Silver Prize: 161
Stinton Award: 62
Suggin Folklife Society Art Show: 160
Summit Art Center Juried Show: 91
Suntan Art Center Open Juried Show: 43
Sweet Briar College: 222
Sydney Moyer Award: 243

T

Tahoe Ehrman Mansion Art Show and Crafts Fair: 92
Tallix Foundry Cast Award: 247
Tarpon Springs Arts and Crafts Festival: 332
Tarpon Springs Chamber of Commerce: 332
Taylor Tuition Scholarships: 241
Tempo Gallery Annual Competitive Graphics Exhibit: 202
Tennessee Annual All-State Artists Exhibition: 79
Tennessee Art League: 72
Tennessee Valley Art Association: 314

Texas Arts and Crafts Foundation (TACF): 8
Texas Fine Arts Association National Exhibition: 66
Texas State Arts and Crafts Fair Young Artist Competition: 8
Texas Watercolor Society Annual Exhibition: 184
50th & France Business & Professional Association: 304
57th Street Art Fair: 337
The Artist Magazine Reader's Pictures Exhibited Contest: 174
The Artist Publishing Company, Ltd.: 174
The Midland Art Council of the Midland Center for the Arts: 98
Three Rivers Arts Festival: 103
Tippecanoe Biennial: 340
Titusville Area Chamber of Commerce: 327
Toledo Area Artists' Exhibition: 104
Toledo Museum of Art: 104
Tolley Galleries Annual Landscape Competition: 171
Trenholm Artists Guild Award: 102
Triangle Communications: 7
Triton Museum of Art Competitive Exhibition: 287
Truro Center for the Arts at Castle Hill Work-Study Program: 237
Tucson Festival Arts and Crafts Fair: 295
Tucson Festival Society: 295
Tyrone Guthrie Centre Creative Artists Residence Grants: 226

U

Union of Bulgarian Artists Prize: 294
Union of Independent Colleges of Art: 207
Union Street Gallery Annual Competition: 194
United Arts Council of Greensboro: 308
United States and Japan Exchange Fellowship Program: 221
University of Delaware: 26
University of Illinois at Urbana-Champaign College of Fine and Applied Arts: 232
University of North Dakota (UND) Visual Arts Department: 111
University of Wisconsin-Superior Art Department: 50
University of Wisconsin-Superior High School Art Scholarship Competition: 9
University of Wisconsin-Superior On-Of Paper Exhibition: 50
University of Wisconsin-Superior Visual Arts Graduate Assistantships: 238
University of Wisconsin-Waukesha (UWW): 114
U.S. International Communication Agency: 211, 212
U.S.-Spanish Joint Committee for Educational and Cultural Affairs Postdoctoral Research Grants: 27

V

VA Art-in-Architecture Program: 131
Vahki Juried Arts and Crafts Competition: 80
Vanderpoel Art Association: 147
Veterans Administration (VA) Art-in-Architecture Program (083): 131
Virginia Center for the Creative Arts (VCCA) Residence Fellowships: 222
Virginia Museum Fellowships: 239
Virginia Museum of Fine Arts: 239
Vizcaya Museum & Gardens: 36
Vogelstein Foundation Grants: 125

W

Wabash Valley Exhibition: 81
Walker Art Gallery: 175

Walt Disney World Festival of the Masters: 333
Walter Lantz Prize: 10
Washington and Jefferson National Painting Show: 172
Washington and Jefferson (W & J) College: 172
Washington Metropolitan Area Exhibition of Paintings and Graphics: 146
Washington Park Art Fair: 298
Washington Square Award: 41
Washington State Arts Commission Art in Public Places Program: 132
Watercolor Art Society-Houston: 178
Watercolor Oklahoma Open Exhibition: 185
Watercolor West Annual Transparent Watercolor Exhibition: 186
Watkins Institute: 79
Waukesha National Print and Drawing Show: 114
West Colorado Springs Commercial Club: 158
West Michigan Juried Art Competition: 288
West Michigan Seaway Festival Juried Art Show: 272
West Saginaw Civic Association (WSCA): 303
Western Art Association (WAA) Art Show and Auction: 311
Western Colorado Center for the Arts: 31
Western Los Angeles Regional Chamber of Commerce: 317
Western New York Exhibition: 82
Westerville Area Chamber of Commerce: 309
Westerville Music and Arts Festival: 309
Westwood Center of the Arts (WCA) National Small Sculpture and Drawing Exhibition: 118
Westwood Center of the Arts (WCA) Open Paintings on Canvas Exhibition: 173
Westwood Center of the Arts (WCA) Open Print Show: 203
Westwood Center of the Arts (WCA) Open Watermedia Exhibition: 187
Westwood Sidewalk Art and Craft Show: 317
White Lake Water Festival Art Exhibition: 44
William E. Lambert, Chair: 117
William Flanagan Center for Creative Persons Residencies: 223
Wind River Valley Artists' Guild (WRVAG): 153
Wind River Valley National Art Exhibit: 153
Winterthur Program in Early American Culture Fellowships: 26
Women's Graphic Center New Moves Scholarships: 240
Women's Studio Workshop (WSW) Facilities Loans: 133
Woolley Scholarships: 225
Works Off Walls: 277
Works on Paper Art Exhibition: 45
Works On Walls: 277
Wright Art Center: 69
WSW Facilities Loans: 133
Wyoming Council for the Arts: 165

Y

Young Sculptor Awards Competition: 10

Z

Zaner Gallery National Watermedia Biennial Exhibition: 188
Zaner Gallery Small Works National Competition: 255

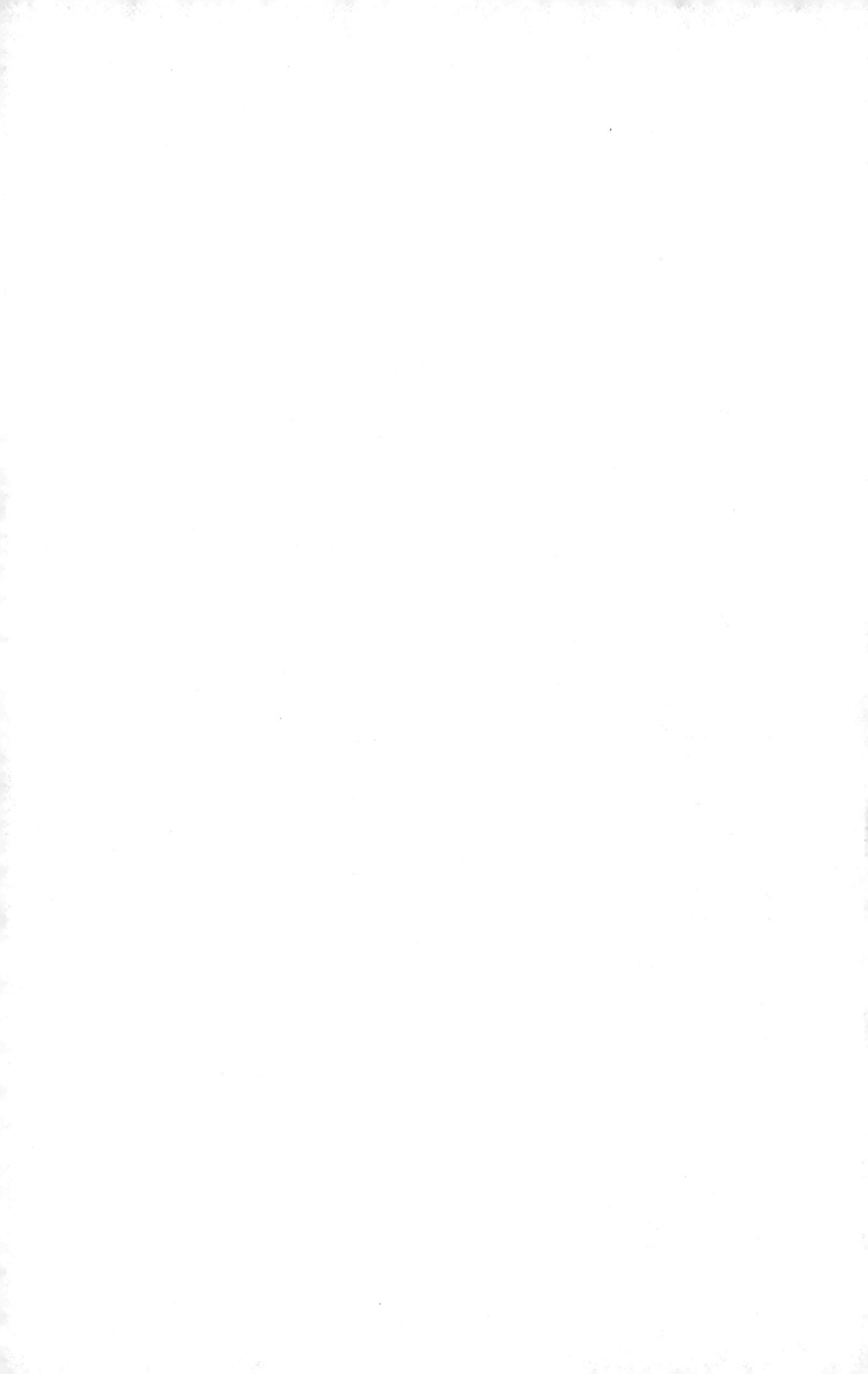

SUBJECT/CATEGORY INDEX

Index to AREAS OF SPECIAL INTEREST (followed by identifying CODE NUMBER of each event).

Abstract: 52, 53
Acrylic: 6, 11, 12, 15, 31, 33, 35, 36, 41, 45, 47, 49, 52, 53, 56, 57, 60, 64, 70, 73, 74, 76, 77, 78, 79, 85, 86, 90, 92, 94, 95, 99, 100, 101, 102, 105, 106, 108, 144, 149, 150, 156, 160, 169, 170, 176, 180, 183, 257, 266, 287
Amateur: 1, 4, 93, 102, 153
Animal: 15, 53
Apprenticeships: 127
Aquatint: 49
Art Fair: 13, 61, 103, 256, 264, 295, 296, 297, 298, 299, 300, 301, 302, 303, 304, 305, 306, 307, 308, 309, 310, 311, 312, 313, 314, 315, 316, 317, 318, 319, 320, 321, 322, 323, 324, 325, 326, 327, 328, 329, 330, 331, 332, 333, 334, 335, 336, 337, 338, 339, 340, 341, 342, 343
Art History: 17, 18, 19, 20, 21, 22, 23, 24, 25, 26, 27
Assistantships: 206, 238
By Women: 95, 120, 133, 240, 247
Casein: 4, 57, 60, 77, 89, 105, 107, 156, 180
Charcoal: 4, 6, 31, 33, 56, 73, 88, 99, 156, 266
Collage: 6, 45, 48, 49, 50, 76, 84, 92, 95, 96, 97, 99, 101, 102, 103, 269, 270
Crayon: 6, 74
Drawing: 1, 3, 4, 14, 15, 28, 29, 30, 32, 36, 37, 38, 39, 40, 41, 43, 44, 45, 46, 47, 48, 49, 50, 51, 53, 54, 55, 58, 59, 60, 61, 62, 64, 65, 66, 67, 68, 69, 70, 71, 72, 73, 75, 78, 79, 80, 81, 82, 83, 84, 85, 86, 87, 90, 91, 93, 94, 95, 96, 97, 98, 99, 100, 101, 102, 103, 104, 109, 110, 111, 112, 113, 114, 115, 116, 117, 118, 157, 258, 264, 272, 273, 275, 280, 287, 288
Engraving: 56, 115
Etching: 15, 49, 56, 64, 73, 76, 77, 92, 99, 257
Fellowships: 127, 232, 239, 241
Gouache: 35, 77, 94, 99, 104, 176, 180
Grants: 119, 120, 121, 122, 123, 124, 125, 126, 127, 128, 129, 131, 132, 135, 136, 137, 138, 139, 140, 141, 142, 234, 239
Graphics: 106, 143, 144, 145, 146, 147, 148, 149, 150, 151, 152, 153, 257, 272, 283
Historical: 154, 156, 158, 159, 160
Humor: 293, 294
Ink: 4, 6, 12, 31, 33, 56, 73, 74, 88, 108, 156, 160, 183, 266
Intaglio: 73, 76, 77, 99
Internships: 18, 21, 22, 236
Landscape: 52, 53, 169, 171, 176
Lithograph: 49, 56, 76, 77, 99
Loans: 130, 133, 134
Miniature: 162, 163, 164, 165, 166
Mixed Media: 6, 12, 14, 15, 31, 33, 45, 46, 47, 49, 56, 74, 76, 77, 79, 84, 85, 86, 87, 88, 89, 90, 91, 93,

94, 98, 100, 101, 107, 149, 150, 169, 273
Mobile: 62
Monoprint: 111, 200, 201, 257
Mosaic: 104, 242
Nature: 14, 16
Oil: 4, 6, 11, 12, 14, 15, 31, 33, 36, 41, 42, 45, 47, 49, 51, 52, 53, 56, 57, 60, 64, 70, 73, 74, 76, 77, 78, 79, 86, 88, 89, 90, 92, 94, 95, 99, 100, 101, 102, 104, 105, 106, 107, 108, 144, 149, 150, 153, 156, 160, 161, 169, 170, 171, 175, 176, 257, 266, 287
Painting: 1, 16, 34, 37, 38, 39, 40, 43, 44, 46, 47, 48, 50, 54, 55, 58, 59, 60, 61, 62, 63, 64, 65, 66, 67, 68, 69, 71, 72, 73, 80, 81, 82, 83, 84, 87, 91, 93, 96, 97, 98, 103, 146, 147, 148, 151, 152, 157, 167, 168, 170, 172, 173, 174, 175, 189, 190, 191, 192, 193, 194, 258, 264, 269, 270, 272, 273, 275, 279, 280, 285, 288, 294
Pastel: 4, 6, 14, 31, 33, 34, 35, 42, 50, 51, 52, 56, 57, 62, 70, 72, 73, 74, 76, 79, 82, 85, 86, 88, 89, 92, 102, 105, 106, 107, 108, 160, 161, 257, 266, 283
Pencil: 4, 6, 12, 31, 33, 56, 73, 74, 76, 88, 99, 156, 266
Portfolio: 6
Portrait: 11, 52, 53, 143
Print: 1, 4, 6, 15, 36, 37, 38, 39, 40, 41, 42, 43, 44, 45, 46, 47, 48, 50, 51, 52, 53, 54, 55, 57, 58, 59, 60, 61, 62, 63, 64, 65, 66, 67, 68, 69, 70, 71, 72, 73, 74, 75, 77, 78, 79, 80, 81, 82, 83, 84, 85, 86, 87, 88, 89, 90, 91, 92, 93, 94, 95, 96, 97, 98, 100, 102, 103, 104, 109, 110, 111, 112, 113, 114, 115, 156, 157, 161, 195, 196, 197, 198, 199, 200, 201, 202, 203, 204, 258, 264, 266, 273, 275, 280, 287, 288
Residence Fellowships: 17, 19, 20, 23, 24, 25, 26, 27, 219, 220, 225
Residence Grants: 205, 207, 209, 211, 212, 213, 214, 216, 217, 221, 222, 223, 224, 226
Residence Scholarships: 208, 210, 215, 218
Scenic: 143, 155, 157, 161
Scholarships: 9, 227, 228, 229, 230, 231, 233, 234, 235, 237, 240, 242
Sculpture: 1, 4, 6, 10, 14, 51, 52, 53, 54, 55, 57, 58, 59, 60, 61, 62, 63, 64, 65, 66, 67, 68, 69, 70, 71, 72, 74, 76, 77, 79, 80, 81, 82, 83, 84, 85, 86, 87, 88, 89, 90, 93, 94, 95, 96, 97, 98, 100, 101, 102, 103, 104, 105, 106, 107, 108, 116, 117, 118, 147, 148, 149, 150, 151, 152, 153, 189, 190, 191, 192, 193, 194, 243, 245, 246, 247, 248, 250, 257, 264, 269, 270, 273, 275, 280, 283, 285, 293
Sculpture (Bronze): 15, 99, 244
Sculpture (Clay): 56, 73, 75, 78, 91, 92, 272, 288
Sculpture (Glass): 91, 244
Sculpture (Medal): 272
Sculpture (Metal): 56, 73, 78, 91, 92, 99, 288
Sculpture (Plaster): 15
Sculpture (Plastic): 56, 244
Sculpture (Stone): 73, 78, 244, 249
Sculpture (Wood): 15, 56, 73, 78, 92, 99, 244, 272, 288
Seascape: 53, 157, 176
Serigraph: 49, 56, 76, 77, 92, 99
Small Works: 97, 251, 252, 253, 254, 255, 285
Still Life: 52, 53, 169
Student: 2, 3, 5, 6, 9, 16, 92, 93
Tempera: 11, 60, 70, 76, 77, 89, 94, 102, 105, 156, 161, 180
Theme: 289, 290, 291, 292, 311
Visual Arts: 2, 5, 7, 8, 9, 94, 154, 155, 257, 258, 259, 260, 261, 262, 263, 264, 265, 266, 267, 268, 269, 270, 271, 272, 273, 274, 275, 276, 277, 278, 279, 280, 281, 282, 283, 284, 285, 286, 287, 288
Watercolor: 4, 6, 12, 14, 15, 31, 32, 33, 35, 36, 41, 42, 45, 47, 49, 51, 52, 53, 55, 56, 57, 58, 60, 62, 64, 66, 70, 73, 74, 76, 77, 78, 79, 85, 86, 88, 89, 90, 92, 94, 95, 99, 100, 101, 102, 104, 105, 106, 107, 108, 144, 149, 150, 153, 156, 160, 161,

169, 170, 172, 176, 177, 178, 179, 180, 181, 182, 183, 184, 185, 186, 187, 188, 257, 266, 279, 283, 287
Wildlife: 12, 13, 143
Woodcut: 56, 76, 257
Youth: 7, 8, 10, 11, 55

Title List

HOW TO ENTER & WIN CONTESTS

By Alan Gadney

The following titles are available in Alan Gadney's series on *How to Enter & Win Contests*. Each title is published in both hardcover and paperback. Most titles are available at your local bookstore.

To order directly, send a check or money order for $7.95 for each paperback copy and $15.95 for each hardcover copy to: Facts On File, 460 Park Ave. So., N.Y., N.Y. 10016. Be sure to add sales tax if your mailing address is in New York or California. We pay postage.

FILM Contests
VIDEO/AUDIO Contests
NON-FICTION WRITING Contests
FICTION WRITING Contests
COLOR PHOTOGRAPHY Contests
BLACK & WHITE PHOTOGRAPHY Contests
DESIGN & COMMERCIAL ART Contests
FINE ARTS Contests
*FABRIC & FIBER CRAFTS Contests
*JEWELRY & METAL CRAFTS Contests
*CLAY & GLASS CRAFTS Contests
*WOOD & LEATHER CRAFTS Contests

* Available in early 1983